P9-DCY-309

11/06

whole grains

EVERY DAY EVERY WAY

OTHER BOOKS BY LORNA SASS

Pressure Perfect

The New Vegan Cookbook

The Pressured Cook: Over 75 One-Pot Meals in Minutes

The New Soy Cookbook

Lorna Sass' Short-Cut Vegetarian

Great Vegetarian Cooking Under Pressure

Lorna Sass' Complete Vegetarian Kitchen
(formerly *Recipes from an Ecological Kitchen*)

Cooking Under Pressure

*In Search of the Perfect Meal: A Collection of the Best Food Writing of
Roy Andries de Groot* (selected and edited)

Christmas Feasts from History

Dinner with Tom Jones

To the Queen's Taste: Elizabethan Feasts and Recipes

To the King's Taste: Richard II's Book of Feasts and Recipes

whole grains

EVERY DAY EVERY WAY

LORNA SASS

Clarkson Potter/Publishers
New York

Library of Congress Cataloging-in-Publication Data
Sass, Lorna J.
    Whole grains every day, every way / Lorna Sass.
        p.   cm.
    Includes index.
1. Cookery (Cereals).   2. Grain.   I. Title.
TX808.S27   2006
641.6'31—dc22   2006009528

ISBN-13: 978-0-307-33672-9
ISBN-10: 0-307-33672-7

Printed in the United States of America

Design by Maggie Hinders

10 9 8 7 6 5 4 3 2 1

First Edition

To the memory of my brother

Philip Gary Sass
1949–1978

And to those who work to restore and sustain the earth

contents

introduction

I'M A LUCKY PERSON.

During the past year, I've stood among amber waves of Kamut grain stretching toward the intense sun of Big Sandy, Montana. And I've wandered through pink, golden, and lavender sprays of quinoa ripening in the highland Andes of Riobamba, Ecuador.

These two experiences changed my life. Before being in those grain fields, I plucked Kamut and quinoa from the shelf of a health food store without giving it a second thought. Now I understand how hard farmers work to grow them, and how long a journey these nutritious kernels make before arriving in our kitchens. I feel grateful having such easy access because whole grains are not only nutritious, but absolutely delicious.

I imagine that for some of you, the whole-grain journey has always seemed long—perhaps interminable—because you've been meaning to get more wholesome food on your table but don't know where to begin. Likely you've read about the health-promoting aspects of whole grains, but aren't sure how to select or cook them. Or perhaps you've had enough brown rice and want to explore more exotic options like black rice from China, green spelt from Lebanon, farro from Italy, or kalijira from the Himalayas.

The choices are thrilling, and I'm here to guide you on an exciting adventure. You may be motivated to begin the trip because you know that grains are good for you. But I am confident that quite soon you will look forward to eating whole grains every day, every way because they taste good.

Happy cooking!

Lorna Sass
New York City

whole grains
EVERY DAY EVERY WAY

whole

grains 101

what is a whole grain?

A kernel of grain is comprised of three edible parts: the bran, the germ, and the endosperm. Some grains have a fourth part—the hull or husk—which is an inedible protective covering.

There are vital nutrients in each of the three edible parts. Let's consider a grain of wheat. The bran is the outermost edible layer—actually seven paper-thin layers—that protects the kernel from insects and bacteria. The bran is a concentrated source of dietary fiber. The largest portion of the bran, the aleurone layer, is an excellent source of B vitamins and has some trace minerals.

The germ is the embryo or vital part of the grain. It contains vitamins B and E, essential fatty acids, phytochemicals, and unsaturated lipids. The germ is located at one end of the kernel near where the kernel connects to the stalk. Since it is just under the bran, if the bran is removed, so is the germ.

The endosperm is the largest portion of the kernel and provides the germ's food supply. It is made up of two types of starch—amylose and amylopectin—and also contains some protein and B vitamins.

In order to qualify as a whole grain, a kernel must have all three parts intact. According to the USDA Dietary Guidelines, when the kernel is cracked into bits, rolled flat for quicker cooking (think of rolled oats, for example), or ground into flour, it must contain the same balance of nutrients found in the original seed to qualify as a whole-grain product. This is the definition also used by the Whole Grains Council, a consortium of scientists, nutritionists, grain producers, and manufacturers whose stated mission is to get more whole grains onto the American table.

When it came to deciding which grains to include in this book, I had to examine each grain's anatomy to see if it qualified. For example, much of the barley grown in this country has to be stripped of its inedible hull in a process called hulling. Barley's hull is so tightly attached to the bran layer that some of the bran is rubbed off in the process. Once any bran is rubbed off, the barley qualifies as pearl or pearled barley. If some of the bran is left intact, the barley is called semi-pearled.

According to the definition above, pearl barley, which has been stripped of all or most of its bran, would not qualify for inclusion in a book on whole grains. However, because of its particular anatomy, barley contains fiber throughout the kernel. So even when you are eating pearl barley, you are still getting a good balance of nutrients. I therefore decided to include pearl barley.

Then there's bulgur, made by parboiling and cracking wheat kernels. Again, during this process some bran is lost. But as parboiling takes place, nutrients from the bran seep into the center. As a result, bulgur offers the range of nutrients available in the whole grain.

Keeping all of these variables in mind, I have included a few processed forms of grains that may not be considered whole in the strictest sense, but give substantial nutritional return. They have the further advantage of being quick-cooking.

I have also included some seeds that are not members of the grain family in botanical terms, but are commonly referred to as "grains" because they are cooked like them and have similar or even better nutritional profiles. These include buckwheat (a member of the rhubarb family), quinoa and amaranth (members of noncereal families of grasses), and wild rice (an aquatic grass).

the health benefits of whole grains

We are fortunate that whole grains are so tasty and versatile because they also happen to promote good health. The word is out that a significant portion of the phytonutrients and phytochemicals in grains are located in the bran and germ, the parts we don't eat when we choose white bread made from refined flour instead of brown bread made from whole grains. And it is now well known that the phytonutrients and phytochemicals play significant roles in disease prevention.

Although most Americans recognize the health benefits of consuming fruits and vegetables, few realize that whole grains have the same or even more disease-fighting compounds. A roundup of scientific literature gathered by the Whole Grains Council (www.wholegrainscouncil.org) offers a significant body of evidence demonstrating the benefits of adding whole grains to the daily diet.

For example, one study conducted by the Harvard School of Public Health revealed that men aged 40 to 75 who had the highest whole-grain intake (about 40 grams a day) lowered their risk

BUYER BEWARE: READ THE LABEL AND LOOK FOR THE WHOLE-GRAIN STAMP
A few years ago, I purchased a seven-grain bread in a bakery. When I sliced it and saw how white the inside was, I realized immediately that I'd mistaken "seven-grain" for "whole grain." Yes, the bread dough may have included the flour of seven different grains, but it sure didn't have any bran or germ.

The word to focus on when shopping for whole grains is the word "whole." Ideally "whole" should be the first word on the label of any whole-grain product, meaning that the most significant ingredient is the whole grain itself.

To facilitate recognition of whole-grain products, the Whole Grains Council has developed special stamps, which many companies now include on their packaging. If you don't spot the stamp, look for labeling that says "100% WHOLE GRAIN Excellent Source."

of heart disease by 20 percent. Another study, conducted by Tufts University, found that those who eat three or more servings of whole grains per day are less likely to develop metabolic syndrome and insulin resistance, two common precursors of type 2 diabetes. Other studies reveal that regular whole-grain intake lowers total cholesterol, reduces the risk of stroke and obesity, and is protective against hormone-related and digestive system cancers.

The good news about whole grains is steadily mounting, and as a result, the American Heart Association and the Dietary Guidelines for Americans recommend the consumption of at least three ounces of whole grains a day. To keep up with the latest findings on the health benefits of whole grains, check the websites listed in Further Reading on page 304.

getting started

SELECTING AND STORING WHOLE GRAINS

Whole grains are living foods that must be treated with respect.

Heat, light, and air are the enemies of the oil in the germ, which slowly becomes rancid if the grain is not stored properly. Since the bran layer acts as a protective coating to the germ, intact grains are not as vulnerable as cracked grains or whole-grain flour.

In the best of all possible worlds, every shop that sells whole grains would store them under refrigeration. Since you are not likely to find refrigerated grains, your best bet is to purchase whole-grain products only from stores that have a good turnover. Alternatively, mail-order your grains from a reliable source (see pages 308 to 313). When buying packaged grains, always check the expiration or "sell-by" date and choose the one that is furthest out. Also check the label to be sure that no preservatives have been added.

If you are shopping from bulk bins, sniff the grains. They should smell faintly sweet, slightly vegetal, or have no aroma at all. If you detect any musty or oily scent, the grains are rancid. Pass them by, and alert the store manager.

Unless you can be assured of their quality, resist any temptation to buy bags of grains wrapped in charming gingham or burlap bags—the kind sold at country fairs or tourist shops full of nick-nacks. It's not likely that they have been stored properly.

Once you bring the grains home, *you cannot store them in a pantry as you would white rice.* Again, the oils in the germ will gradually turn rancid, particularly in hot weather. For example, no whole grains, even those in unopened packages, ever survived a New York City summer in my pantry. So be sure to *refrigerate or freeze whole grains in tightly sealed containers as soon as they enter your kitchen.*

Forgive my micromanaging, but let me share with you how I store uncooked grains. I open the sealed packages by snipping off the top corner. When I've poured out what I need, I fold over the top once or twice and put a rubber band around the package. Then I put the package into a zipper-topped bag and mark the date of purchase. If there's room in my freezer, I store the grains there. Otherwise, I put them into the refrigerator. I try to use the grains within 6 months, but I have had some grains for well over a year and they've remained fresh when stored as described.

EQUIPMENT

The most essential piece of equipment you'll need for successful whole-grain cooking is a heavy, well-made round pot commonly called a Dutch oven. My first choice is the Le Creuset round oven. It has a tight-fitting lid so little to no water escapes in the form of steam, and it has a heavy bottom so the grains rarely stick and never scorch. The round oven also offers you the valuable option of stove-top or oven cooking. Since many grains like to be cozy when they cook, I recommend a 2-quart pot for preparing 1 to 2 cups of dry grain.

Another useful piece of equipment is an electric coffee grinder, reserved for the purpose of grinding spices and small batches of grain. All freshly ground spices taste more vibrant than preground, and the same may be said for freshly ground flour. I was surprised to discover that a small coffee grinder does a fine job of making coarse meal and grits from whole kernels, and flour from rolled grains.

I love the vibrant essential oils in citrus zest and use zest in a lot of my recipes. If you share my passion, invest in a Microplane, a long, rasp-like, ruler-shaped strip of stainless steel that makes child's play of zesting citrus fruits. (It also does an admirable job of grating cheese.)

And finally, treat yourself to an immersion blender with a mini-chopper component. The immersion blender makes quick work of pureeing soup that is still in the pot. The mini-chopper is convenient for making salad dressings and grinding seeds into flour.

TO RINSE OR NOT TO RINSE

Over the years, I've gone back and forth about the necessity to rinse grains, and here is what I've concluded: The vast majority of grains sold in this country, whether imported or not, are very clean and do not require rinsing. On occasion, a batch of grain contains foreign matter like twigs and tiny stones and must be carefully picked over and rinsed in several changes of water. You will be able to tell at a glance if you have dusty or dirty grains on your hands.

If you need to rinse them, the best way is to pour the grains into a large strainer. Place the strainer in a bowl and run water over the grains until they are submerged. With your fingers, rub the grains against the strainer in a swirling motion for about 30 seconds. Raise the strainer, empty the bowl, and repeat the process until the water remains fairly clear. (There will always be some starchy white residue.)

In the basic recipes, I let you know if a particular grain requires rinsing. If you feel more comfortable giving all grains a quick rinse, go for it. But rinse only the amount of grains that you are planning to cook; moist grains either sprout or become moldy.

THE EFFECTS OF SOAKING AND SALT

Overnight soaking is often recommended as a way to cut down on the cooking time of dense grains like wheat berries. I have not found the time saving to be significant—perhaps it shaves off about 10 minutes. But I do recommend overnight soaking for some grains because the slow softening and penetration of the bran results in more even cooking and a plumper final product. In the basics chapter, I always indicate when presoaking is preferred.

"Soaking overnight" is a loose term and can be interpreted as about 8 hours. If you don't have time to cook the grains after they've soaked, just refrigerate them in the water for up to 24 hours.

When it comes to salt, grains react very much like beans. Ideally one would add salt to enhance flavor, but time and again I have found that if the salt is added early on, the bran layer toughens and does not allow even penetration of liquid. For this reason, I rarely add more than a pinch of salt. Truth be told, I have come to appreciate and prefer the mild, sweet taste of unsalted grains.

All of the recipes have been tested with fine sea salt. I like the taste of sea salt and appreciate the fact that it has trace minerals. If you are using another type of salt, adjust the amount accordingly.

MOLDING GRAINS INTO DECORATIVE SHAPES

Most cooked grains have enough surface starch to stick to each other when pressed together. For very little extra effort, you can present individual portions very attractively in molded shapes called timbales. Use ½- to 1-cup ramekins or small molds of varying sizes intended for fancy pastries. A coffee cup or clean tuna can also does just fine.

There's nothing to it: Just press the hot, seasoned grains firmly into the mold. Turn them out immediately onto a plate. The smaller grains, like quinoa and bulgur, also mold well when they are cold. If nuts and dried fruits or vegetables are cut small enough and tossed with the grains, they don't interfere with the molding process.

Here's the truth, pure and simple: No two batches of grain cook up exactly the same way.

And how could they? They've been grown in different soils, harvested at different moisture contents, stored under diverse conditions, and displayed on the store's shelf for who knows how long.

Because of these unknown variables, you can never trust a recipe that gives you a precise amount of liquid and tells you the grain will be done when the liquid is absorbed. The best an honest grain recipe can do is to suggest a reasonable amount of liquid and an approximate cooking time, then advise you how to determine when the grain is done.

Flexibility is the key. You'll need to add a bit of water if the grain isn't done and all of the liquid has been absorbed. Or you'll have to drain off a bit of liquid when the grain is done and there's some left.

Because of this variability, it's practical to cook the grains first, then prepare the recipes with already cooked grains. There is another important reason for taking this approach: When grains are raw, the bran layer acts as a barrier to seasonings. That's why when you try to make a curried brown rice pilaf from scratch, the rice doesn't absorb much of the curry flavor. Once the grains are cooked and the bran layer is either softened or split, the grains will absorb added flavors very quickly.

And that's the whole truth about cooking whole grains.

the grain bank: whole grains as fast food

In the basic recipes, I've given liquid-to-grain ratios for preparing from 2 cups to as much as 6 cups of cooked grain. Even though you might need only 3 cups for a given recipe, I encourage you to make extra to store in your Grain Bank. My intention is for you to create leftovers on purpose, with the goal of having a variety of cooked grains on hand for future meals.

The Grain Bank is conveniently located in your refrigerator and freezer. You can refrigerate cooked grains for up to 5 days. Often the starch gelatinizes as the grains chill, leaving them stiff and unpleasantly dry. To restore grains to their former suppleness, place them in a bowl lightly covered with a paper towel. (There is no need to add water.) Microwave the grains until steaming hot, stirring once or twice for even heat distribution. Alternatively, place the grains in a heavy pot with about $1/4$ inch of water, cover, and steam them over medium-low heat until they are soft, adding more water if needed. See also the Keeping and Reheating instructions in specific recipes for any information that may vary somewhat from this.

Cooked grains can also be frozen for at least 3 months. Before freezing, cool them completely. Store them in 2- or 3-cup quantities in labeled zipper-top bags. Most frozen grains will clump together in a block, but if you need a smaller amount than that contained in the bag, just bang the bag against the kitchen counter to release the quantity you require. Or remove the entire batch from the plastic bag and microwave or steam to defrost as directed above. You can also defrost the grains at room temperature or overnight in the refrigerator.

The point is that once the Grain Bank is full of cooked grains, you'll be able to prepare most of the recipes in this book quickly. You'll also have the option of adding frozen grains directly to simmering soups or stews to create fast one-pot meals.

I know it's hard to believe, but properly stored and reheated leftover grains taste as good as freshly cooked and are terrific ingredients for quick meals.

■ ■ ■

grain
profiles

and
basic
recipes

In the pages that follow you will find a great deal of information about each grain, including its nutritional highlights, appearance, and taste. You'll also learn what forms of the grain are available (e.g., wheat berries, cracked wheat, bulgur) and where you can purchase them. Then you'll find my preferred way to cook each form. For example, in the millet section, you'll learn how to cook hulled millet, kibbi millet, and millet grits.

Take a look at the Cook's Notes following many of the basic recipes if you'd like to understand more about the pros and cons of various cooking techniques I tried. This section also includes incidental information. Anyone wanting suggestions for seasoning the grains or creating a quick dish after cooking the basic recipe can check the section called Compatible Foods and Flavors. The ingredients suggested here pair well with the grain. For example, if you make a batch of Basic Amaranth (page 18) and don't want to serve it plain, you can stir in some of the compatible ingredients listed.

IN MY KITCHEN LABORATORY

ALTHOUGH I've been cooking whole grains for over three decades, I began this book with "beginner's mind." I cooked each grain every way I could think of to determine its unique qualities and to evaluate which cooking technique resulted in the best taste and texture. I ran many tests twice for each grain, first without salt and then with salt. It became clear that there is no universal formula for all grains. Rather, there is an optimal way to cook each one that maximizes its own qualities, which I provide, grain by grain, in the basic recipes in this chapter. Here are the tests I ran:

1. Bring the grain to a boil in 3 times the amount of water. Cover and simmer until tender. Drain and measure unabsorbed water.
2. Bring 3 times the amount of water to a boil first, then add the grain. Cover and simmer until tender. Drain and measure unabsorbed water.
3. Bring a large pot of water to a boil, then add the grain. Cook uncovered until tender. Drain and return the grains to the hot pot. Cover and steam in the residual heat for 10 minutes.
4. Bring a large pot of water to a boil with the grain. Cook uncovered until tender. Drain and set in a strainer over 2 cups of water. Cover and steam for 7 minutes.
5. Toast uncooked grains in a dry skillet. Repeat test number 1.
6. Toast uncooked grains coated with oil in a skillet. Repeat test number 1.
7. Repeat test number 2 in a pressure cooker.

If you are new to whole grains, please don't feel intimidated by all of this information. Start by trying a few of the quick-cooking, very easy-to-love varieties. These include quinoa, Chinese black rice, bulgur, buckwheat, and cornmeal polenta. Try the basic recipes and then check the index to find simple dishes incorporating them. As your repertoire grows, so will your confidence.

amaranth

While bubbling in the pot, this ancient Andean grain sends forth a scent reminiscent of corn. But there the similarity ends.

Amaranth's taste and texture are unique: It has an earthy, faintly grassy taste. As the tiny seeds cook, they release a viscous starch (amylopectin) that creates a silken sauce—like risotto, but with the slippery, go-down-easy quality of okra. The grain never completely softens, so each mouthful delivers a delicate crunch.

Like its South American compadre quinoa (page 56), amaranth is considered a "supergrain" because it contains all of the essential amino acids and is therefore an excellent source of high-quality protein. High in fiber and rich in calcium, phosphorus, iron, and vitamins E and B, these minuscule seeds are worth your acquaintance.

I've come to love amaranth, but it was definitely an acquired taste. Once I gave up the idea that the grain could be transformed into a fluffy pilaf, this nutritional powerhouse began to reward me with some very enjoyable eating.

In fact, amaranth has turned out to be much more versatile and delicious than I anticipated. Cooked into a glistening porridge and laced with honey, it makes a comforting, nutrition-dense breakfast cereal (page 249). Include amaranth in soups (page 118) or stews for body and a nutritional boost. Marry it with porcini for a rich, earthy polenta-like side dish (page 223). Or try the coarsely ground seeds in a savory pie crust for quiche (page 196).

Amaranth has a slightly herbal taste so, for the most part, it works best in savory dishes. As a featured ingredient, opt for pale beige amaranth rather than black; the latter looks stunning but has a high proportion of bran and can taste gritty. Use black amaranth as you would poppy seeds, for texture or as a garnish.

The great news for cooks is that it's virtually impossible to overcook amaranth; it always maintains an appealing crunch. I have tested the recipes only with beige amaranth, which is the most readily available.

AMARANTH AT A GLANCE

FORM	DESCRIPTION/PROCESSING	AVAILABILITY	COMMENTS
WHOLE, BEIGE	Minuscule disc-shaped seeds ranging from beige to golden, slightly larger than poppy seeds	Health food stores, mail-order	Some batches have stray black seeds, which is fine
WHOLE, BLACK	Minuscule ebony seeds, same shape as golden but often smaller	Mail-order	High proportion of bran makes these taste gritty; best to use them raw as a high-protein substitute for poppy seeds
FLAKES	Steamed, pressed, and rolled for ready-to-eat breakfast cereals; look like miniature snowflakes	Health food stores, mail-order	Available both plain (unsweetened) and flavored (with sweetenings)
PUFFED	Tiny, whitish, bead-shaped morsels created by placing the seeds under pressure that is suddenly released	Health food stores, mail-order, some supermarkets	Available unsweetened and unsalted; makes a nice casserole topping or salad garnish
FLOUR	Finely ground cream-colored flour	Health food stores, mail-order	See page 264

basic amaranth

This method produces a thick polenta-like side dish. Toasting the amaranth darkens the seeds and deepens the flavor, but is optional.

CUPS DRY	CUPS WATER	SALT	POT SIZE	APPROXIMATE CUP YIELD
1	1¾	Add to taste after cooking	3-quart	2
1½	2½	Add to taste after cooking	4-quart	3
2	3½	Add to taste after cooking	4-quart	4

Set a heavy Dutch oven or saucepan over medium heat and toast the amaranth, stirring frequently, until it begins to pop, jump around, and smell toasty, 2 to 4 minutes.

Turn off the heat. Stand back to avoid splattering, and add the water. The grains will float to the top and clump together. Stir in any grains clinging to the sides of the pot. Return to a boil, then cover and simmer over low heat until most of the water is absorbed, 7 to 9 minutes. Stir once. Turn off the heat and let sit, covered, for 10 minutes.

When fully cooked, amaranth looks pearlescent and the grains are tender, with just a hint of crunch. Upon close inspection the germ, which is a thin filament around the circumference, should be visible and still attached. If necessary, stir in additional water, cover, and simmer until done. Add salt and other seasonings to taste. (See Compatible Foods and Flavors, opposite.) Serve hot.

KEEPING AND REHEATING: Refrigerate for up to 5 days in a tightly sealed container. Reheat in a microwave or in a heavy saucepan, covered, over very low heat. Stir in more water, if needed. Does not freeze well.

cook's notes

- It isn't practical to rinse amaranth since the grains are so small, but I have never come across a batch that required cleaning.

- Cooking amaranth with salt or in an acidic base (such as fruit juice) increases cooking time and the grains don't ever become fully tender.

- Amaranth polenta thickens as it cooks, but it is too crumbly to cut into squares and fry or bake, as you would corn polenta. Once in a while you will mysteriously find yourself with a batch that does set up firmly. If so, cut it into pieces, brush the surface with olive oil, and bake in a 400°F oven until crisp.

compatible foods and flavors

- Savory: butter, olive oil, sun-dried tomatoes, mushrooms, oregano, corn, sesame seeds, fresh ginger

- Sweet: honey, vanilla, chocolate, cinnamon, banana, winter squash

basic amaranth porridge

This approach creates a thick, creamy porridge suitable for breakfast.

CUPS DRY	CUPS WATER	SALT	POT SIZE	APPROXIMATE CUP YIELD
1	3	Add to taste after cooking	2-quart	2
1½	4½	Add to taste after cooking	2-quart	3

Bring the water to a boil in a heavy Dutch oven or saucepan. Add the amaranth. The grains will float to the top and clump together. Stir in any grains clinging to the sides of the pot. Cover, reduce the heat, and simmer, stirring occasionally, until the mixture thickens and the amaranth is tender and looks pearlescent, about 22 minutes.

When done, the grains will be soft, with just a hint of crunch. Upon close inspection the germ, which is a thin filament around the circumference, should be visible and still attached. If necessary, stir in more water and cook a few more minutes. If there is excess water, gently boil the mixture uncovered to achieve the desired consistency. Serve hot.

KEEPING AND REHEATING: Refrigerate for up to 5 days in a tightly sealed container. Reheat in a microwave or in a heavy saucepan, covered, over very low heat. Stir in more water, if needed. Does not freeze well.

basic "dry" amaranth

Cooked amaranth is never dry enough to fluff up, but this method creates grains that are sufficiently dry to add to batters or sprinkle into salads. You can also stir the crunchy cooked seeds into soups and stews for added texture and a boost of protein.

CUPS DRY	CUPS WATER	SALT	POT SIZE	APPROXIMATE CUP YIELD
½	6 (1½ quarts)	Add to taste after cooking	3-quart	1¼
1	10 (2½ quarts)	Add to taste after cooking	4-quart	2½

Bring the water to a boil in a heavy Dutch oven or saucepan. Add the amaranth. The grains will float to the top and clump together. Stir in any grains clinging to the sides of the pot. Cook uncovered at a gentle boil, stirring occasionally, until the grains are tender, 14 to 16 minutes. When done, the grains will be soft, with just a hint of crunch. Upon close inspection the germ, which is a thin filament around the circumference, should be visible and still attached.

Drain through a fine-meshed strainer. Run cold water over the grains to wash away surface starch. Bounce the strainer up and down to drain off all water. Spread the grains out on a large plate to cool.

KEEPING AND REHEATING: See The Grain Bank, page 10.

cook's notes

■ Although many sources give instructions for popping amaranth, I've tried many different techniques and not experienced much success. At best, about 20 percent of the seeds pop.

■ I've had no luck cooking amaranth in a ratio of 1 cup water to 1 cup grains to create a pilaf-style dish.

■ If you locate a bunch of black amaranth, use the Basic Amaranth recipe (page 18) with a ratio of 2 parts water to 1 part grain. Be prepared for a longer cooking time.

popped amaranth crunch

Here is a crunchy topping made by popping amaranth and tossing it with pumpkin seeds and spices. It's great scattered on stews and green salads.

Choose a heavy-bottomed pot about 4 inches deep to prevent the popping amaranth from going AWOL.

MAKES ABOUT $1/2$ CUP

3 tablespoons amaranth

3 tablespoons raw, hulled pumpkin seeds

1 teaspoon cumin seeds

$1/4$ teaspoon dried oregano

$1/8$ teaspoon chili powder

$1/8$ teaspoon salt

Heat a large pot over high heat. When a bead of water dropped on the bottom immediately sizzles, stir in the amaranth. Lower the heat to medium. Stir constantly until the grains turn a shade or two darker and about 20 percent of the amaranth has popped. (The popped grains will look like tiny white beads.) Stir in the pumpkin and cumin seeds and continue stirring for another 30 seconds. Turn off the heat and continue stirring until the amaranth stops popping.

Immediately transfer the mixture to a small bowl. Stir in the oregano, chili powder, and salt. Let cool and then store in a jar in a cool place until ready to use or for up to 1 month.

NOTE: If you'd like to double or triple this recipe, make it in batches. It's difficult to prevent the amaranth from burning when you try to pop more than 3 tablespoons at a time.

barley

Chewy, juicy barley is so versatile that it could be called the chicken of the grain world: With its mild, faintly sweet taste, barley goes with just about anything. It's a thirsty and generous grain, absorbing whatever cooking liquid you provide and expanding to three times its original volume. No wonder it is one of the most familiar and best-loved grains.

Unfortunately, the nomenclature used to describe the various forms of barley can be a bit confusing. The variety of barley most commonly available is called covered barley because each kernel is enclosed in two layers of inedible hull. To remove the hulls, the grains undergo an abrasive process called hulling. Once the hulls are removed, the grains are called hulled barley. Because the hull is so tightly attached to the protein-rich bran layer (technically called the *aleurone*), some bran is inevitably lost during processing, but most of it is retained. You will find hulled barley in health food stores. It has a distinctly tan color and looks larger than pearl barley.

Once the grains are hulled, they are usually further refined by another abrasive polishing process called pearling. Because pearling strips off the germ and most or all of the bran, pearl barley kernels are paler, smaller, and less nutritious than hulled barley. Virtually all of the barley available in supermarkets is pearl barley, and since the industry has no standardized regulations, the degree of pearling varies from brand to brand and batch to batch.

You can also find pearl barley in health food stores, and it almost always has some bran intact, which means that the grains will look darker and plumper than supermarket pearl barley. For accuracy, it should be labeled semi-pearled, but it isn't. Keep in mind that the more bran, the better, because the bran layers include protein, fiber, and B vitamins.

A new type of barley has become available over the past few decades. It's called hull-less barley because the hulls simply fall off when the grains are harvested, leaving the bran intact. Since hull-less varieties require no pearling, no nutrients are lost.

Bud Clem, a small Montana grower of various hull-less varieties that he markets as NuBarley, is rightfully proud of his grains, which range in color from straw-gold to deep bronze to purplish black. More slender and elegant than hulled barley, they are a special treat to eat.

All barley is high in amylopectin, the type of starch that makes Barley, Beef, and Mushroom Soup (page 120) thick and gives it a beautiful sheen. The amylopectin also makes barley an ideal candidate for creamy Barley Risotto with Wild Mushrooms (page 148).

Barley's sweetness marries well with carrots when baked into a casserole such as the Barley-Carrot Kugel with Honey Glaze on page 208. Barley holds its shape well and remains soft and pliant in a refreshing, nubbly tabbouleh (page 130). And it makes a comforting pudding when cooked with rhubarb (page 301). Barley flour adds appealing moisture to savory muffins flecked with thyme (page 270).

Barley's nutritional profile is similar to wheat's when it comes to protein, vitamin, and mineral content. Of special note, barley contains a heart-healthy soluble fiber called beta-glucan that has been shown to lower cholesterol. So barley has everything going for it. It's not only good, but good for you.

BARLEY AT A GLANCE

FORM	DESCRIPTION/PROCESSING	AVAILABILITY	COMMENTS
HULLED (also called pot, Scots, Scotch, and barley groats)	Chubby tan grain whose inedible hull is removed by abrasion; some bran lost during processing	Health food stores, mail-order	Hearty, chewy, and full-flavored; great for soups and stews. Packages are labeled "hulled."
HULL-LESS (also called naked)	Elongated grain whose hull falls off when harvested, obviating the need for pearling, so no nutritious bran is lost	Health food stores, mail-order	Pleasing chewiness. Specialty varieties of hull-less barley include Bronze Nugget, Golden Nugget, Golden Waxy, Ethiopian, and Treasure State; they are especially tasty.
BLACK (purple) barley	A hull-less variety with a dark purplish bran layer	Mail-order	Handsome and tasty, but usually too "branny" and dense to serve alone; for attractive specks of dark color and textural variety, use in a mixed grain salad or add a few tablespoons when cooking hulled or hull-less barley or brown rice
PEARL (pearled) barley	Hull and some or all bran removed by abrasion; supermarket brands are usually more pearled (therefore smaller and paler) than those available in health food stores	Health food stores, mail-order, supermarkets	Best for barley risotto and puddings, and other dishes where bran detracts from texture
GRITS	Whole or pearled grains cut into bits of uneven size	Health food stores, mail-order	Cooks quickly, but more prone to rancidity than whole grain

BARLEY AT A GLANCE (continued)

FORM	DESCRIPTION/PROCESSING	AVAILABILITY	COMMENTS
ROLLED (also called flakes)	Light tan flakes similar in appearance to rolled oats; kernels are steamed and pressed through rollers to flatten	Health food stores, mail-order	Cooks quickly, retains chewy texture, and maintains shape well
FLOUR	Pale beige; finely milled from whole grain	Health food stores, mail-order	Contains an oil prone to rancidity once ground; best to grind your own from barley flakes or whole grain, or buy in small amounts and use immediately (see page 264)

basic pearl, hull-less, and hulled barley

Use the same cooking technique for these three forms of the whole kernel. The more refined the barley, the shorter the cooking time; therefore, pearl barley takes less time to cook than hull-less or hulled.

CUPS DRY	CUPS WATER	TEASPOONS SALT	POT SIZE	APPROXIMATE CUP YIELD
1	3	Pinch	2-quart	2 (hull-less, black) 3 (hulled, pearl)
1½	4½	⅛	3-quart	3 (hull-less, black) 4 (hulled, pearl)
2	6	¼	3-quart	4 (hull-less, black) 6 (hulled, pearl)

Bring the water and salt (see Cook's Notes, page 26) to a rolling boil in a heavy Dutch oven or saucepan. Turn off the heat to avoid boil-overs. Add the barley and return to a boil over medium heat. Reduce the heat, cover, and simmer until the barley is tender—it will still be chewy—and one color throughout when sliced in half crosswise, 30 to 40 minutes for pearl or 40 to 55 minutes for hull-less, hulled, and black. Drain off any unabsorbed water. Immediately return the barley to the hot pot. Cover and steam off the heat for 5 or 10 minutes.

OVEN-BAKED: Once you've added the barley, set the covered pot in the middle of an oven preheated to 350°F.

PRESSURE-COOKED: See page 112.

KEEPING AND REHEATING: See The Grain Bank, page 10.

cook's notes

■ You can add more than the recommended amount of salt to the cooking water when preparing pearl barley, but salt toughens the bran layer and interferes with proper absorption of water when cooking hulled or hull-less varieties, so add only the recommended amount.

■ Barley foams as it cooks. Keep an eye on the pot to avoid boil-overs. Alternatively, to subdue foaming, stir a little oil or butter into the water before adding the barley.

■ For a stickier result, sometimes desirable for a risotto or breakfast porridge, bring the barley, water, and salt to a boil together.

■ Because of its inherent stickiness, barley molds beautifully. Press it into ramekins and unmold onto plates for an attractive presentation.

■ If the cooked barley is sticky and you prefer separate grains, pour boiling water over the grains to rinse off surface starch. Drain well. Reheat, if necessary.

■ Most types stay soft and pliant, even when chilled, so barley makes a fine base for grain salads.

■ Since it's virtually impossible to overcook, barley is extremely versatile and makes an agreeable companion to ingredients like tough cuts of meat that have an unpredictable cooking time.

compatible foods and flavors

■ Savory: butter, browned onions, mushrooms, lamb, beef, celery, tomatoes, green peas, root vegetables, dill, oregano

■ Sweet: dried fruit, honey, cinnamon and other sweet spices, apples

basic barley grits

Because slicing the barley into bits exposes the grains' starchy endosperm, grits cook in about 50 percent less time than the whole grain. Toasting enhances their flavor. Mellow, porridgy barley grits make a nice alternative to mashed potatoes and go especially well with beef and lamb stews and roasts.

CUPS DRY	TABLESPOONS BUTTER OR OIL	CUPS WATER	TEASPOONS SALT	POT SIZE	APPROXIMATE CUP YIELD
1	1	3	$^3/_4$	2-quart	3
1$^1/_2$	1$^1/_2$	4$^1/_2$	1	2-quart	4$^1/_2$

Toast the barley grits in a heavy Dutch oven or saucepan over medium heat, stirring constantly, until they emit a fragrant aroma, about 3 minutes. Stir in the butter.

Turn off the heat to avoid boil-overs. Stir in the water and salt. Bring to a boil over high heat. Cover, reduce the heat, and simmer until the grits are tender, 16 to 20 minutes.

Turn off the heat and let sit for 5 minutes. Drain off any unabsorbed water or boil uncovered, stirring frequently, until evaporated.

KEEPING AND REHEATING: Refrigerate for up to 5 days in a tightly sealed container. Reheat in a lightly covered bowl in the microwave or in a heavy saucepan over low heat, stirring occasionally and adding a little water if needed. Does not freeze well.

cook's notes

■ Use barley grits instead of whole barley in soups and stews that have short cooking times.

■ Use barley grits as the base for sweet dessert puddings.

■ For a breakfast porridge, consider cooking the grits in part milk and part water.

buckwheat

With its distinctly earthy taste and aroma, buckwheat is a love-it-or-leave-it grain. Many people have a passing acquaintance with kasha, the toasted buckwheat favored in Eastern Europe. Probably the best-known use of kasha is in the Ashkenazi Jewish dish of buckwheat, mushrooms, and bowtie pasta known as *kasha varnishkes*. Those who love Japanese food have probably enjoyed soba, the highly esteemed buckwheat noodles.

If you, like me, have rejected kasha in the past because of its assertive flavor, try pale untoasted buckwheat groats and you may be pleasantly surprised by their mild taste. In any case, buckwheat is definitely worth a second glance. It's a fast-cooking grain that is high in protein (especially lysine, which is uncommon in most cereal grains) and a fine source of minerals including iron, phosphorus, and potassium. It also has impressive amounts of vitamins B and E.

Despite its name, buckwheat is not related to wheat. In fact, it's not a cereal grass at all, but a flowering plant related to rhubarb. (The flowers are beloved by bees, who produce distinctively flavored buckwheat honey.)

Cooks can easily find many imaginative uses for buckwheat. Little Buckwheat Pancakes with Smoked Salmon and Dilled Yogurt Cheese makes a fetching appetizer or brunch entrée (page 238). For a side dish or vegetarian entrée, try the Buckwheat and Cottage Cheese Casserole (page 214). For a most unusual breakfast, consider Buckwheat Hash with Bacon and Eggs (page 254).

BUCKWHEAT AT A GLANCE

FORM	DESCRIPTION/PROCESSING	AVAILABILITY	COMMENTS
WHOLE GROATS, TOASTED (also called kasha)	A pyramidal grain with a deep brown color; inedible black hull removed; toasted to deepen flavor	Supermarket, health food stores	Toasted groats are usually labeled kasha
WHOLE GROATS, UNTOASTED	A pyramidal grain of greenish ivory; inedible black hull removed; mild taste	Supermarkets, health food stores	Untoasted groats are labeled "whole buckwheat groats" or "dehulled buckwheat kernels"
GRANULATED	Groats cut into grits for quicker cooking	Supermarkets	Available in coarse, medium, and fine granulations (packages labeled accordingly); toasted (kasha) most commonly available
CREAM OF BUCKWHEAT	Untoasted, finely granulated buckwheat	Supermarkets, health food stores	Use for breakfast cereal or savory polenta
DARK FLOUR	Toasted groats ground into flour	Health food stores	A dark, heavy flour; purchase or grind at home in a spice grinder
LIGHT FLOUR	Untoasted groats ground into flour	Not readily available	Purchase whole or granulated untoasted buckwheat and grind it to flour in a spice grinder

basic whole buckwheat

This recipe works for both toasted and untoasted buckwheat groats, though untoasted often take a few minutes longer. To keep the grains from disintegrating, buckwheat is traditionally coated with egg or some kind of fat. One large egg is enough to coat up to 1½ cups of buckwheat. Though I usually cook grains in water, buckwheat is especially delicious when cooked in chicken broth. Use the higher amount of liquid for a moist, stuffing-like final product. Use the lower amount of liquid for drier grains.

CUPS DRY	TABLESPOONS BUTTER OR NUMBER OF EGGS	CUPS LIQUID	TEASPOONS SALT	POT SIZE	APPROXIMATE CUP YIELD
1	1	1¾ to 2	½	2-quart	3½
1½	1	2¾ to 3	¾	2-quart	5 to 6

IF USING BUTTER: Heat the butter in a heavy Dutch oven or saucepan. Add the buckwheat and toast over medium heat, stirring frequently, for 2 to 3 minutes. Turn off the heat. Stir in the liquid gradually to avoid boil-overs. Add the salt (omit if using salted broth) and bring to a boil over high heat. Lower the heat, cover, and simmer until the liquid is absorbed, 10 to 12 minutes. Turn off the heat and let stand for 5 minutes.

IF USING EGG: In a small bowl, lightly beat the egg. Toss in the buckwheat and coat thoroughly. Heat a nonstick skillet over medium heat. Add the buckwheat and cook, stirring occasionally, until the egg coating is dry. Bring the liquid and salt (omit if using salted broth) to a boil in a heavy Dutch oven or saucepan. Stir in the coated buckwheat. Cover and simmer until the liquid is absorbed, 10 to 12 minutes. Turn off the heat and let stand for 5 minutes.

KEEPING AND REHEATING: Refrigerate for up to 5 days in a tightly sealed container. Reheat in a lightly covered bowl in the microwave or in a heavy saucepan over low heat, stirring occasionally and adding a little water if needed. Does not freeze well.

cook's notes

■ You can use egg whites instead of whole eggs to coat the buckwheat.

compatible foods and flavors

■ Savory: fresh and dried mushrooms, bacon, sausage, chicken, browned or caramelized onions, butter, sour cream, cottage cheese, salmon, roasted cashew nuts, dill, thyme

■ Sweet: dried apples

basic buckwheat grits and cream of buckwheat

You can buy buckwheat in various granulations, all of which develop a porridge-like consistency. Use the proportions and directions for Basic Whole Buckwheat (opposite). Cooking time is 8 to 11 minutes for coarse granulation, 7 to 10 for medium granulation, and 5 to 6 for fine granulation (cream of buckwheat). Let stand off the heat for 5 minutes.

KEEPING AND REHEATING: Refrigerate for up to 5 days in a tightly sealed container. Reheat in a lightly covered bowl in the microwave or in a heavy saucepan over low heat, stirring occasionally and adding a little water if needed. Does not freeze well.

the corn family

Is there anything as good as fresh corn, lightly steamed, eaten with melted butter and a sprinkle of salt? The answer is a resounding yes! Corn is the only grain eaten both fresh and dried, and the dried versions are every bit as memorable as the fresh—though about as different as you can imagine. Fresh corn is sweet corn, one of five varieties available today. The other four are popcorn, field, flint, and flour.

Each type of corn has a different use, depending upon its structure and composition. For example, although any corn kernel will pop, the variety classified as popcorn has the highest moisture content and therefore pops the best. Field corn, also called dent corn (because a little pocket of waxy starch at one end causes an indentation when the kernels are dried), is preferred by Southerners for hominy and grits, while ground flint corn has been favored by Northerners for making johnny-cakes. To some degree, regional preferences have been dictated by local growing conditions rather than a gourmet selection process. For example, Northerners could just as easily use flour corn for their johnnycakes, but the flint variety grows better in the climate and soil of New England.

The flavor and nutritional properties of corn vary according to type and processing. According to food historian Betty Fussell, author of *The Story of Corn*,

> *Varietal flavor depends on texture (hard, soft, chalky, flaky, crisp, moist), aroma (fruity, earthy, herby) and the relative proportion of starch to sugar to oil in the kernel. Color is not a major factor of taste, though it gives clues about the nutritional content. For example, yellow corns contain carotene (vitamin A) and white corns do not. Both types are rich in vitamins B and C and potassium.*

The protein in most varieties of corn lacks two essential amino acids: lysine and tryptophan. However, when corn is combined with beans, dairy, or meat, those missing amino acids are supplied. It's fascinating to think that some intuitive understanding made corn and beans companions in so many parts of the world.

We have the Native Americans of both North and South America to thank for the imaginative and delicious ways they found to process and store corn. Whoever first thought of boiling the large ripe kernels with an alkali (such as lye from wood ash or lime) to release the tough hulls was a genius. The whole hulled kernels are called hominy. When the hominy is cut into small bits, it is called grits. On the downside, when the hull is removed, the oil-rich germ goes along with it. But the loss of the volatile oils in the germ makes hominy a very good keeper at room temperature.

Fortunately there are numerous corn products that have not been degerminated, but you must inquire or check the labels carefully. Speckled grits and whole-grain, stone-ground cornmeal are extremely perishable because the oil-rich germ is intact. A major treat is blue cornmeal, a delicious blue-gray flour ground from a special variety of corn grown by Native Americans of the Southwest.

For optimum taste and nutrition, mail-order freshly stone-ground cornmeal and grits, and refrigerate or freeze them immediately. Use these corn products as soon as possible, and you will be rewarded with memorable taste. Alternatively, purchase whole-grain stone-ground grits or cornmeal in sealed packages from a health food store; look for the furthest-out expiration date.

You'll find delicious recipes for many forms of corn in this book. Even though I'm a Yankee, I'm very proud of my Spoonbread (page 210), Cornmeal Biscuits with Sage Butter (page 276), Corn Bread (page 274), Blue Cornmeal Pancakes (page 240), and Corn Muffins (page 275). For main dishes, try the hearty Posole (page 188), Popcorn-Crusted Catfish (page 174), Corn Grits with Collard Greens and Andouille (page 170), and the Masa Harina–Beef Casserole (page 194).

CORN AT A GLANCE

FORM	DESCRIPTION/PROCESSING	AVAILABILITY	COMMENTS
CORN ON THE COB	Fresh unshucked sweet corn; see basic recipe on page 37	Everywhere in season; otherwise frozen	Lamentably many of the heirloom, nonhybridized varieties have all but disappeared; gardeners can obtain seeds from Seed Savers Exchange or Native Seeds
DRIED SWEET CORN	Air-dried immature sweet corn traditionally eaten in Pennsylvania Dutch country	Mail-order, health food stores	The heritage John Cope's brand is still available; Sensible Foods' salted organic variety is more widely distributed
PARCHED CORN	Dried, toasted yellow, blue, and red kernels	Mail-order	Eaten as a snack by Native Americans of New Mexico
CHICOS (chicos hornos)	Oven-roasted immature sweet corn kernels	Mail-order	Popular in the Southwest; intensely sweet, sometimes have a faint smoky flavor; soak overnight before adding to soups or stews; traditionally cooked with beans
HOMINY (posole)	Dried flint, dent, or flour-type corn cooked with an alkali to separate the tough hulls; see basic recipe on page 36	Mail-order, some supermarkets	Posole is the Spanish name for hominy and also the name of a slow-cooked stew containing hominy and meat; available in red, white, and blue varieties
HOMINY GRITS	Whole hominy cut into bits	Supermarkets, mail-order	Degerminated

FORM	DESCRIPTION/PROCESSING	AVAILABILITY	COMMENTS
MASA HARINA	Flour ground from the dried dough used for making corn tortillas	Mail-order, health food stores, some supermarkets	Has a robust corn taste; highly recommended for use in pancakes and as a thickener; stays fresh longer than whole-grain cornmeal; yellow, blue, and red corn masas available
CORN GRITS	Dried yellow and white corn kernels cut into bits	Mail-order, health food stores	Available in various grades from coarse to fairly fine; opt for stone-ground that contains the germ; refrigerate or freeze and use as soon as possible
SPECKLED-HEART CORN GRITS/MEAL	Ground from whole kernels, including tiny black dots of germ tip	Mail-order	Available in yellow and white varieties
QUICK CORN GRITS	Dried corn kernels ground into small particles for quicker cooking	Mail-order	Best are stone-ground from the whole grain
INSTANT CORN GRITS	Degerminated hominy ground into fine particles for quick cooking	Supermarkets	Don't have much taste or texture
CORNMEAL (also called corn flour)	Flour ground from dried white, yellow, or blue corn	Mail-order, health food stores	Opt for whole-grain, stone-milled
TOASTED CORNMEAL (also called atole)	Toasted blue corn, very finely ground	Mail-order	A specialty of Native Americans of the Southwest; can be made into a drink or a cooked cereal
POLENTA	Cornmeal ground medium-fine	Gourmet shops, mail-order	Imported cornmeal which costs more and may not be as fresh as stone-ground American cornmeal
POPCORN	Dried corn kernels hybridized for a high moisture content, hard endosperm, and tough hull; when heat is applied, internal steam pressure builds and forces the hull to burst	Health food stores, supermarkets	Avoid batches with broken kernels; makes a terrific garnish for Southwest soups and stews
PUFFED CORN	Moistened kernels that have puffed up after being placed under pressure that is suddenly released	Health food stores	Available without sugar for use as a breakfast cereal; also can be used to garnish soups and stews

basic corn grits

T hose who grew up on traditionally prepared grits don't consider them cooked unless they've simmered in the top of a double boiler for at least an hour—until they are meltingly soft and every last molecule of flavor has been coaxed out of them. I'm presenting an unconventional method that doesn't require a double boiler, but does take as much time. You must use a heavy-bottomed pot—like a Le Creuset Dutch oven—or the grits will stick like crazy.

This method works with yellow or white corn grits. Use the lower amount of salt if serving the grits for breakfast.

CUPS DRY	CUPS WATER	TEASPOONS SALT	POT SIZE	APPROXIMATE CUP YIELD
1	4½	¼ to ½	3-quart	4
1½	6	½ to ¾	3-quart	6

Bring the water and salt to a boil in a heavy Dutch oven or saucepan. Whisk in the grits and return to a boil. Cover, lower the heat, and simmer, stirring occasionally to prevent the grains from sticking to the bottom of the pot. Continue cooking until the grits swell and are tender, and the mixture is creamy and thick, 50 to 60 minutes. Stir in more water, if needed, to prevent the mixture from becoming too dry before the grits are thoroughly cooked.

KEEPING AND REHEATING: Refrigerate for up to 5 days in a tightly sealed container. Reheat, lightly covered, in the microwave. Alternatively, heat in a heavy covered saucepan over low heat, adding a little water if needed. Do not freeze well.

cook's notes

- Soaking the grits overnight does not reduce the cooking time.

- For richer grits, use half water and half milk, and stir in butter after cooking.

- After cooking, stir in ½ to 1 cup grated Cheddar cheese.

compatible foods and flavors

- Chile peppers, bell peppers, ham and pork, tomatoes, cumin, corn, beans

basic hominy

Eating home-cooked hominy is a major treat. It takes many hours to prepare, but there's no labor involved. Use this recipe for white, red, or blue hominy. I don't advise cooking them together since the blue and red varieties often need more cooking time than the white. Since hominy takes so long to cook, it makes sense to prepare a big batch and freeze the extra.

CUPS DRY	CUPS WATER	SALT	POT SIZE	APPROXIMATE CUP YIELD
1	8 (2 quarts)	Add to taste toward the end of cooking	3-quart	2¼
1½	10 (2½ quarts)	Add to taste toward the end of cooking	4-quart	3½
2½	16 (4 quarts)	Add to taste toward the end of cooking	5-quart	6

Place the hominy in a pot and cover with the water. Soak overnight.

Bring to a boil. Reduce the heat, cover, and simmer until the hominy is puffy and tender, 1 to 3 hours. Although cooked hominy remains slightly chewy, the internal texture should be creamy, without any hint of mealiness. A visual check for doneness is to cut a kernel in half crosswise: It should be one color throughout.

When done, cover the pot and let the hominy rest in the cooking liquid until needed, up to 4 hours. Reheat, if necessary. Drain. (Save the liquid for making soup or stew or for reheating, if you wish.) Always eat hominy hot or it will taste stodgy.

PRESSURE-COOKED: See page 112.

KEEPING AND REHEATING: See The Grain Bank, page 10.

cook's notes

■ Hominy cooks most evenly when first soaked overnight. I tried quick-soaking it in hot water for 2 hours, but the grains cooked unevenly.

- You can add salt once the grains look puffy. Adding it sooner can retard cooking.

- Adding a halved onion and a few cloves of garlic to the cooking liquid gives flavor to the hominy and provides a bonus broth for your next soup.

compatible foods and flavors

- Chile peppers, bell peppers, ham and pork, tomatoes, cumin, corn, beans

basic sweet corn on the cob

The best and most convenient way I have found to cook fresh corn is to steam it in the microwave, leaving the husk and silk completely intact. Set the corn directly on the carousel. Cook at high power for 2 minutes (1 cob) or 5 minutes (2 cobs). Let rest in the microwave for 5 minutes. Peel back the husks and silks and serve hot, with butter and salt, if desired.

basic soft polenta

Many people around the world eat cornmeal porridge. The Romanians love their *mamaliga* and the Kenyans their *ugali,* and of course, the Italians their polenta.

Americans have never really gotten into cornmeal porridge in a big way and I think most of the problem is that we call it *mush.* The trouble with the word mush is that it just doesn't sound as if the cook put any love into it. Polenta is corn mush that sounds delicious, so it tastes better. Let's call it polenta.

This method works with both coarse stone-ground cornmeal and imported polenta. Stirring the cornmeal into cold water and then adding the mixture to boiling water prevents lumping and makes the whole process simple and foolproof. Try the oven-baked method if you don't want to do a lot of stirring.

CUPS DRY	CUPS WATER	TEASPOONS SALT (OPTIONAL)	POT SIZE	APPROXIMATE CUP YIELD
1	4 (1 quart)	½ to 1	3-quart	4 cups
2	8 (2 quarts)	1½ to 2	3-quart	8 cups

In a large glass measuring cup, stir the cornmeal into two times its volume of cold water until smooth. Bring the remaining water and the salt to a rolling boil in a heavy Dutch oven or saucepan. (For example, if you're using 1 cup of dry cornmeal, stir it into 2 cups of water. Meanwhile, bring the remaining 2 cups of water to a boil.) Gradually stir the cornmeal mixture into the boiling water. Cook uncovered, adjusting the heat so that the mixture simmers with big bubbles puffing up here and there on the surface.

As the mixture thickens, stir frequently, taking care to scrape up grains sticking to the bottom and sides of the pot. It will thicken fairly quickly and appear to be done, but it needs longer simmering for the cornmeal to be thoroughly cooked and lose its grittiness. The polenta will be done when it becomes thick and creamy, and the bits of cornmeal swell and become translucent, 20 to 30 minutes total cooking time, depending upon how fine or coarse the cornmeal. Stir in more water, about ½ cup at a time, if the polenta becomes very thick before the cornmeal tastes cooked. Serve hot.

OVEN-BAKED: Once the cornmeal mixture is stirred into the boiling water, transfer the mixture to a shallow buttered baking dish. Bake uncovered in the upper third of an oven preheated to 350°F for 40 minutes. Stir in grated cheese to taste, if desired, and continue cooking until creamy and thick, about 10 minutes more. Let stand for 5 minutes before serving.

KEEPING AND REHEATING: Refrigerate for up to 6 days in a tightly sealed container. Reheat, lightly covered, in the microwave. Alternatively, cut into squares and bake or fry in a little butter or oil. Does not freeze well.

cook's notes

■ For a richer polenta, substitute one quarter milk for the equivalent amount of water.

■ In parts of Northern Italy, a small amount of buckwheat meal is mixed with the cornmeal. Use about one quarter untoasted buckwheat (fine granulation) or mail-order imported Polenta Taragna.

■ When the polenta is done, stir in butter or olive oil plus grated Parmesan or Romano (or a mixture) to taste.

■ For crostini: While still hot, pour the polenta into a baking pan and smooth off the top. It will stiffen and set up as it cools. Cut the polenta into squares. Fry or bake the squares until crisp.

compatible foods and flavors

■ Braised meats, tomatoes, cheese (Parmesan, Romano, Gorgonzola), butter, olive oil, black pepper

basic popcorn

It's easy, fun, and economical to make popcorn at home. Here is a fast and foolproof way to do the job in the microwave. You must coat the kernels with little bit of oil before popping, or they will burn.

Some microwave manufacturers advise against popping corn in the microwave. If in doubt, call your microwave's customer service department and inquire, particularly if you have an older model or one that does not have a rotating carousel.

MAKES 5 TO 6 CUPS POPPED CORN

¼ cup popcorn kernels
1 tablespoon olive or other vegetable oil
Olive oil spray
Salt

In a small bowl, combine the popcorn and oil. Stir to coat the kernels thoroughly. Empty the mixture into a brown paper sandwich bag (6 by 10 inches). Fold the top over twice to seal.

Cover the microwave carousel with a paper towel to absorb oil. Lay the bag on its side on the paper towel. Use the popcorn setting or microwave on high until the popping subsides, usually about 2 minutes (Pay close attention as timing will vary from one microwave to another.) Once the popping subsides, immediately press stop. Let the bag sit in the microwave for 1 minute. Unfold the bag carefully in case there is any residual steam.

Transfer to a large bowl and mist with olive oil spray. Sprinkle on salt to taste.

KEEPING: Cool completely. Store in an airtight container in a cool place (but not the refrigerator) for up to 5 days.

cheesy popcorn

After spraying on olive oil, toss the popcorn with ¼ to ⅓ cup grated Parmesan or Romano cheese.

cajun popcorn

After spraying on olive oil, toss the popcorn with a mixture of 1 teaspoon chili powder, ½ teaspoon paprika, and ⅛ teaspoon ground cumin.

cinnamon spice buttered popcorn

Omit the salt. Melt 2 to 3 tablespoons butter. Blend in 1 tablespoon honey, ½ teaspoon ground cinnamon, ¼ teaspoon ground nutmeg, and ¼ teaspoon ground allspice. Drizzle over the popped corn and toss to coat.

cook's notes

■ To flavor popcorn with salt or spices, a good low-fat way to make the seasonings stick is to spray the popped kernels with olive oil. Rather than use an aerosol pan spray, you can use a little pump made by Cuisipro designed specifically to do this. Once the popcorn is sprayed with a thin mist of oil, sprinkle on salt, spices, or grated cheese to taste.

■ Store unpopped corn kernels in the refrigerator to maintain moisture. If they dry out, they won't pop since it's the expansion of moisture in the form of steam that forces the kernels to pop.

■ I tried seasoning the popcorn before popping by stirring salt and spices into the initial tablespoon of oil, but the salt and flavorings didn't stick.

■ Avoid the temptation to purchase different colored popcorns at a premium price. Once popped, all of the kernels look the same.

job's tears

I fell in love with Job's tears when I was writing my first vegan cookbook, *Recipes from an Ecological Kitchen*, during the early 1990s. At that time, organic Job's tears were available in any well-stocked health food store. Then they seemed to disappear, and the only ones I could find were in Asian groceries and were of inferior quality.

When I started collecting grains for this book, I remembered Job's tears and was delighted to discover that I could mail-order organically grown grains. Chewy and creamy, with a mild corn taste reminiscent of hominy, they were every bit as good as I remembered. Use Job's tears as you would hominy or barley, adding the grains to soups and stews whose flavors match that of corn.

Job's tears are a good source of protein, potassium, and magnesium. They are much prized by the Japanese, who call them *hato mugi,* which translates as "beauty pearls," referring to their reputation for clearing the complexion and to their puffy, irregular, cartoonish teardrop shape. The Japanese also make a vinegar from the grain.

Much of the Job's tears sold in the United States is grown in Thailand and cleaned for export in Japan. In Asian groceries the packages are mistakenly labeled wild barley or pearled barley, although Job's tears are not botanically related to the barley we know and love. Barley and Job's tears don't look alike, but both offer a silken richness to soups and stews.

JOB'S TEARS AT A GLANCE

FORM	DESCRIPTION/PROCESSING	AVAILABILITY	COMMENTS
JOB'S TEARS (also called *hato mugi* and *Juno's tears*)	An ivory, roundish, teardrop-shaped grain with a distinct dark crease down the center of one side; most imported Job's tears have been pearled	Mail-order; some health food stores and Asian markets	Look for batches that have few dark or discolored grains
BROWN-SKINNED JOB'S TEARS (*yuuki hato mugi*)	As above, but less refined, with some bran intact	Mail-order	More fiber and stronger flavor than refined Job's tears
ROLLED JOB'S TEARS (*oshi mugi*)	Rolled and pressed into flakes for quicker cooking	Asian markets	Taste resembles rolled oats, but slightly chewier; holds shape well; use instead of pasta in cold salads or soups

basic job's tears

Use this recipe for both pearled *(hato mugi)* and brown-skinned *(yuuki hato mugi)* Job's tears. Soaking the grains overnight reduces cooking time and creates a creamier texture, but is optional.

CUPS DRY	CUPS WATER	TEASPOONS SALT	POT SIZE	APPROXIMATE CUP YIELD
1	2	Pinch	2-quart	2½
1½	3	Pinch	2-quart	3¾
2	4	¼	2-quart	5

Sort through the grains and discard any that look grayish or have deeply tan areas. (These usually have an off-taste.) Rinse well by swishing in several bowls full of water until the water remains clear. If time permits, soak overnight in ample fresh water to cover. Drain.

Bring the water to a boil in a heavy Dutch oven or saucepan. Add the Job's tears. Cover, reduce the heat, and simmer 20 to 40 minutes for grains that have been soaked or 45 to 60 minutes for unsoaked grains, until the grains are pleasantly chewy, the internal texture is creamy (rather than mealy), and the grain is one color throughout when cut in half crosswise. If all of the water has been absorbed before the grain is tender, add more hot water as needed.

When the grains are tender, turn off the heat and let sit for 10 minutes. Drain off any excess water.

OVEN-BAKED: Once you've added the Job's tears, set the covered pot in the middle of an oven preheated to 350°F.

PRESSURE-COOKED: See page 112.

KEEPING AND REHEATING: See The Grain Bank, page 10.

cook's notes

■ Pretoasting is not advised; it causes the grains to absorb water unevenly.

■ Job's tears are best when freshly cooked. They harden after overnight refrigeration; reheat them in a microwave, lightly covered with a paper towel or waxed paper.

■ Using the recipe for basic short-grain brown rice (page 66), try cooking a mixture of one quarter pearled Job's tears and three quarters brown rice. Once the water has come to a boil, add the Job's tears and simmer covered for 12 minutes. Stir in the brown rice and continue cooking as for brown rice.

compatible foods and flavors

■ Chipotle, bell peppers, parsley, cilantro, and other ingredients that are compatible with corn

■ ■ ■

basic rolled job's tears (*oshi mugi*)

Stir in some butter, salt, and pepper to taste for a good, quick side dish.

CUPS DRY	CUPS WATER	TEASPOONS SALT	POT SIZE	APPROXIMATE CUP YIELD
½	1	Pinch	2-quart	1¼
1	2	Pinch	2-quart	2½
1½	3	⅛	3-quart	4

Bring the water and salt to a boil in a heavy Dutch oven or saucepan. Stir in the rolled Job's tears. Cover, reduce the heat, and simmer until tender, 8 to 10 minutes. Drain off any unabsorbed liquid.

KEEPING AND REHEATING: Refrigerate in an airtight container for up to 5 days. Reheat in the microwave or in a covered saucepan, adding a little water if needed. Does not freeze well.

millet

Millet is one of the thirstiest grains I know, and if it's not given all the water it requires, it ends up tasting dry and mealy. So, despite the fact that it is extremely nutritious, quick cooking, easily digested, and quite inexpensive, millet suffers from a serious image problem and most people consider it "for the birds."

Millet is a good source of protein, B vitamins, iron, phosphorus, manganese, and copper. It is a staple food in many parts of Africa, where it is primarily made into a thick porridge—and it certainly makes a pleasant hot breakfast cereal. But there are many other ways to prepare it.

I describe three techniques in the next few pages. One results in a fluffy grain that is a fine stand-in for couscous. Another creates a sticky grain that can be seasoned and molded into croquettes, stuffed into peppers, or incorporated into layered casseroles. And the third is a porridge that can be served sweet for breakfast and dessert or savory as a side dish for dinner.

Millet's flavor is mild, making it a good backdrop for exciting seasonings and textures, as in Millet with Gingered Beets and Orange (page 218) or Millet Pie with Spinach and Feta (page 193). It makes a memorable alternative to mashed potatoes when blended with buttermilk and chives (page 226). And puffed millet can be coated with chocolate and transformed into a crunchy confection that kids will love (page 287).

Cathy Roberts, a dear friend who tests every recipe I create before it gets published, reported to me that her husband, Neil, loves millet. When I asked why, Neil reported, "It has a pleasant but not dominating flavor. It is firm but not tough. It looks good. In summation, it has many of the things I like about white rice but apparently lacks the sins that have driven white rice from my dinner table." Amen.

MILLET AT A GLANCE

FORM	DESCRIPTION/PROCESSING	AVAILABILITY	COMMENTS
HULLED	Small, round, straw-yellow beads; outer inedible hull removed	Health food stores, some supermarkets	Prone to rancidity; buy in sealed packages and check expiration dates
KIBBI	Golden beads about same size as hulled	Mail-order	A sweet glutinous variety imported from Japan; worth seeking out for its creamy texture and faint corn flavor
GRITS/MEAL	Whole grain ground into bits or to a coarse flour	Some health food stores, mail-order	To ensure freshness, use a spice grinder to make your own as needed; see Grits with Cranberries, Toasted Almonds, and Orange Zest, page 248; good for making a breakfast porridge or polenta
FLOUR	Whole grain ground to a fine flour	Some health food stores, mail-order	Mild taste. Best to grind your own and use immediately.
PUFFED	Moistened kernels that have puffed up after being placed under pressure that is suddenly released	Cereal section of some health food stores	Mild corn flavor, pleasantly crunchy. A good breakfast cereal and garnish for soups and salads; available salt- and sugar-free; add some to pancake batter; see Millet-Chocolate Crunch, page 287.

basic hulled millet

Here is a foolproof technique for making moist, fluffy millet from the hulled whole grain. Millet will surprise you by bursting open like flower buds on a very sunny day. The humble little seed drinks up every drop of liquid and quadruples in size, transforming into bouncy fluff. Toasting enhances the flavor of this mild grain, and the texture improves when it is cooked with a little butter.

CUPS DRY	CUPS WATER	TEASPOONS SALT	TABLESPOONS BUTTER OR OIL	POT SIZE	APPROXIMATE CUP YIELD
1	2¼	¼	½	2-quart	4
1½	3½	½	1	3-quart	6

Inspect the millet and remove any black (unhulled) or broken grains. Swish the millet in several changes of water until the water remains fairly clear.

Bring ample water to a boil in a kettle so that you will have enough ready to add after toasting the grains.

Set a heavy Dutch oven or saucepan over medium heat. Add the millet and stir frequently until it dries out, begins popping, turns slightly golden, and emits a rich toasted aroma, 4 to 6 minutes. If the millet threatens to burn, immediately transfer it to a bowl and let the pot cool a bit before putting the millet back into it.

When the millet is toasted, turn off the heat. Stand back and stir in the suggested amount of boiling water gradually to avoid boil-overs. Stir in the salt and butter. Cover and simmer over low heat until most or all of the water has been absorbed, usually 13 to 18 minutes. Turn off the heat and let stand for 10 minutes or until ready to serve. If the millet tastes dry or gritty, stir in a few tablespoons of hot water and continue steaming off the heat for another few minutes. Fluff up before serving. Serve immediately.

If you can't serve the cooked millet piping hot, straight out of the pot, stir in a little more butter or oil to help retain moisture and separation of grains. Keep it covered to prevent drying out. If necessary, reheat it in the microwave before serving.

OVEN-BAKED: Follow directions above, but instead of simmering, bake on the center rack in an oven preheated to 350°F until the water is absorbed, 15 to 18 minutes. Remove from the oven and let stand for 10 minutes. Fluff up before serving.

KEEPING AND REHEATING: See The Grain Bank, page 10.

cook's notes

■ The majority of millet available in the U.S. is proso millet, imported from China. I have been told that the foxtail millet grown in Canada is tastier, but I have not been able to locate any.

■ Perhaps because of poor turnover or improper storage conditions, a particular batch of millet may be bitter or rancid. When buying millet from bins, sniff to make sure it has either no aroma or a slightly sweet one. If buying from packages, check the expiration date. In either case, refrigerate or freeze the grain as soon as you get home. If you cook a batch that turns out to be bitter, set it in a strainer or steaming basket and steam covered over hot water for 5 to 10 minutes. All or most of the bitterness will disappear.

■ For added flavor, it's nice to cook millet in broth instead of water. However, adding more than a modest amount of salt accentuates any bitterness, so use the low-sodium variety.

■ Millet tends to cook unevenly, with some grains very soft and others slightly crunchy. Many people enjoy this textural variation.

■ Millet dries out as it cools, so don't ever plan to serve it in a room-temperature salad.

compatible foods and flavors

■ Savory: butter and oil, eggs, fresh herbs (especially thyme), mushrooms, browned onions, sour cream, crème fraîche, buttermilk, black pepper, chives and scallions, feta cheese

■ Sweet: squash, carrots, beets, honey, sweet spices such as cinnamon, anise seeds, and nutmeg

basic sticky millet

Use this method for making millet that you'd like to shape into croquettes or press into a pan for a savory grain layer. Do not toast the grains. Refer to the chart on page 48, but increase the water to $2\frac{3}{4}$ cups for 1 cup of dry millet and 4 cups for $1\frac{1}{2}$ cups dry millet. Bring the water, salt, and millet to a boil together. Reduce the heat, cover, simmer, and continue as directed.

KEEPING AND REHEATING: Refrigerate in a well-sealed container for up to 5 days. Reheat in the microwave or in a heavy saucepan over low heat, stirring occasionally. Stir in a little water if needed. Does not freeze well.

basic kibbi millet

Do not toast the grains. Refer to the chart on page 48. Bring the water, salt, and millet to a boil together. Reduce the heat, cover, and simmer until the water is almost absorbed, 13 to 15 minutes. Turn off the heat. Stir a few times to release the grains sticking to the bottom of the pot. Cover and let sit undisturbed for 10 minutes.

KEEPING AND REHEATING: Refrigerate in a well-sealed container for up to 5 days. Reheat in the microwave or in a heavy saucepan over low heat, stirring occasionally. Stir in a little water if needed. Does not freeze well.

basic creamy millet grits/meal

Millet prepared in a generous quantity of water becomes porridgy and develops a beautiful sheen. If the grits aren't too fine, the mixture will remain nubbly and toothsome, good for a wholesome hot breakfast cereal or a polenta-like base for chilis and other savory stews.

You can either purchase grits or make your own by grinding whole millet into a coarse meal, ½ cup at a time, in a spice grinder.

CUPS DRY	CUPS WATER	TEASPOONS SALT	TABLESPOONS BUTTER	POT SIZE	APPROXIMATE CUP YIELD
½	2½	¼	1 to 2	2-quart	2½ cups
1	5	½	2 to 3	2-quart	5 cups

Do not rinse the grits. Toast them, if you wish, according to instructions for Basic Hulled Millet (page 48).

Bring the water and salt to a boil in a heavy Dutch oven or saucepan. Gradually whisk in the millet and return to a boil. Cover, lower the heat, and simmer, stirring occasionally, until the grits are tender, 15 to 30 minutes, depending upon the size of the grits. If the mixture is thin, boil it uncovered over medium heat, stirring frequently, until it reaches the desired consistency. Stir in the butter and more salt, if needed. Serve hot.

KEEPING AND REHEATING: Refrigerate in a well-sealed container for up to 5 days. Reheat in the microwave or in a heavy saucepan over low heat, stirring occasionally. Stir in a little water if needed. Does not freeze well.

cook's notes

■ For a breakfast porridge, cook in part milk and part water. Toss in some raisins or other dried fruit, and add sweet spices such as cinnamon and nutmeg.

■ For a savory polenta, cook in part broth and part water. After cooking, stir in olives, rosemary, and Parmesan or Romano.

oats

Because of the popularity of oatmeal, oats are arguably the best-known and most commonly eaten whole grain in the American diet. That's good news, because oats are higher in protein than whole wheat, and contain B vitamins. Plus, oats are unique among the commonly eaten whole grains because they have substantial amounts of both soluble and insoluble fiber. Oats' soluble fiber helps lower blood cholesterol levels, and their insoluble fiber helps promote digestive regularity.

Although it's likely that most Americans never get beyond oatmeal and oatmeal cookies, with their mild flavor, delicate sweetness, and pleasing texture, oats can easily play a much larger role in everyday meals. When cooked, they are equally chewy and creamy, a felicitous combination. The bran layer is so soft that it calls no attention to itself, making oats a welcome component of dessert puddings as well as savory dishes. All forms of oats—from whole to rolled to flour—are considered whole grain, which means that they contain the same proportion of bran, germ, and endosperm as the oat kernel.

The soluble fiber in oats that has been shown to lower blood cholesterol is the very ingredient that gives body, smooth texture, and a beautiful sheen to soups, as in Oat and Turkey Soup with Tex-Mex Flavors (page 126). In pilafs, oats add a chewy heartiness that is at home with sweet vegetables such as carrots and beets (pages 206 and 219). Lovers of oatmeal owe it to themselves to try 5-Minute Steel-Cut Oats with Gingered Fruit Compote (page 247), which makes a superb breakfast porridge. In the dessert category, rolled oats are ideal for crisp toppings, chewy bottom crusts, and superlative cookies, and oat flour creates delightful scones (page 272) and light muffins (page 265).

Wheat and Oat Scones
with Cranberries (p. 272)

Farro Salad with Prosciutto and
Asparagus (p. 134)

Shrimp, Corn, and Quinoa Soup (p. 119)

Thai Chicken Soup with
Chinese Black Rice (p. 127)

Wheat Berry Salad with Apples and Mint (p. 139)

Hominy with Shredded Chicken
and Peppers (p. 176)

Millet with Gingered Beets and Orange (p. 218)

spelt kernels

forbidden black rice

brown basmati rice

wheat berries (winter)

Thai sticky black rice

Wehani rice

cracked wheat

farro

Colusari red rice

puffed corn

popcorn

Kamut kernels

green spelt kernels

short-grain brown rice

fine white corn grits

medium-grain sweet brown rice

puffed Kamut

blue cornmeal

red hominy

wheat berries (summer)

long-grain brown rice

masa harina

yellow corn grits

blue hominy

white hominy

bulgur (medium grind)

red and black quinoa

rye berries

sorghum

amaranth

triticale kernels

rolled oats

ivory quinoa

Job's tears

black (purple) barley

golden waxy barley

untoasted buckwheat groats

steel-cut oats

toasted buckwheat groats

brown teff

wild rice

millet

oat groats

pearl barley

Wild and Brown Rice with Sesame-Soy Glazed Salmon (p. 162)

Masa Harina–Beef Casserole (p. 194)

Kamut, Broccoli Rabe, and Sausage Medley (p. 175)

Quinoa and Chili-Scented Pork Chops
with Roasted Red Pepper
Dressing (p. 156)

Teff Waffles with Caramelized
Bananas (p. 244)

Cornmeal Biscuits with Sage Butter and Prosciutto (p. 276)

Pumpkin Pie with Pumpkin Seed Crust (p. 294)

OATS AT A GLANCE

FORM	DESCRIPTION/PROCESSING	AVAILABILITY	COMMENTS
WHOLE OATS (also called oat groats)	A slender, tan grain with a distinct crease down the middle; inedible outer hulls removed; steamed and roasted to prevent rancidity	Health food stores	Take about 45 minutes to cook and have the chewiest texture
STEEL-CUT OATS (also called Irish, pinhead, or Scotch oats)	Whole groats cut into bits with steel blades	Health food stores, some supermarkets	Take about 30 minutes to cook and have a chewy, wholesome texture; for quick cooking, soak overnight (see page 247)
ROLLED OATS (also called old-fashioned oatmeal)	Flakes made from whole groats that are put through a roller to flatten the kernel	Readily available	Take about 5 minutes to cook. The type used for oatmeal, oatmeal cookies, and dessert toppings; see Oatmeal for Connoisseurs (page 246).
QUICK OATS	Small, thin flakes made from steel-cut oats that are rolled thinner than old-fashioned	Supermarkets	Take about 1 minute to cook. Have a milder taste and less hearty texture than rolled.
OAT FLOUR	Finely ground from whole groats	Health food stores	Easy to make at home by grinding rolled oats in a spice grinder

basic whole oats

It's a treat to eat whole oats. They taste "oatier" than any other form of the grain. Cooking oats in lots of salted water (like pasta) followed by a brief steaming over boiling water results in plump, separate, tasty grains that keep their shape and are not sticky.

CUPS DRY	CUPS WATER	TEASPOONS SALT	POT SIZE	YIELD IN CUPS
1	10 (2½ quarts)	¾	4-quart	3
1½	14 (3½ quarts)	1	5-quart	4½
2	18 (4½ quarts)	1½	6-quart	6

In a large pot, bring the water and salt to a rapid boil. Add the oats and lower the heat slightly to prevent boil-overs. Boil uncovered until the oats are tender, 25 to 35 minutes. To determine doneness, cut an oat groat in half. If it is one color throughout (i.e. there is no opaque center), it is done. Drain the oats through a strainer that will sit comfortably on the pot.

Pour 2 cups of fresh water into the empty pot and bring to a boil. Set the strainer containing the oats over the boiling water. Set a piece of paper towel on top of the oats. Place the pot lid on top of the strainer. Boil for 7 minutes. Use immediately or cool to room temperature and store as directed in The Grain Bank (page 10).

PRESSURE-COOKED: See page 112.

KEEPING AND REHEATING: See The Grain Bank, page 10.

cook's notes

■ Overnight soaking reduces cooking time but softens the bran. The softened bran causes the grains to burst open during cooking. Therefore, overnight soaking is not recommended.

■ Toasting oats before cooking reduces the cooking time somewhat but cracks the delicate bran layer and results in burst-open grains. I have not experienced increased flavor in toasted whole oats and do not see any reason for toasting.

■ Adding salt to the cooking water hardens the delicate bran layer just enough to keep it intact, preventing most of the grains from bursting open.

■ The final steaming washes starch from the surface and plumps the grains, resulting in chewy kernels that do not stick together. The paper towel on top of the oats absorbs any liquid that would otherwise condense on the lid and drip back into the oats.

compatible foods and flavors

■ Savory: thyme, carrots, celery, mushrooms, walnuts

■ Sweet: dried and fresh fruit, cinnamon, sugar, maple syrup

quinoa

Quinoa was called "the mother grain" by the Incas because it was the major protein source of their powerful empire. But I can think of another good reason for giving it this name. Like most mothers, quinoa is great at multitasking.

Pronounced KEEN-wa, this tiny, disc-shaped seed is so versatile that one could easily write a soup-to-nuts cookbook featuring it in every recipe. As if that weren't enough reason to recommend it, quinoa is an excellent source of protein (it contains all of the essential amino acids), cooks in under 15 minutes, and is light and easy to digest. It is one of my favorite grains.

Numerous visionaries have been responsible for quinoa's long journey from the land of the Incas to the American dinner table. Among them are the late Dave Cusick, a botanist dedicated to making protein-rich foods available to impoverished peoples everywhere; Ernie New, who continues to experiment with growing quinoa on his Colorado heirloom potato farm; and Marjorie and Bob Leventry, a retired couple who were introduced to quinoa during their stint in the Peace Corps in Ecuador and now import organic grains from a farmers' cooperative in Riobamba.

There are over a hundred varieties of quinoa grown in the Andes, and any given batch is likely to contain dozens of types. In more general terms, though, quinoa can be distinguished by the color of its seed coat: ivory/tan, red, and black. Ivory/tan quinoa is imported primarily from Ecuador and Bolivia, with a small amount grown in Colorado and distributed by the Quinoa Corporation. Red and black quinoas are imported from Bolivia, and a small amount of black quinoa is grown by Ernie New in Colorado.

The taste of quinoa varies considerably from one batch to the next. Good quinoa has a slightly sweet, subtly herbal taste. The depth of flavor has a good deal to do with how the harvested seeds are processed. Quinoa seeds are naturally coated with an insect-repelling coating called saponin. Saponin has a bitter, soapy taste—it's used as detergent in the Andes—and must be removed. Washing is the traditional way to remove the saponin and has the advantage of leaving the flavor- and fiber-rich seed coat intact. However, washing is labor-intensive and expensive, so many producers use an abrasion process to rub off the saponin. Abrasion removes some of the seed coat and germ along with the saponin, resulting in grains with less nutrition, flavor, and fiber.

Judging from the dozens of samples I've tasted, the ivory/tan quinoa processed by rinsing is technically the only quinoa that is truly whole grain. Grown organically by indigenous farmers in Ecuador, this quinoa is a mixture of many varieties and therefore has an appealing, complex flavor. It is also highest in iron, calcium, and fiber. This is the quinoa imported by the Leventrys through their company, Inca Organics.

Red quinoa, imported primarily from Bolivia, is processed by the abrasion method. It is beautiful but quite bland. The black quinoa currently grown by Ernie New in Colorado is actually a mix between black quinoa and a related plant called lamb's quarters. It's variegated in color and full of flavor—though the flavor varies from one harvest to the next. Pure black quinoa, imported from the Andes, has more bran than starch and can taste quite gritty.

Unfortunately, labels do not indicate how the grains have been processed and often don't reveal where they've been grown, but if two brands are available, compare the nutritional information and purchase the one with the higher fiber content.

Keep in mind, however, that any quinoa is better than no quinoa, so don't hesitate to buy whatever brand of this nutritional powerhouse is sold in your local store. Try Amaranth, Quinoa, and Corn Chowder (page 118) for an experience of quinoa's lightness, or Quinoa-Beef Picadillo (page 178) for a sense of how well it marries with tomatoes and lime juice. Quinoa with Summer Squash and Basil (page 220) reveals how quinoa is also delicious with the flavors of the Mediterranean. Perhaps most surprising is the Quinoa Cake with Crystallized Ginger (page 271), which exemplifies the appealing texture of this bouncy, slightly crunchy grain.

QUINOA AT A GLANCE

FORM	DESCRIPTION/PROCESSING	AVAILABILITY	COMMENTS
IVORY/TAN QUINOA	Tiny, pale ivory to tan beadlike seeds, slightly larger and rounder than sesame seeds; saponin coating must be removed	Health food stores and some supermarkets	Considerable range in flavor, depending upon source
RED QUINOA	As above, but with reddish-brown seed coat	Health food stores and some supermarkets	Generally less flavor than the best ivory/tan varieties; best cooked with ivory/tan quinoa in small amounts for dots of color
BLACK QUINOA	Generally smaller than ivory seeds, with dark mahogany-colored seed coat	Mail-order	Some batches remain gritty; best cooked with ivory/tan quinoa in small amounts for color and texture
QUINOA FLAKES	Steamed and roller-pressed; the size of small snowflakes	Health food stores, mail-order	Used for breakfast cereal; mild, faintly vegetal taste; soften almost immediately in liquid
QUINOA FLOUR	Ground from ivory seeds, light in color and texture	Health food stores, mail-order	For best texture, use in combination with whole-wheat flour; slightly herbal taste, so best to use in savory baked goods; easy to process from seeds in a spice grinder
QUINOA PASTA	Spaghetti and various other shapes	Health food stores, mail-order, some supermarkets	Totally gluten-free products can be soft; pasta texture best when product contains some whole-wheat flour

basic quinoa

Most recipes call for cooking 1 cup of grain in 2 cups of water until the water is absorbed. Since there is no way to know in advance how much water a batch of quinoa will absorb, nor how long it will take for the quinoa to become tender, this approach often results in quinoa that is overcooked and mushy.

After years of trial and error, I have concluded that the only foolproof way to cook quinoa is in an abundance of boiling water—like pasta. Using this approach, the cook is guaranteed perfectly cooked quinoa every time. This method also diminishes quinoa's characteristic grassiness, which some find unappealing.

Use this method for ivory, red, and black quinoas. Although red and black quinoas usually take a few minutes longer to become tender, you'll have good results if you cook 1 or 2 tablespoons along with ivory quinoa for a variety of color and texture.

Nowadays almost all packaged quinoa is thoroughly cleaned and requires little more than a quick rinse.

CUPS DRY	CUPS WATER	SALT	POT SIZE	APPROXIMATE CUP YIELD
1	10 (2½ quarts)	Add to taste after cooking	4-quart	3 1½ (black)
1½	14 (3½ quarts)	Add to taste after cooking	5-quart	4½ 2¼ (black)
2	16 (4 quarts)	Add to taste after cooking	5- or 6-quart	6 3 (black)

Pour the water into a large pot and bring to a boil over high heat.

Meanwhile, rinse the quinoa: Pour the grains into a fine-meshed strainer set over a large clear or white bowl and run water over it. Swish the grains around with your hand. Raise the strainer. If the water is clear and there are no bubbles, no more rinsing is needed.

If the water is cloudy or sudsy, fill the bowl with fresh water and repeat until the water remains clear and there are no bubbles on the surface. (Red and black quinoa may bleed color, not to be mistaken for dirt or other impurities.)

When the water is boiling, add the quinoa. Boil uncovered over medium-high heat until there is no white "dot" of starch evident in the center, 11 to 14 minutes. Taste a few grains: ideally, there should still be a little crunch. With most batches, some or all of the germs (little white comma-shaped filaments) will release from the seeds and unfurl; this is a sign that the grains are either done or very close.

Drain well. Let the grains sit in the strainer for 5 minutes. Fluff up and serve hot. Or, if making a salad, spread out the quinoa on a large platter or baking tray to cool.

KEEPING AND REHEATING: Refrigerate for up to 5 days in a tightly sealed container. Quinoa tastes great cold, straight out of the refrigerator. To heat, place in a bowl, cover lightly with a paper towel, and microwave. Alternatively, heat in a heavy saucepan, covered, over low heat. Add a little water if necessary, but take care that the quinoa does not become mushy. Does not freeze well.

cook's notes

■ Unless making porridge, avoid stirring while cooking, which causes stickiness.

■ Toss cooked quinoa with olive oil, fresh herbs, lemon or lime juice, and one or more of the other compatible savory foods listed below. Serve warm or at room temperature.

■ To make porridge, lightly toast the quinoa in a saucepan over medium heat. Add double the amount of water as you have quinoa, and a pinch of salt and allspice, if you wish. Simmer covered until tender, about 12 minutes. Thin with milk or additional water. Uncover and boil gently, stirring frequently, until the quinoa is cooked and the mixture reaches the desired consistency. Sweeten with honey.

compatible foods and flavors

■ Savory: corn, black beans, avocado, olive oil, lemon and lime juice, oregano, chile peppers, cilantro, tomatoes, red bell pepper

■ Sweet: fresh ginger, honey

the rice family

Whole-grain rice is white rice with its bran and germ intact. This is a good thing, because the lion's share of nutrients is located in the germ and bran, which are rich in vitamins, minerals, and fiber. To be more precise, when the kernels are polished and transformed from brown rice into white, the refining process destroys 67 percent of the vitamin B3, 80 percent of the vitamin B1, 90 percent of the vitamin B6, half the phosphorus and manganese, 60 percent of the iron, and all of the dietary fiber and essential fatty acids. Fortunately, because of the growing interest in whole grains, it is now very easy to buy the nutrition-packed "brown" counterparts of all the familiar varieties, such as long-grain white rice and white basmati.

One of the ways rice is categorized is by the length of the grains. Long-grain rices are three to five times longer than they are wide. Medium- and short-grain rices are more oval and pudgy, less than twice as long as they are wide. These categorizations are important to the cook because each type of rice lends itself to different uses and benefits from a specific cooking technique.

All rices (and all grains, for that matter) contain two kinds of starch: amylose (nonsticky starch) and amylopectin (sticky starch). The long-grain varieties have a higher proportion of amylose and therefore cook up light and fluffy. The short- and medium-grain rices have more amylopectin. As the rice cooks, the released starch binds the grains together into a sticky mass. Particularly sticky varieties are labeled glutinous, an odd choice of adjective since all rice is gluten-free.

Some rices are considered aromatic because they give off a nutty or popcorn-like aroma as they cook. Basmati and jasmine are two good examples of aromatic rices. These aromas have no effect upon cooking but usually foretell good flavor.

My attempts to use the traditional pilaf method—coating the rice with oil or butter and cooking it with aromatics—have not brought good results with whole-grain rice. The fat coats the bran layer and retards penetration of the liquid, resulting in uneven cooking. The bran layer also acts as a barrier to the infusion of flavor. Therefore, the cook's best strategy is to prepare the rice as directed in the basic recipe, then toss it with seasonings and other ingredients afterwards. The Brown Rice Pilaf with Walnuts and Dried Cranberries on page 203 is a good example of this approach, and you'll find many others throughout the book.

I love using fragrant brown basmati rice in Asian-inspired dishes like Brown Basmati Rice and Thai Coconut Shrimp (page 182). Chewy short-grain brown rice holds up well in a stir-fry of beef and vegetables (page 168) and in a salad with peanut dressing that makes an unusual accompaniment for flank steak (page 150).

For newcomers to whole grains, there are numerous rices available that are good for making the transition because their bran layer is either thin or partially removed. One sensational example,

Chinese black rice, is stunning in a chicken soup (page 127). Or try Bhutanese red rice or kalijira, light and fluffy varieties that cook quickly and make delicious pilafs (see pages 202 and 205). Thai black sticky rice makes a fetching, creamy coconut rice pudding (page 299).

Because the rice family is so large, I've grouped the basic recipes into three categories according the color of the bran: brown, red, and black. The cook has many exciting choices!

BROWN RICES AT A GLANCE

FORM	DESCRIPTION/PROCESSING	AVAILABILITY	COMMENTS
BROWN BASMATI	A slender long-grain aromatic rice	Health food stores, supermarkets, Indian groceries, mail-order (imported from Pakistan or India)	California-grown basmati can pale in comparison to best-quality imported; however, imported is not as well cleaned and quality varies
BROWN JASMINE	A slender long-grain aromatic rice	Health food stores, mail-order	Originally from Thailand, now grown organically by Lowell Farms in Texas; cooks in about 30 minutes
BROWN KALIJIRA	Tiny, aromatic, with a very thin bran layer	Gourmet shops, mail-order	Grown in Bangladesh; cooks in about 30 minutes
BROWN LONG-GRAIN	A long, slender tan grain with some greenish grains interspersed	Health food stores, supermarkets	Cooks up light and fluffy; less chewy than short-grain; good for pilafs
BROWN MEDIUM-GRAIN	Shorter and plumper than long-grain	Health food stores, mail-order	Slightly moister and sweeter than long-grain
BROWN SHORT-GRAIN	Dense and chubby tan grain with some greenish grains interspersed	Health food stores, supermarkets	Moist and slightly sticky; Southern Brown Rice, Ohsawa Pearl, Akito-machi, and Lundberg Golden Rose are particularly tasty examples
BROWN, SWEET	Dainty, flat, pale tan, short-grain variety	Health food stores, mail-order	Sticky, mild, and slightly sweet; good for sushi, rice balls, and desserts
BROWN RICE GRITS	Brown rice cut into small bits	Health food stores	Sometimes labeled farina but not all farina is whole-grain; cooks into a hot breakfast cereal
BROWN RICE, QUICK-COOKING	Parboiled brown rice that cooks in about 15 minutes	Supermarkets	Avoid. It's a faint shadow of the real thing.

BROWN RICES AT A GLANCE *(continued)*

FORM	DESCRIPTION/PROCESSING	AVAILABILITY	COMMENTS
PUFFED BROWN RICE	Mottled brown puffs created when moistened grains are placed under pressure that is suddenly released	Health food stores	Nice taste and crunch; available without sugar for use as a cereal
BROWN RICE CAKES	Crisp cracker-like discs produced when kernels in a pressurized mold puff up and stick together when pressure is suddenly released	Health food stores, supermarkets	Lundberg Organic has best taste and texture

compatible foods and flavors

- Savory: beef, lamb, chicken, beans, nuts, milk, fresh and dried herbs, avocado, sesame seeds, nuts

- Sweet: maple syrup, honey, coconut milk, dried fruit, cinnamon and other sweet spices

■ ■ ■

basic brown basmati and long-grain brown rice

For optimal texture and appearance, soak brown basmati and long-grain brown rices for 30 minutes before cooking. This soaking time softens the bran layer, allowing the grains to absorb water evenly.

CUPS DRY	CUPS WATER	TEASPOONS SALT (OPTIONAL)	POT SIZE	APPROXIMATE CUP YIELD
1	1¾	Pinch	2-quart	3
1½	2½	Pinch	2-quart	4½
2	3¼	¼	2-quart	6

In a heavy Dutch oven or saucepan, combine the rice and cold water. Let sit for 30 minutes. Add salt (if using). Bring to a boil. Cover, reduce the heat, and simmer until tender (a grain halved crosswise should be one color throughout), 30 to 40 minutes.

If all of the water has been absorbed and the rice is undercooked, sprinkle 2 to 3 tablespoons of water on top (do not stir) and continue cooking over very low heat for another 5 minutes. When the rice is tender or just short of done, turn off the heat and let sit for 5 minutes. Fluff up and serve.

OVEN-BAKED: Once the grains and water have come to a boil, cover and bake in the center of an oven preheated to 350°F.

PRESSURE-COOKED: See page 112.

KEEPING AND REHEATING: See The Grain Bank, page 10.

basic brown jasmine rice

Brown jasmine is a slender, aromatic long-grain rice with a light bran layer, so it cooks in about 30 minutes. It is slightly sweet and mildly fragrant, with an easygoing chewiness—a good choice for those new to whole grains.

Jasmine rice was grown and eaten primarily in Thailand until 1989, when L. G. Raun, a third-generation rice farmer in Texas, produced an organically grown, lightly milled brown jasmine. This is the brown jasmine rice currently grown by Lowell Farms and available in the bulk bins of many health food stores.

CUPS DRY	CUPS WATER	TEASPOONS SALT	POT SIZE	APPROXIMATE CUP YIELD
1	2	Pinch	2-quart	3
1½	2½	Pinch	2-quart	4½
2	3½	1/4	2-quart	6

Rub the rice gently in a large bowl of water. Discard any bits of black hull that float to the top. Drain. Bring the rice, water, and salt to a boil in a heavy Dutch oven or saucepan. Cover, reduce the heat, and simmer until the rice is tender (it should be one color throughout when cut in half crosswise), about 30 minutes. It overcooks and becomes sticky in a flash, so pay attention and keep tasting toward the end of the cooking time.

As soon as the rice is tender, drain off any unabsorbed water by bouncing the rice up and down in a strainer. Serve immediately.

KEEPING AND REHEATING: See The Grain Bank, page 10.

basic kalijira brown rice

Although kalijira is a diminutive brown rice, it quadruples to almost the size of basmati when cooked—though it is not quite as long. It has the sweetness and nutty, popcorn-like aroma of basmati.

CUPS DRY	CUPS WATER	TEASPOONS SALT	POT SIZE	APPROXIMATE CUP YIELD
1	1¾	Pinch	2-quart	3½ to 4
1½	2½	Pinch	2-quart	5 to 6

Place the rice in a bowl and cover with cold water. Rub between your fingers. Skim off any hulls that rise to the top. Drain. Repeat until there are no more loose hulls and no grit at the bottom of the bowl. Drain again.

Bring the rice and water to a boil in a heavy Dutch oven or saucepan. Cover, reduce the heat, and simmer until the water has been absorbed and the rice is tender, about 30 minutes. If the rice is unevenly cooked and the water has all been absorbed, add 3 tablespoons hot water (do not stir), cover, and let steam off the heat for 5 minutes. Fluff and serve.

KEEPING AND REHEATING: Refrigerate for up to 5 days in a tightly sealed container. Reheat, lightly covered, in the microwave. Alternatively, reheat in a heavy saucepan over low heat, stirring occasionally. Add a little water if needed. Does not freeze well.

basic medium- and short-grain brown rices

These rices are slightly sticky since they have a high proportion of amylose starch and a high ratio of starch to bran. They are moister and chewier than long-grain rices. To my palate, they also have more character. Good for sushi and stir-fries.

CUPS DRY	CUPS WATER	TEASPOONS SALT (OPTIONAL)	POT SIZE	APPROXIMATE CUP YIELD
1	2	Pinch	2-quart	3
1½	2¾	Pinch	2-quart	4½
2	3½	¼	2-quart	6

Rinse and drain the rice. Bring the water and salt (if using) to a boil in a heavy Dutch oven or saucepan.

Add the rice. Cover, reduce the heat, and simmer until the rice is tender (it should be one color throughout when cut in half crosswise) and most or all of the water has been absorbed, 30 to 35 minutes for medium-grain and 40 minutes for short-grain.

If all of the water has been absorbed and the rice is undercooked, sprinkle 2 to 3 tablespoons of water on top (do not stir) and continue cooking over very low heat for another 5 minutes. When the rice is tender or just short of done, turn off the heat. Let stand, covered, for 5 minutes (medium-grain) or 10 minutes (short-grain). Fluff up and serve.

OVEN-BAKED: Once you've added the rice, cover and set the pot in the middle of an oven preheated to 350°F.

PRESSURE-COOKED: See page 112.

KEEPING AND REHEATING: See The Grain Bank, page 10.

basic sweet brown rice

In Asia, this glutinous rice is traditionally steamed over boiling water and used for dessert. My experiments revealed that when toasted first and then steamed in a limited amount of water, sweet brown rice maintains a pleasant chewiness and is delightful in savory preparations.

Because this rice is sticky, it works particularly well in sushi and molds nicely into small balls that can be stuffed with smoked fish or chopped, cooked vegetables and rolled in toasted sesame seeds. And since the bran layer is thin and unobtrusive, sweet brown rice cooked as directed below is also a good choice for rice puddings and other desserts.

CUPS DRY	CUPS WATER	TEASPOONS SALT	POT SIZE	APPROXIMATE CUP YIELD
1	2	Pinch	2-quart	2½
2	3¾	Pinch	2-quart	5

Bring the water to a boil in a kettle. Meanwhile, set a heavy Dutch oven or saucepan over medium heat. Add the grains and toast, stirring frequently, until they emit a fragrance, about 3 minutes. Stand back to avoid splattering and add the boiling water and salt.

Cover, reduce the heat, and simmer until the rice is tender, about 25 minutes. Drain off any unabsorbed water. Cover and let steam off the heat until ready to serve, or transfer to a bowl, season, and mold into desired shapes.

KEEPING AND REHEATING: Best when freshly made.

FORM	DESCRIPTION/PROCESSING	AVAILABILITY	COMMENTS
BHUTANESE RED RICE	An unevenly pearled, small grain with a thin reddish-brown bran layer intact; some spots of white endosperm are exposed	Gourmet shops, mail-order, supermarkets	Because the grains are small and some of the endosperm is exposed, the rice cooks in 20 minutes
CAMARGUE RED RICE	A semi-pearled, oval, slightly flat grain	Available on and off by mail-order and in gourmet shops	The batch I had disappointed: minimal flavor and grains did not hold their shape; use recipe for Basic Italian Wild Red Rice, page 72
COLUSARI RED RICE	A handsome, deep mahogany, slightly chubby grain with bran intact	Mail-order	Adds nice dots of color when cooked with brown rice; probably too branny to eat on its own
HIMALAYAN RED RICE	A long, slender, partially pearled rice with most of its russet bran intact; some grains in the batch are white because all of the bran has been removed	Mail-order, gourmet shops	Cooks in about 30 minutes
ITALIAN WILD RED RICE	A medium-grain, chestnut-colored, unevenly pearled rice	Mail-order, gourmet shops	Grown by organic farmers in Pavia, Italy; brands include La Gallinella and Aironi
THAI RED RICE	A medium-grain, chestnut-colored, unevenly pearled rice	Thai groceries, sporadically via mail-order from Asian sources	Pleasingly sweet; see Cook's Notes, opposite
WEHANI RICE	A slender, russet, aromatic, long-grain hybrid of brown rice crossed with Indian basmati rice	Health food stores, many supermarkets	Developed by Lundberg Family Farms; use instead of wild rice as an inexpensive way to add color and texture to pilafs

basic bhutanese red rice

This delicate, mild-flavored, quick-cooking rice is grown at an altitude of 8,000 feet in the Himalayas. Because the rice has been fairly vigorously pearled, leaving only a thin layer of bran intact, it's an excellent choice for those who are transitioning to whole grains. The cooked grain has the soft chewiness of well-cooked white rice and a mild sweetness suggesting honey. Because some endosperm is exposed, most of the grains burst open and triple in size. The color given off by the bran as the grains cook "dyes" the endosperm red.

CUPS DRY	CUPS WATER	TEASPOONS SALT (OPTIONAL)	POT SIZE	APPROXIMATE CUP YIELD
1	1½	⅛	2-quart	3
1½	2	¼	2-quart	4½

Rinse the rice; it will bleed. Combine the rice, water, and salt in a heavy Dutch oven or saucepan. Bring to a boil. Cover, reduce the heat to low, and simmer until the rice is tender and there is no opaque white dot in the center when a grain is cut in half crosswise, 18 to 21 minutes. If there is any unabsorbed water, drain it off. For a drier, fluffier finish, return the rice to the pot, cover, and set over low heat for 1 minute. Turn off the heat and let rest for a few minutes. Serve hot.

KEEPING AND REHEATING: Refrigerate for up to 5 days in a tightly sealed container. Reheat, lightly covered, in the microwave. Alternatively, reheat in a heavy saucepan over low heat, stirring occasionally. Add a little water if needed. Does not freeze well.

cook's notes

■   Follow this recipe to prepare Thai red rice, but increase cooking time to 30 minutes and standing time to 10.

compatible foods and flavors

■   Beef, lamb, chicken, pork, garlic, scallions, toasted sesame oil, soy sauce, coconut milk

basic colusari red rice

A gorgeous, bold rice, Colusari is perhaps too intense to eat on its own. There is some tannin in the bran, which gives this rice its strong personality. I like to cook a few tablespoons of Colusari with short-grain brown rice, or to cook it separately and toss it with cooked pearl barley or oat groats.

CUPS DRY	CUPS WATER	TEASPOONS SALT	POT SIZE	APPROXIMATE CUP YIELD
1	1¾	Pinch	2-quart	3½ to 4
1½	2½	Pinch	2-quart	5 to 6

Bring the water and salt to a boil in a heavy Dutch oven or saucepan. Add the rice. Return to a boil, cover, and simmer until there is no opaque white dot in the center when a grain is cut in half crosswise (the endosperm will be whitish but should be the same color throughout) and the rice tastes tender, 40 to 45 minutes. Turn off the heat, cover, and let sit for 10 minutes. Drain off any unabsorbed water. Serve hot.

OVEN-BAKED: Once you've added the grains, cover and set the pot in the middle of an oven preheated to 350°F.

PRESSURE-COOKED: See page 112.

KEEPING AND REHEATING: See The Grain Bank, page 10.

cook's notes

■ Cooking with more than a pinch of salt hardens the bran and prevents proper absorption. Season the rice after it is tender.

basic himalayan red rice

This handsome deep mahogany grain has the long, slender shape of basmati when raw. As it cooks, the rice bursts open and curls to reveal a pale ivory endosperm. The best way to cook Himalayan red rice is like pasta, in lots of water. Using this technique, the bran becomes soft and the starch very creamy. Although the cooking water turns red, the cooked rice retains good color.

CUPS DRY	CUPS WATER	TEASPOONS SALT	POT SIZE	APPROXIMATE CUP YIELD
1	10 (2½ quarts)	1	4-quart	2
1½	14 (3½ quarts)	1¼	5-quart	3
2	18 (4½ quarts)	1½	5-quart	4

Rinse the rice. Bring the water and salt to a boil in a large pot. Add the rice. Return to a boil. Boil uncovered over high heat until the rice is tender and there is no opaque white dot in the center when a grain is cut in half crosswise, 20 to 24 minutes. Drain well. Serve hot.

KEEPING AND REHEATING: Refrigerate for up to 5 days in a tightly sealed container. Reheat, lightly covered, in the microwave. Alternatively, reheat in a heavy saucepan over low heat, stirring occasionally. Add a little water if needed. Does not freeze well.

cook's notes

■ When cooked in 2 parts water to 1 part rice as some instructions suggest, the rice develops a mealy texture.

basic italian wild red rice

The bran layer on the two types I tried was the color of chestnuts. The grains burst to reveal a tan endosperm and were pleasantly chewy.

CUPS DRY	CUPS WATER	TEASPOONS SALT	POT SIZE	APPROXIMATE CUP YIELD
1	10 (2½ quarts)	¾	4-quart	1½
2	14 (3½ quarts)	1	5-quart	3
3	16 (4 quarts)	1¼	6-quart	4½

Rinse the rice. Bring the water and salt to a boil in a large pot. Add the rice. Return to a boil. Boil uncovered over high heat until the rice is tender and there is no opaque white dot in the center when a grain is cut in half crosswise, 35 to 38 minutes. Drain. Immediately return the rice to the hot pot. Cover and let steam in the residual heat for 10 minutes. Serve hot.

KEEPING AND REHEATING: See The Grain Bank, page 10.

■ ■ ■

basic wehani rice

This long-grain, reddish-brown rice is a hybrid of Indian basmati and long-grain brown rice developed by the Lundberg Brothers on their Richvale, California, farm. There is a hint of chestnut flavor, and the rice holds its shape and color nicely when cooked, making it a welcome addition to most any pilaf.

Wehani has the density and slight woodiness of wild rice, and many will find it too intense when served on its own. Try cooking about one quarter of Wehani with short-grain brown rice (page 66) for nice flecks of color and textural variety.

CUPS DRY	CUPS WATER	TEASPOONS SALT	POT SIZE	APPROXIMATE CUP YIELD
1	2	None	2-quart	3
1½	3	None	2-quart	4½
2	4	None	2-quart	6

Rinse the rice. Combine the rice and water in a heavy Dutch oven or saucepan. Bring to a boil. Cover, reduce the heat to low, and simmer until the rice is tender and there is no opaque white dot in the center when a grain is cut in half crosswise, about 45 minutes. Stir quickly to distribute the grains. Turn off the heat and let rest for 10 minutes to even out cooking. Drain off any unabsorbed water.

OVEN-BAKED: Once the grains and water have come to a boil, cover and set the pot in the middle of an oven preheated to 350°F.

PRESSURE-COOKED: See page 112.

KEEPING AND REHEATING: See The Grain Bank, page 10.

cook's notes

■ Don't presoak Wehani as the bran layer separates and the cooked rice loses its shape and becomes mushy.

■ Never cook Wehani with salt, which hardens the bran layer and prevents proper absorption of water.

BLACK RICES AT A GLANCE

FORM	DESCRIPTION/PROCESSING	AVAILABILITY	COMMENTS
CHINESE BLACK (also called Forbidden Black Rice)	A medium-grain Chinese rice with a very dark, deep purple bran layer	Gourmet shops, mail-order	Cooks in 30 minutes; full of flavor and striking visual appeal
BLACK JAPONICA	A blend of a medium-grain red rice and a short-grain black rice; gorgeous color	Health food stores, some supermarkets	Developed and grown by the Lundberg family; highly recommended blend with creamy texture and nutty aroma
THAI BLACK STICKY	Slender grain with a very dark bran layer	Asian groceries, mail-order	Works well for savory dishes as well as sweet
ITALIAN BLACK (also called *riso nero venere*)	An ebony medium-grain cross between Italian and Chinese varieties	Mail-order	Use recipe for Basic Italian Wild Red Rice, page 72, cooking for about 30 minutes, but omit final steaming; nutty, with delightful texture

basic chinese black rice

A very high-quality Chinese black rice is distributed by Lotus Foods under the registered trademark name "Forbidden Black Rice." This rice bleeds beet-red when you rinse it and, once cooked, ends up a striking deep burgundy. It holds its shape very well and is pleasantly chewy. With a subtle sweetness and a rich taste, it's a stunning rice that has everything going for it. Put it high on your list of rices to try.

CUPS DRY	CUPS WATER	SALT (OPTIONAL)	POT SIZE	APPROXIMATE CUP YIELD
1	$1^3/_4$	Pinch	2-quart	$3^3/_4$
$1^1/_2$	$2^1/_4$	Pinch	2-quart	$7^1/_2$

Rinse the rice. Combine the rice, water, and salt (if using) in a heavy Dutch oven or saucepan. Over high heat, bring to a boil. Skim off any foam floating on the surface. Cover, reduce the heat, and simmer until the rice is tender, 30 to 35 minutes. Let sit, covered, for 5 minutes. Drain off any excess water.

KEEPING AND REHEATING: See The Grain Bank, page 10.

compatible foods and flavors

■ Savory: shiitake mushrooms, soy sauce, toasted sesame oil, star anise, garlic, ginger, beef, pork, chicken

■ Sweet: coconut milk, honey, cinnamon

basic black japonica

Developed, grown, and distributed by the Lundberg brothers of Richvale, California, this is a handsome blend of two rices, both of Japanese origin: a short-grain black rice and a medium-grain mahogany rice. The Lundbergs grow them in the same field, and the proportion of one rice to the other varies from harvest to harvest. I prefer the method below to the one offered on the package.

There is a subtle sweetness and earthiness to the duo, and they look extremely attractive on a plate. You'll also find Black Japonica mixed into numerous other Lundberg grain blends.

CUPS DRY	CUPS WATER	TEASPOONS SALT	POT SIZE	APPROXIMATE CUP YIELD
1	2	Pinch	2-quart	3½
1½	3	Pinch	2-quart	5
2	3¾	¼	3-quart	7

Rinse the rice; it will bleed somewhat. Bring the water and salt to a boil in a heavy Dutch oven or saucepan. Stir in the rice. Reduce the heat, cover, and simmer until some of the grains have burst open and the rice is tender, about 45 minutes. Turn off the heat and let sit for 10 minutes.

OVEN-BAKED: Once the grain and water have come to a boil, cover and bake in the center of an oven preheated to 350°F.

PRESSURE-COOKED: See page 112.

KEEPING AND REHEATING: See The Grain Bank, page 10.

cook's notes

■ The rice loses some of its color as it cooks, ending up a reddish brown.

■ It's nice to cook half Black Japonica with half short-grain brown rice.

■ If you find the cooked rice too sticky, run some hot water over it and drain well by bouncing the strainer up and down.

basic thai black sticky rice

Although labeled sticky rice and traditionally steamed over liquid, this rice works surprisingly well when cooked in the standard way and used for a savory pilaf. It marries especially well with mushrooms.

CUPS DRY	CUPS WATER	TEASPOONS SALT	POT SIZE	APPROXIMATE CUP YIELD
1	1¾	Pinch	2-quart	2¼
1½	2¾	Pinch	2-quart	3¼
2	3½	Pinch	2-quart	4½

Rinse the rice; the color will bleed. In a heavy Dutch oven or saucepan, bring the water and salt to a boil. Add the rice and return to a boil. Cover, reduce the heat, and simmer until the rice is tender, 25 to 30 minutes. Drain off any unabsorbed water. Return the rice to the pot and let steam, covered, until ready to use.

KEEPING AND REHEATING: See The Grain Bank, page 10.

rye and triticale

Rye hasn't had much of a life beyond bread and whisky, and triticale—a cross between rye and wheat—hasn't had much of a life at all. Eaten as whole grains, neither kernel has a strong personality, though it's fun to use rye berries with ingredients that evoke Eastern European kitchens, as I've done in Rye Berry Soup with Cabbage and Dill Sour Cream (page 128) and Rye Berry Slaw with Smoked Trout and Dill (page 138). However, truth be told, if you used wheat berries instead of rye, probably only a supertaster would be the wiser, though rye isn't as sweet as wheat and you'll notice a hint of sourness if you eat it plain and pay close attention.

When it comes to nutrition and appearance, however, rye and wheat part ways. Whole-grain rye contains more protein, phosphorus, iron, potassium, and B vitamins than whole wheat. Rye kernels look quite different from wheat. They are long and slender—elegant, in fact—and distinctly khaki green, even when cooked.

Triticale (pronounced trit-i-KA-lee) is a bit pudgier than rye, with a brownish, slightly wrinkled bran layer. The strange name derives from the Latin botanical names for wheat *(Triticum)* and rye *(Secale)*. Triticale existed first as a natural hybrid, which was eventually (after some difficulty) replicated in the laboratory by plant scientists. The goal was to create a grain that combined wheat's high yield and fine baking qualities with rye's nutritional profile and ability to withstand harsh growing conditions.

Triticale indeed has both more protein and a better amino acid profile than either wheat or rye, but it has never caught on. For the cook, it has a mild, pleasing personality and can be used interchangeably with wheat and rye berries in recipes.

RYE AND TRITICALE AT A GLANCE

FORM	DESCRIPTION/PROCESSING	AVAILABILITY	COMMENTS
RYE BERRIES (also called rye kernels, rye groats)	Slender grain with a distinct olive green hue	Health food stores, mail-order	Fairly bland, with a pleasing chewiness; can be substituted for wheat berries in any recipe
RYE GRITS (also called cracked rye)	Whole grain cut into small bits	Health food stores, mail-order	Makes a quick-cooking breakfast cereal or a moist pilaf
RYE FLAKES	Whole berry pressed through rollers to flatten into flakes	Health food stores, mail-order	Good for breakfast cereal, soften quickly; do not hold their shape as well as oatmeal when cooked; can easily be ground into flour
RYE FLOUR	A dark flour finely ground from the whole grain	Health food stores, mail-order	Heavy for quick breads; better for bread-baking
TRITICALE	A smallish, plump grain with a wrinkled, tan bran layer	Health food stores, mail-order	Bland, without the hint of sweetness characteristic of wheat; can be substituted for wheat berries in any recipe
TRITICALE FLAKES	Whole berry pressed through rollers to flatten into flakes	Health food stores, mail-order	Good for breakfast cereal, soften quickly; do not hold their shape as well as oatmeal when cooked; can easily be ground into flour

basic whole rye and triticale berries

Both rye and triticale kernels (berries) benefit from presoaking, which softens the bran and allows the grains to cook more evenly.

CUPS DRY	CUPS WATER	SALT	POT SIZE	APPROXIMATE CUP YIELD
1	2½	Add to taste toward the end of cooking	2-quart	2½
1½	3¼	Add to taste toward the end of cooking	2-quart	3¼
2	4½	Add to taste toward the end of cooking	2½-quart	5

Soak the grains in the water overnight in a heavy Dutch oven or saucepan. Alternatively, do a quick-soak: Bring the water to a rapid boil. Stir in the grains. Turn off the heat, cover, and let stand for 1 hour.

Bring the water and grains to a boil in the soaking liquid. Cover, reduce the heat, and simmer until tender, 25 to 40 minutes. Add salt toward the end of cooking, if you wish.

Once a few of the grains have burst open or you detect the whitish starchy endosperm peeking through one end of some grains, start checking for doneness: Cut a few grains in half and see if they are one color throughout. If so, taste a few grains and see if they are juicy and the bran and starchy center are soft. Remove from the heat. Rye gets plumper if left to soak in the cooking liquid for an extra 10 to 15 minutes. Triticale should be drained once tender.

After draining, if you wish to reduce surface moisture, return the grains to the hot empty pot, cover, and let steam in the residual heat for 5 to 10 minutes. Keep the grains covered after cooking as they quickly dry out and stiffen.

OVEN-BAKED: Once the grains and water have come to a boil, cover and set the pot in the center of an oven preheated to 350°F.

PRESSURE-COOKED: See page 112.

KEEPING AND REHEATING: See The Grain Bank, page 10.

cook's notes

■ Don't be tempted to toast either grain before cooking. Toasting cracks the bran layer and the grains will cook unevenly and get mushy.

compatible foods and flavors

■ Cabbage, beets, raisins, mustard, dill, sage, rosemary, caraway, sweet-and-sour dressings

basic rye grits (cracked rye)

Rye grits take longer to cook and require more water than most other cracked grains. Rye's sour undertone is accentuated when the grain is prepared in this form, so it's a good idea to balance the mix with a flavorful sweetish nut oil such as walnut. I'm not sure any but the most die-hard rye lovers would enjoy rye grits on their own, but they make a delicious, starchy side dish when cooked with bacon and potatoes (page 230).

After overnight refrigeration, rye grits prepared this way mold easily into a patty. Season well with salt, pepper, and spices or finely chopped fresh herbs. Mold into patties, and brown in oil for a tasty and nourishing vegan burger.

CUPS DRY	TABLESPOONS OIL	CUPS WATER	TEASPOONS SALT	POT SIZE	APPROXIMATE CUP YIELD
1	1	2	Pinch	2-quart	2½
1½	1½	3½	¼	2-quart	3¼

Bring ample water to boil in a kettle so that you will have enough ready to add after toasting the grains.

Heat the oil in a heavy Dutch oven or saucepan. Stir in the cracked rye. Toast over medium heat, stirring frequently, until the grains emit a toasty aroma, 2 to 3 minutes. Stand back and pour in the suggested amount of boiling water gradually to avoid boil-overs. Stir in the salt. Return to a boil.

Cover and reduce the heat to low. Cook for 5 minutes and then stir once or twice. Continue cooking until the grains are almost tender and the water has been mostly or entirely absorbed, 5 to 7 minutes longer. If the grits are still quite hard, evenly distribute ¼ to ½ cup additional boiling water over them and cook over low heat for another minute or two. Turn off the heat and steam, covered, until the grits are tender, 15 to 20 minutes longer.

KEEPING AND REHEATING: Refrigerate for up to 5 days in a tightly sealed container. Reheat, lightly covered, in the microwave. Alternatively, heat in a heavy, covered saucepan over low heat, adding a little water if needed. Does not freeze well.

BASIC RYE FLAKES: See Rolled Grain Porridge with Currants, Apple, and Walnuts, page 252.

sorghum

Although sorghum is a staple in parts of Africa and India, it is hardly known in America. However, now that there is such a rapidly growing interest in gluten-free grains, you are likely to be hearing more about it. Since there are many varieties, it's difficult to generalize about nutritional content, but most sorghum is a good source of protein and an excellent source of phosphorus and potassium.

Sorghum is a bland, starchy grain that resembles millet in taste and character. Because of an inherent dryness, it benefits by being associated with juicy ingredients like tomatoes, such as in Sorghum with Cherry Tomatoes and Corn (page 221). Cracked into a coarse meal and toasted, sorghum makes a delicious breakfast porridge (page 250).

Sorghum syrup, also called sorghum molasses, is known in the South. It is made from the sweet juice that accumulates in the stalks of a nongrain variety of sorghum.

SORGHUM AT A GLANCE

FORM	DESCRIPTION/PROCESSING	AVAILABILITY	COMMENTS
WHOLE SORGHUM (also called milo and kafir)	Inedible hull removed, revealing a roundish tan/ivory grain with a deep crease; slightly larger than millet	Health food stores, mail-order	Best when freshly cooked
SORGHUM GRITS	Whole grains cracked into small bits in a coffee grinder	Not commercially available	Easily made at home from the whole grain
SORGHUM FLOUR	A fine beige flour milled from whole grain	Health food stores, mail-order	Easy to grind at home in a spice grinder. Toast flour before use. Bland taste; gluten-free bakers extol its virtues.

basic sorghum (milo)

Sorghum's mild taste is enhanced by toasting the grains before cooking. The slow, even heat of the oven softens the bran layer more effectively than stove-top simmering, and cooks the internal starch more evenly.

CUPS DRY	CUPS WATER	TEASPOONS SALT (OPTIONAL)	POT SIZE	APPROXIMATE CUP YIELD
1	2	Pinch	1½- or 2-quart	2½
1½	3	⅛	2-quart	3¾

Place a rack in the middle of the oven and preheat the oven to 350°F.

Bring ample water to a boil in a kettle so that you will have enough ready to add after toasting the grains.

Rinse the sorghum and drain well. Set a heavy Dutch oven or saucepan over medium-high heat. Add the sorghum and toast, stirring frequently, until the grains dry off. Reduce the heat to medium and continue toasting, stirring frequently, until some of the kernels darken slightly, usually 1 to 3 minutes more.

Stand back and stir in the suggested amount of boiling water gradually to avoid boil-overs. Cover and bake for 50 minutes. To test for doneness, slice open a few grains: They should be one color throughout. If they are not done and the mixture seems dry, stir in ¼ cup boiling water and return to the oven. When done, remove from the oven and let sit covered and undisturbed for 10 minutes. Drain off any excess liquid. Serve hot.

PRESSURE-COOKED: See page 112.

KEEPING AND REHEATING: Though it can be reheated and rehydrated by heating in a covered bowl in the microwave, the texture of sorghum is optimum when the grains are freshly cooked. The texture of leftovers is better preserved if you toss them in a little oil before refrigeration or freezing.

cook's notes

- Cook sorghum in chicken or beef broth for enhanced flavor.

- Never serve sorghum at room temperature or chilled: It is unpleasantly dry and mealy.

- Toss cooked sorghum with a little walnut oil and some chopped toasted walnuts for an easy side dish.

- Toss fresh mushrooms in olive oil and season with salt and pepper. Roast them until tender in a separate dish alongside the sorghum. When the sorghum is done, toss in the mushrooms and some chopped fresh herbs. Season to taste with salt and pepper.

compatible foods and flavors

- Savory: sesame seeds, yogurt, buttermilk, mushrooms, walnuts

- Sweet: molasses, banana

teff

If you've eaten the large spongy flatbread bread called injera at an Ethopian restaurant, you've had a taste of teff. Although the grains have not ventured far beyond the Ethiopian kitchen, it's time they did.

Teff is a minuscule grain. To give you some idea of just how minuscule, it takes 50 grains of teff to equal the weight of a single grain of wheat.

Wayne Carlson discovered teff when he spent time in Ethiopia. He was so impressed with its taste and wonderful nutrient profile that he founded The Teff Company and began growing it in Caldwell, Idaho, both to serve the Ethiopian community in America and to introduce the grain to a wider public. Teff is a source of high-quality protein since it contains all eight of the essential amino acids. It is also high in fiber, calcium, phosphorus, iron, copper, and other minerals. Ethiopian athletes credit teff for their stamina and prowess.

At present both ivory and brown teff are available in the United States. Both have a mild corn, slightly herbal taste. Ivory teff is milder in flavor than the darker variety. Teff adds body and sheen to soups and stews. Ground into flour, the brown grain makes a cocoa-colored waffle that looks elegant with a garnish of caramelized bananas (page 244). Teff also makes a delicious breakfast porridge and a savory polenta, which can be served as the side dish starch for an Ethiopian Chicken Stew (page 164). Teff polenta sets up beautifully and can be cut into shapes and fried for Teff Polenta Triangles with Caramelized Apples (page 231), an interesting side dish for poultry and game.

Cooking with teff has been one of the most rewarding aspects of writing this book. For such a tiny grain, it offers big surprises.

TEFF AT A GLANCE

FORM	DESCRIPTION/PROCESSING	AVAILABILITY	COMMENTS
WHOLE GRAIN	Minuscule seeds, ivory or chestnut brown	Health food stores, mail-order	Lighter seeds have lighter taste
FLOUR	Fine flour ground from the whole grain; light and dark available	Health food stores, mail-order	Great in pancakes and waffles (page 244); produces a slightly grainy texture in quick breads; see page 264

basic dry-cooked teff

Cooking 1 cup of teff in 1 cup of water results in a grain that has the texture of poppy seeds. In fact, a good use of teff prepared this way is to add a boost of protein crunch to pancake, waffle, and quick-bread batters. Since the cooked grains clump together, for best distribution stir them into the wet ingredients. You can also blend dry-cooked teff into peanut butter or fruit preserves for added texture.

Even when enriched with butter or mixed with chopped nuts or fresh herbs, the texture of dry-cooked teff is too intensely gritty to serve on its own as a side dish, but the grains make an attractive chestnut-colored sprinkle for steamed green vegetables.

CUPS DRY	CUPS WATER	TEASPOONS SALT	POT SIZE	APPROXIMATE CUP YIELD
1	1	1/8	2-quart	1 1/4

Bring ample water to a boil in a kettle so that you will have enough ready to add after toasting the grains.

Set a heavy Dutch oven or saucepan over medium heat. Toast ivory or brown teff, stirring almost continuously, until the grains begin to pop, usually 3 to 6 minutes. (You may not hear any popping, but will notice little white dots of popped grain in the pot.)

Stand back and stir in the boiling water gradually to avoid boil-overs. Reduce the heat and stir in the salt. Cover and simmer, stirring every few minutes to prevent the grains from sticking to the bottom of the pot. Cook until the water is absorbed, 6 to 7 minutes. Let stand off the heat, covered, for 5 minutes.

KEEPING AND REHEATING: Store in the refrigerator for up to 5 days or freeze for up to 4 months. Defrost at room temperature.

basic teff polenta (soft and firm)

Teff makes a very delicious breakfast porridge when perked up with sweet spices and enriched with butter. Or serve it seasoned with salt and pepper as a soft polenta with spicy stews. The polenta will set up as it cools and can be cut into pieces and pan-fried or baked. When you use the dark brown grain, the polenta looks like molten chocolate.

CUPS DRY	CUPS WATER	TEASPOONS SALT	POT SIZE	APPROXIMATE CUP YIELD
1	3	½	2-quart	3 cups
2	5½	1	3-quart	6 cups

Bring ample water to a boil in a kettle so that you will have enough ready to add after toasting the grains.

Set a heavy Dutch oven or saucepan over medium heat. Add the teff and toast it, stirring frequently, until the grains emit a mild toasty aroma and begin to pop, 3 to 6 minutes. (You will notice little white dots of popped grain but may not hear the popping.)

Stand back and add the boiling water gradually to avoid boil-overs. Stir in the salt. Reduce the heat, cover, and cook at a gentle boil until the grains are tender and the mixture is fairly smooth and thick, 15 to 20 minutes. Stir every few minutes to prevent the grains from sticking to the bottom of the pot. Break up any lumps by smashing them against the side of the pot. If the grains are cooked and the mixture is still thin, boil uncovered while stirring to achieve a thick porridge consistency. Mound onto plates and serve hot, like soft corn polenta.

KEEPING AND REHEATING: Refrigerate for up to 5 days in a tightly sealed container. Reheat, lightly covered, in the microwave. Alternatively, heat in a heavy, covered saucepan over low heat, adding a little water if needed. Does not freeze well.

FOR CHILLED FIRM POLENTA: Use 1 cup teff and proceed as directed on the preceding page. Reduce the heat to low and cook until slightly thicker, another minute or two. Meanwhile, oil a rectangular pan, about 12 by 8 inches. Pour the hot polenta into the pan and spread it out to an even thickness. Smooth off the top. Cover lightly with a kitchen towel and cool to room temperature, about 2 hours. If the polenta isn't firm enough to cut, refrigerate for a few hours or overnight. Cut into pieces and fry in butter or oil until crisp on both sides. Makes enough to serve as a side dish for 6.

KEEPING AND REHEATING: Chilled firm polenta (before frying) can be refrigerated for up to 5 days in a tightly sealed container. Fry as directed above just before serving. Does not freeze well.

compatible foods and flavors

- Savory: chicken, beef, cardamom, black pepper, chile peppers

- Sweet: apples, dates, cloves

the wheat family

Even though wheat is the major American grain, most people are acquainted with it only in the form of refined white flour in breads, cakes, and cookies. Once a door opens onto the vast and varied family of whole-grain wheats, the cook's palette of ingredients is dramatically expanded.

The name wheat berries is someone's idea of a marketing gimic, and it looks like we're stuck with it. The grains are not berries at all, but kernels. However, I'll go on calling them berries so you'll know what I'm talking about.

Wheat is "the staff of life" in so many cultures because it is a nutrient-dense grain that contains a wide spectrum of vitamins and minerals, including B_6 and E, magnesium, niacin, folacin, pantothenic acid, thiamin, chromium, manganese, iron, and zinc.

Jane Brody, in her *Good Food Book,* calls milling "the rape of the wheat berry" because both the bran and the germ are discarded when the wheat berry is milled into white flour. Together the bran and germ contain 28 percent of the grain's protein, 94 percent of the vitamin B_6, 97 percent of the thiamin, and 58 percent of the riboflavin. The bran contains 86 percent of the niacin and the germ has all of the vitamin E. Do those statistics encourage you to give whole-grain wheat a try?

Depending upon when the grains are planted, the berries are labeled either winter or spring wheat. Both are harvested during the summer. Spring wheat is generally about 20 percent higher in protein than winter wheat.

Wheat berries are also divided into types according to density, color, and variety. There are hard wheats and soft wheats—you can actually bite through a kernel of raw soft wheat. The flour ground from most hard wheat varieties is generally used for making bread, except for varieties of durum, which are used for making pasta. Soft wheat flour, also called whole-wheat pastry flour, has less protein and gluten and is therefore better for making quick breads, cookies, and cereals.

Wheat kernels are also grouped by the color of the bran layer, which varies from reddish to pale tan to white. All of the distinctions just mentioned are of critical importance when working with whole-grain wheat flour, but for the cook using the whole grain, there is hardly any detectable difference among the varieties. Indeed, any type can be used in recipes that call for wheat berries, such as the Wheat Berry Salad with Apples and Mint (page 139).

The wheat family includes spelt, Kamut, and farro, three types of wheat that are botanically closer to ancient varieties than the grains we label wheat berries today. Some people who are allergic to wheat can tolerate them.

For the cook, these grains provide handsome and tasty options. Spelt grains are slightly larger than wheat berries and are recognizable by their reddish bran, which plumps up and deepens to a rich caramel as it cooks. Spelt has a characteristic "wheaty" sweetness, but its flavor is milder than that of wheat berries. Use it interchangeably with wheat berries in stews and casseroles, such as Any-Grain and Honeyed Squash Casserole with Hazelnuts on page 207. For a special treat, try immature green spelt (page 97). As you will see in the quick-breads section, whole-grain spelt flour makes sensational quick breads and cookies, such as Lemon–Poppy Seed Muffins (page 268) and Spelt Gingersnaps (page 285).

Kamut is the registered trademark used to market a type of wheat that was first grown and promoted by the visionary Montana farmer Bob Quinn. The trademark guarantees that all Kamut is grown organically. You may read that the seeds were found in an ancient Egyptian tomb, but that's a myth. Nevertheless, Kamut's heritage is ancient and it is an unhybridized relative of modern durum wheat.

More important for the cook, Kamut is a large, gorgeous bronze grain, more slender than other varieties of wheat and about twice the length. When cooked, the kernels become firm and full, like wheat berries that have been lifting weights. Each grain is full and juicy and squishes between your teeth like a ripe cherry tomato. Because they are twice the size of the average wheat berry, Kamut grains have an imposing presence in such dishes as Kamut with Mussels in Tomato Broth (page 183) or Kamut, Broccoli Rabe, and Sausage Medley (page 175).

Recently farro has become a trendy grain, cropping up on restaurant menus in soups and salads. Chefs love farro with good reason: It cooks quickly, is pleasantly chewy, has a distinct sweet "wheaty" taste, doesn't harden when refrigerated, and is extremely versatile. In short, to taste it is to love it. Try it in Farro Salad with Prosciutto and Asparagus (page 134), Farro Soup with Kale and Cannellini (page 124), and even in dessert, Farro Parfait with Ricotta, Oranges, and Mint (page 302).

Bulgur is made by parboiling wheat kernels, then drying and grinding them into various granulations. Bulgur-making is an ancient technology, a way of transforming a slow-cooking food into a fast-cooking one; bulgur requires little to no cooking.

Bulgur is user-friendly, making an excellent base for pilafs and savory salads such as Bulgur and Chickpea Salad with Parsley Dressing (page 133). It's also very comforting in a dessert like Bulgur Pudding with Honey and Dates (page 296).

After the Wheat-at-a-Glance chart, you'll find basic recipes for each type of whole-grain wheat, as well as the more processed versions like cracked wheat and bulgur. Directions for sprouting wheat are at the end of this section.

WHEAT AT A GLANCE

FORM	DESCRIPTION/PROCESSING	AVAILABILITY	COMMENTS
WHEAT BERRIES (also called wheat kernels)	Medium-size kernels with the bran intact; bran color varies from whitish to pale tan to reddish brown	Health food stores, mail-order	Many types available; see page 90 and Basic Wheat Berries, page 94
CRACKED WHEAT	Whole-wheat kernels cut or crushed into grits for faster cooking	Health food stores, mail-order	More prone to rancidity than whole; buy sealed and check expiration date; often confused with bulgur; see Basic Cracked Wheat, page 104
BULGUR (also called burghul)	Whole kernels parboiled, dried, and either left whole or cracked into different particle sizes	Health food stores, mail-order, super-markets (Goya pack-ages fine and coarse)	Available in four grades from fine to coarse; look for darkest available; see Basic Bulgur, page 98
WHOLE-WHEAT COUSCOUS	Tiny, dried pale golden pellets of whole-wheat dough made from the flour of hard durum wheat	Health food stores, supermarkets, mail-order	A whole-grain, quick-cooking vari-ant of couscous traditionally made from refined flour
ROLLED WHEAT (also called wheat flakes)	Whole kernels moistened to increase flexibility, then rolled into flakes	Health food stores, mail-order	Similar to rolled oats; see Rolled Grain Porridge, page 252
PUFFED WHEAT	Mottled brown puffs created when moistened whole grains are placed under pressure that is suddenly released	Health food stores, supermarkets	Available unsweetened for use as breakfast cereal; requires no cooking
WHOLE-WHEAT FLOUR	Whole kernels ground into flour; includes bran and germ	Health food stores, supermarkets, mail-order	Divided into two categories: whole-wheat flour (for bread) and whole-wheat pastry flour (for quick breads, cookies, and pancakes)
FARINA	Finely ground wheat kernels	Health food stores, mail-order	Most cereals labeled farina are not whole-grain; content label should read "Whole Wheat"
FARRO	Emmer wheat that has had some bran removed (semi-perlato) or most bran removed (perlato)	Gourmet shops, mail-order	All authentic farro is imported from Italy; farro grains are larger than spelt berries, with which they are often confused

WHEAT AT A GLANCE

FORM	DESCRIPTION/PROCESSING	AVAILABILITY	COMMENTS
WHOLE KAMUT KERNELS	A large, golden, elongated grain	Health food stores, mail-order	The trademarked name of an ancient, unhybridized form of organic whole wheat
CRACKED KAMUT (also called Kamut grits)	Whole kernels cut into bits for faster cooking	Health food stores, mail-order	Often sold as cereal; prone to rancidity; buy in sealed packages and check expiration date
PUFFED KAMUT	Mottled tan puffs created when moistened whole grains are placed under pressure that is suddenly released	Health food stores, mail-order	Available unsweetened for use as breakfast cereal; especially tasty; require no cooking
ROLLED KAMUT	Whole kernels steamed and rolled into flakes	Health food stores, mail-order	Sometimes labeled flakes, but require cooking; see Rolled Grain Porridge, page 252
KAMUT FLOUR	Ground from whole grain; contains bran and germ	Health food stores, mail-order	Good for bread-making, pasta, quick breads, cookies, and pancakes
WHOLE SPELT KERNELS	A slender grain with reddish bran; an ancient form of wheat	Health food stores, mail-order	A chewy, versatile grain similar to wheat berry, but blander in taste
CRACKED SPELT (also called spelt grits)	Whole grain cut into pieces for faster cooking	Health food stores, mail-order	Prone to rancidity; buy in sealed packages and check expiration date
ROLLED SPELT (also called spelt flakes)	Whole kernels steamed and rolled into flakes	Health food stores, mail-order	Sometimes labeled flakes, but require cooking; see Rolled Grain Porridge, page 252.
GREEN SPELT KERNELS (also called *frika* and *gruenkern*)	Spelt harvested before maturity and smoked while burning away chaff; whole grain with olive green bran intact	Mail-order	Highly recommended for its beautiful looks and smoky taste; gruenkern generally better sorted and cleaned than the frika I've sampled
CRACKED GREEN SPELT (also called green spelt grits)	Whole green spelt cut into pieces for faster cooking	Mail-order	Highly recommended for its smoky taste; cooks faster than whole kernels but the latter are more
attractive SPELT FLOUR	Whole grain milled into flour; bran and germ intact	Health food stores, mail-order	Excellent for whole-grain quick breads, cookies, and pancakes

basic wheat berries, whole kamut kernels, and whole spelt kernels

Presoaking the grains is optional but recommended. It saves some cooking time, but more important, presoaking results in a softer bran layer, more even cooking, and plumper grains. The cooking time of these grains is wildly unpredictable, so allow at least an hour in case you have a recalcitrant batch.

CUPS DRY	CUPS WATER	SALT	POT SIZE	APPROXIMATE CUP YIELD
1	2½	Add to taste toward end of cooking	2-quart	2 (spelt) 2¼ (Kamut) 2½ (wheat berries)
2	4½	Add to taste toward end of cooking	2-quart	4 (spelt) 4½ (Kamut) 5 (wheat berries)

If time permits, soak the grains in the water overnight. Alternatively, do a quick-soak: Bring the water to a rapid boil in a Dutch oven or heavy saucepan. Stir in the grains. Turn off the heat, cover, and let stand for 1 hour.

Bring the water and grains to a boil. Cover, reduce the heat, and simmer until tender.

Once a few of the grains have burst open or you detect the whitish starchy endosperm peeking through one end of some grains, start checking for doneness: Cut a few grains in half and see if they are one color throughout. If so, taste a few grains and see if they are juicy and the starchy center is soft. Cooking time is typically 30 to 40 minutes for soaked grains, about an hour for unsoaked. If the water is absorbed before the grains are done, add more as needed.

When the grains are tender, drain them thoroughly. To plump them slightly more and reduce surface moisture, return the grains to the hot empty pot and cover them. Let them steam in the residual heat for 5 to 10 minutes.

OVEN-BAKED: Instead of simmering on the stove top, bring to a boil, then cover and place in the center of an oven preheated to 350°F. Start checking for doneness after 30 minutes.

PRESSURE-COOKED: See page 112.

KEEPING AND REHEATING: See The Grain Bank, page 10.

cook's notes

■ I don't recommend dry-toasting wheat berries, spelt, and Kamut as a first step. Dry-toasting creates fissures in the bran layer and results in burst-open, soggy grains.

■ Adding salt hardens the bran layer and slows down cooking, so it's best added when the grains are close to tender.

compatible foods and flavors

■ Just about anything!

■   ■   ■

basic farro

Farro is the Italian word for emmer wheat. Most farro cooks quickly because it has been agressively pearled so little to no bran remains. If the grains are quite white, virtually all of the bran has been removed and it will be labeled *perlato*. If the grains are streaked with tan, some bran remains and it will be labeled *semi-perlato*. The timing below is for farro that has been partially pearled since this is the only type I have seen sold in the United States. If you have a batch of farro with the bran intact, it will take longer to cook and you should add the salt after cooking. Farro is a great transitional grain for cooks and eaters new to whole grains. It is very user-friendly and easy to love.

CUPS DRY	CUPS WATER	TEASPOONS SALT	POT SIZE	APPROXIMATE CUP YIELD
1	1¾	Pinch	2-quart	2½
1½	2½	Pinch	2-quart	3¾
2	3	¼	3-quart	5

Bring ample water to boil in a kettle so that you will have enough ready to add after toasting the grains.

Set a Dutch oven or heavy saucepan over medium heat. Toast the farro lightly, stirring frequently, until it emits a toasty aroma, about 3 minutes. Turn off the heat. Stand back and add the suggested amount of boiling water gradually to avoid boil-overs. Add the salt.

Return the mixture to a boil. Cover and simmer over low heat until tender, 20 to 30 minutes. To test for doneness, cut a few grains in half horizontally. If the interior of the grain is one color throughout, the batch is done. Let rest off the heat for 10 minutes. Drain off any excess water. Fluff up and serve hot.

OVEN-BAKED: After adding the boiling water, set in the middle of an oven preheated to 350°F. Start checking for doneness after 20 minutes.

KEEPING AND REHEATING: See The Grain Bank, page 10.

basic whole green spelt (frika, gruenkern)

There is a long-standing tradition of harvesting immature green spelt kernels by burning away the leaves, stems, and chaff to leave the kernels with a winning smoky flavor like Lapsang souchong tea. There are numerous theories about the origin of this technique. One is that the method was discovered by accident, when a field of immature spelt caught on fire and the roasted grains were found to be delicious. Another is that to save the crop from being destroyed by hail, it was harvested early and quickly dried over an open fire to store.

Green spelt from the Middle East is called *frika, faraykee,* or *freka*, while that produced in a small area of southern Germany is called *gruenkern*—green kernel. Of the samples I tried, the *frika* was daintier and required considerable rinsing. The *gruenkern* was plump and ready to throw into the pot. You can add cooked green spelt to soups and stews, but the grain's taste is so interesting that you may prefer just to toss it in a little olive oil, season with salt, and serve it on its own.

CUPS DRY	CUPS WATER	SALT	POT SIZE	APPROXIMATE CUP YIELD
1	2	Add to taste after cooking	2-quart	2
2	3¾	Add to taste after cooking	2-quart	4

Place the grains in a strainer and place the strainer in a bowl. Cover with ample water. Swirl with your hand, rubbing the grains against the strainer. Pour off the water and repeat the rinsing process until the water has a greenish tint but shows no sign of dirt. Drain.

Bring the water to a boil. Add the grain, cover, and reduce the heat to a simmer. Cook until tender, 14 to 18 minutes for frika and 20 to 30 for gruenkern. Check for doneness by cutting a grain in half crosswise. If it's one color throughout, it's done. Drain off any unabsorbed water. Return to the pot, cover, and let stand off heat for 5 minutes. Serve hot.

OVEN-BAKED: After adding the boiling water, set in the middle of an oven preheated to 350°F. Start checking for doneness after 14 minutes for frika and 20 minutes for gruenkern.

KEEPING AND REHEATING: See The Grain Bank, page 10.

compatible foods and flavors

- Pine nuts, cinnamon, butter and oil, lamb, tomatoes, lemon

basic bulgur

Bulgur is a staple food in the Middle East, the Balkans, and North Africa. It is an extremely clever invention that transforms long-cooking wheat kernels into fast food. To make bulgur in the traditional way, wheat kernels are boiled until tender, then spread out and parched until dry, after which they are coarsely ground. The bulgur is then passed through sifters to separate the various particle sizes. Nowadays the same basic process is done by machines.

Bulgur has less fiber than whole wheat kernels since some bran is lost during processing. (However, when compared to brown rice, bulgur still has more than twice as much fiber.) Nutrient loss during processing is minimal, according to Mike Orlando, president of Sunnyland Mills, which started out as the Sunnyland Bulgur Wheat Company when it was founded by two Syrian immigrants in 1935. Orlando explains that "the boiling process allows the nutrients from the outer layers of the wheat kernels to migrate to the inner core."

Bulgur is available in four grinds, all of which are quick-cooking. The two most commonly available are fine (the type that comes in packaged tabbouleh mixes) and coarse (distributed in 1-pound packages by Goya). Sunnyland Mills produces all four sizes, which are available by mail-order.

Because of variations in age and storage conditions, as well as no firm regulation on the size of each grind, no two batches of bulgur require exactly the same amount of water for rehydration. Below you'll find general formulas and strategies, followed by a section in Cook's Notes that tells you how to rescue less-than-perfect batches.

All cooked bulgur molds beautifully when pressed into a ramekin or small cup and turned out.

fine and medium bulgur
(grinds #1 and #2)

Before steeping, fine bulgur (#1) is slightly flaky and looks somewhat like wheat germ. Medium (#2) looks like grits. After steeping, fine bulgur resembles instant couscous. It is light and delicate, with a bit of crunch, and makes a quick breakfast cereal or a good base for tabbouleh. It also works well as a last-minute thickener for soups and stews.

Steeped medium bulgur looks like couscous on steroids. It is chewier and has more of a grain presence than fine. Use cooked bulgur instead of rice as the base for chili, or add small amounts to pancake, waffle, or quick-bread batter for interesting texture. Fine and medium bulgur triple in size when cooked.

CUPS DRY	CUPS WATER	TEASPOONS SALT	POT SIZE	APPROXIMATE CUP YIELD
1	1 + 1 tablespoon	½	2-quart	3
1½	1½	¾	2-quart	4½
2	2	1	2-quart	6

Bring the water and salt to a boil in a heavy Dutch oven or saucepan. Stir in the bulgur. Cover and turn off the heat. Let steam for 10 minutes. Fluff up and serve hot, or spread out on a large plate to cool.

KEEPING AND REHEATING: See The Grain Bank, page 10.

coarse bulgur (grinds #3 and #4)

Coarse bulgur (#3 and #4) is about double the size of fine. While some recipes call for steeping it for 30 to 60 minutes, I find it more efficient and prefer the results when it is briefly cooked and then steamed off the heat. Coarse bulgur quadruples in size when cooked and is ideal for making pilafs and casseroles, and for stuffing vegetables or chicken.

In Middle Eastern groceries you may run across Lebanese coarse bulgur. The sample I tried from Kalustyan's (available by mail-order) is a handsome deep reddish color and slightly smaller than the #3 coarse bulgur from Sunnyland Farms. I cooked it according the instructions for #3 and it cooked up nice and fluffy. The flavor was slightly nuttier than standard bulgur.

Coarse bulgur cooks up double the size of fine and medium. Grain lovers who appreciate chewiness and texture will favor this granulation, particularly in pilafs (see the recipe on page 152). Coarse bulgur also makes a good meat substitute in chili, and a nicely textured patty when mixed with ground meat.

CUPS DRY	CUPS WATER	TEASPOONS SALT	POT SIZE	APPROXIMATE CUP YIELD
1	2	$\frac{1}{2}$	2-quart	3
$1\frac{1}{2}$	3	$\frac{3}{4}$	2-quart	$4\frac{1}{2}$
2	$3\frac{3}{4}$	1	3-quart	6

Bring the water and salt to a boil in a heavy Dutch oven or saucepan. Add the bulgur and stir once. Cover and reduce the heat to low. Cook for 10 minutes for #3 or 20 minutes for #4. Taste. If the grains are tender, drain off any unabsorbed liquid, fluff up, and serve. If just short of tender, turn off the heat and steam, covered, for 5 minutes. If not serving hot, spread out on a plate to cool. When cool, if not using immediately, cover with a kitchen towel or transfer to an airtight container to prevent the grains from drying out.

KEEPING AND REHEATING: See The Grain Bank, page 10.

cook's notes

■ When the bulgur is not tender in the time suggested: If the mixture is moist, cover and continue steaming off the heat for another 5 to 10 minutes. If the mixture is dry, drizzle 1 to 2 tablespoons boiling water on top and continue steaming until the grains reach the desired consistency.

■ When the bulgur doesn't fluff cooperatively or is overcooked and mushy: Transfer it to a large colander and run hot water over the grains to rinse off surface starch. Drain well by bouncing the colander up and down. Spread out on a large sheet pan lined with a kitchen towel and let sit at room temperature until the surface is dry. If necessary, reheat briefly in the microwave or a skillet.

compatible foods and flavors

■ Savory: parsley, tomatoes, scallions, lemon juice, olives, lamb, toasted nuts

■ Sweet: dried fruit, cinnamon and other sweet spices

basic whole-wheat couscous

In 1993, as part of an Oldways International Symposium in Tunisia, I had the great fortune to visit a couscous factory in the town of Sfax. There I saw traditionally dressed Berbere women drizzling salted water onto a bowl of flour and rolling tiny pellets of couscous by hand from the dough. Later I toured the factory, where machines turn out couscous in great quantity since few North Africans eat hand-rolled couscous anymore.

The extraordinary versatility of couscous was revealed to us in a lavish buffet table that contained more than a dozen hot and cold savory dishes as well as sweet desserts.

CUPS DRY	CUPS WATER	TEASPOONS SALT	POT SIZE	APPROXIMATE CUP YIELD
1	2	½	2-quart	3
1½	3	¾	2-quart	4½
2	3¾	1	3-quart	6

Traditional couscous is made from a refined form of hard durum wheat ground into flour, but whole-wheat couscous is an excellent option. Quick-cooking and mild tasting, whole-wheat couscous is terrific to use as the base for a saucy stew or a last-minute grain salad—or to toss some into a soup that needs thickening.

Bring the water and salt to a boil in a heavy pot that has a tight-fitting lid. Add the couscous and stir once. Cover and reduce the heat to low. Cook for 1 minute. Turn off the heat and steam, covered, until all of the liquid is absorbed and the particles are tender, 5 to 10 minutes. Fluff up. If not using immediately, cover with a kitchen towel or transfer to an airtight container to prevent the grains from drying out.

KEEPING AND REHEATING: Refrigerate for up to 5 days in a tightly sealed container. Reheat, lightly covered, in the microwave. Alternatively, heat in a heavy, covered saucepan over low heat, adding a little water if needed. Does not freeze well.

cook's notes

■ Package directions for preparing whole-wheat couscous may differ from those above, but my experience is that they often call for too much water.

■ Steep the couscous in low-sodium broth instead of water. Alternatively, use half water and half tomato or fruit juice.

compatible foods and flavors

■ Savory: lamb, olive oil, saffron, almonds, tomatoes, cucumbers, fresh herbs

■ Sweet: unsalted butter, raisins and other dried fruits, cinnamon and other sweet spices

basic cracked wheat

The advantage to cooking cracked wheat rather than the whole wheat kernels (wheat berries) is that cracked grains cook in about 20 minutes while whole kernels take three times as long.

Don't let anyone tell you that cracked wheat is the same as bulgur. It's not! And the two have different cooking requirements. The way to recognize the difference is that uncooked cracked wheat reveals the starchy white endosperm where the kernel has been cut. Bulgur is one color on all sides.

The best way to cook cracked wheat is to toast it in oil and cook it in minimal water as directed below. The resulting grain is chewy and slightly moist, with a pronounced toasted flavor.

CUPS DRY	TABLESPOONS OIL	CUPS WATER	SALT	POT SIZE	APPROXIMATE CUP YIELD
1	1	1¼	Pinch	2-quart	2¼
1½	1½	2	Pinch	2-quart	3½
2	1½	2¼	Pinch	2-quart	4½ to 5

Bring ample water to boil in a kettle so that you will have enough ready to add after toasting the grains.

Heat the oil in a heavy Dutch oven or saucepan. Stir in the cracked wheat. Toast over medium heat, stirring frequently, until the grains emit a toasty aroma, 2 to 3 minutes. Stand back and stir in the suggested amount of boiling water gradually to avoid boil-overs. Stir in the salt. Return to a boil. Cover and reduce the heat to low. Cook until the grains are almost tender and the water has been mostly or entirely absorbed, 5 to 8 minutes. (If the grains are still quite hard, evenly distribute ¼ cup additional boiling water over them and cook over low heat for another minute or two.) Turn off the heat and steam, covered, until tender, 10 to 15 minutes. Serve hot.

KEEPING AND REHEATING: Refrigerate for up to 5 days in a tightly sealed container. Reheat in a bowl, lightly covered, in the microwave. Does not freeze well.

cook's notes

■ If you cook cracked wheat in the commonly suggested proportions of 2 or 3 parts water to 1 part grain, the result will be porridge.

■ Cooked cracked wheat makes a nice base for stuffing.

■ Toss it with butter or a fragrant oil and nuts or herbs for a simple side dish.

■ Mix cooked cracked wheat with browned onions, and season with salt and pepper and a little balsamic syrup.

basic cracked green spelt

Imported from Germany, this product is quick-cooking and is a good choice for making moist pilafs and stuffings. With its distinctly smoky flavor, cracked spelt marries well with game and pork.

I have found the product to be very clean, but give it a quick rinse and drain well. Then follow the recipe for Basic Cracked Wheat, opposite. Cooked cracked green spelt has the texture of cracked wheat but looks unique, with its olive green bran and ivory endosperm.

basic kamut grits

Kamut grits are whole kernels that have been cut into pieces of uneven size. Kamut grits are usually labeled Kamut cereal, but if you cook the grits in less water than the package suggests, they can be fluffed up and served as a couscous-like pilaf.

Because the cracked grain's starchy center (endosperm) is exposed, the grits absorb water quickly and become tender in about 25 minutes—little more time than it takes to prepare white rice. Kamut grits cook up like cracked wheat except that they absorb more water and triple in size.

CUPS DRY	TABLESPOONS OIL	CUPS WATER	TEASPOONS SALT	POT SIZE	APPROXIMATE CUP YIELD
1	1	1½	Pinch	2-quart	3
1½	1½	2¼	¼	2-quart	4½
2	1½	3	½	2-quart	6

Bring ample water to a boil in a kettle so that you will have enough ready to add after toasting the grains.

Heat the oil in a heavy Dutch oven or saucepan. Stir in the cracked Kamut. Toast over medium heat, stirring frequently, until the grains emit a toasty aroma, 2 to 3 minutes. Stand back and pour in the suggested amount of boiling water gradually to avoid boil-overs. Stir in the salt. Return to a boil.

Cover, and reduce the heat to low. Cook until the grains are almost tender and the water has been mostly or entirely absorbed, 7 to 8 minutes. (If the grains are still quite hard, evenly distribute ¼ cup additional boiling water over them, cover, and cook over low heat for another minute or two.) Turn off the heat and steam, covered, until tender, 15 to 20 minutes. Serve hot.

KEEPING AND REHEATING: See The Grain Bank, page 10.

sprouting wheat

It's fun and easy to sprout all types of wheat kernels—including whole spelt and Kamut—and you don't need any special equipment. As sprouting takes place, the starch in the kernels transforms to sugar and the grains become sweet and chewy, with a touch of fresh crunch. Kamut sprouts are particularly tasty.

Sprouts are delicious to snack on. Add them to salads, sandwiches, or even waffle and pancake batters. Try adding them at the last minute to soups and stews.

Place ¼ cup of spelt, Kamut, or wheat berries in a large, wide-mouthed jar and add ample water to cover. Soak for 8 to 12 hours.

Hold a strainer close to the rim of the jar and drain off the soaking water. Add fresh water, shake the jar gently, and drain again.

Set the uncovered jar on its side in a dark, warm place for 24 hours. A turned-off oven with a pilot light is ideal.

Rinse and drain daily. Keep the uncovered jar in a dark, warm place until the sprouts are about ¼-inch long. The process usually takes 2 or 3 days. Refrigerate the sprouts for up to 5 days.

cook's notes

■ Sprouted grains are always ground before they are added to batters. If included whole, they dry out and become hard when baked.

■ It's possible to sprout various other whole grains, but I've found wheat to be the easiest and most reliable. For further information, instructions, and recipes, visit www.sproutpeople.com.

wild rice

Slender, long, and dark, wild rice always seems elegant and exotic. And then there's the matter of price. Until recently wild rice has been quite expensive and was always saved for special occasions.

Nowadays only about 15 percent of what we call wild rice actually grows wild in the place of its origin, the western Great Lakes. The remainder is cultivated in Minnesota, Wisconsin, California, and more recently Oregon. Even though the mystique of pricey, hand-harvested wild rice has persisted, experts claim that postharvest processing has more effect on flavor and texture than how or where the rice is grown.

Although an aquatic grass and not a true grain, wild rice has a nutritional profile similar to grains. It offers good-quality protein and is high in minerals, fiber, and B vitamins. Unlike most grains, it is low in fat, making it a good keeper. (You can store it at room temperature.)

Originally, Native Americans harvested wild rice by bending the long stalks over their canoes and, using sticks, beating the seed heads to release the immature, green grains into the boat. These days, air boats push collection trays that mechanically dislodge and catch the kernels. Once the rice is harvested, it goes through four processing steps before distribution: drying, parching, hulling, and winnowing to separate the hulls from the edible grain.

In the past, parching was done over an open fire, so if you purchase traditionally processed wild rice, be prepared for it to have a distinct smokiness. Since the taste of the grain resides primarily in the bran, the most flavorful grains will be those with the most bran intact. If you look closely and compare several brands, you'll see variations of color from deep mahogany to goldish brown. The more uniformly dark grains have more of their bran intact and will have more intense woodsy flavor. The lighter grains have had more of their bran removed in a mechanized scratching process called scarification. If you prefer a bigger flavor and crunchier grain, choose the darker batch. If you prefer a milder taste and texture, choose the lighter product.

The mechanization of harvesting and processing, plus the fact that so much wild rice is cultivated, has made wild rice quite affordable—especially given the fact that it triples or quadruples in volume when cooked. Now that the festive grain no longer has to be saved for special occasions, you will quickly understand how versatile it is. Try it in Wild Rice and Turkey Salad with Pear Dressing (page 141) or Wild and Brown Rice with Sesame-Soy Glazed Salmon (page 162). Substitute cooked wild rice for some of the brown in Brown Basmati Rice Custard Pudding (page 298) or Stir-Fried Beef and Vegetables (page 168). For more traditional Thanksgiving fare, enjoy Wild Rice and Chestnut Stuffing (page 212) or Wild Rice with Gingered Squash (page 222).

I find wild rice too intense to eat on its own and always like to combine it with either another grain or a vegetable.

WILD RICE AT A GLANCE

FORM	DESCRIPTION/PROCESSING	AVAILABILITY	COMMENTS
GIANT OR LONG	Each grain is about 1 inch long	Gourmet shops, mail-order	Few broken grains, fairly costly
EXTRA-FANCY OR MEDIUM	Each grain is about ½-inch long	Gourmet shops, mail-order, some supermarkets	Few broken grains, moderately expensive
SELECT	Short and broken grains of unequal size	Supermarkets, mail-order	Good for soups and stews when appearance is not important
TRADITIONAL OR HAND-PICKED WILD RICE	Naturally seeded and manually harvested in the Great Lakes region of Michigan and Canada	Gourmet shops, mail-order	The genuine item; considerable range of taste, color, and cost. Shop around.
CULTIVATED WILD RICE	Mechanized planting and harvesting in areas beyond the Great Lakes region	Gourmet shops, mail-order, supermarkets	Considerable range of taste, color, and cost. Shop around.

basic wild rice

Wild is a good name for this grain since every batch presents a wild card to the cook. However, as a general rule, the darker and more uniform the bran layer, the longer the grains will take to cook.

Allow for 65 minutes of cooking time, but start checking for doneness after only 35 minutes.

CUPS DRY	CUPS WATER	SALT	POT SIZE	APPROXIMATE CUP YIELD
3/4	1 3/4	Add to taste toward end of cooking	2-quart	2 1/4 to 3
1	2 1/2	Add to taste toward end of cooking	2-quart	3 to 4
1 1/2	3 1/4	Add to taste toward end of cooking	2-quart	4 1/2 to 6

Rinse the rice. Bring the rice and water to a boil in a heavy Dutch oven or saucepan. Cover, reduce the heat, and cook until some of the rice splits open and some of the grains have "butterflied" (split open and curled), 35 to 65 minutes. The internal texture of the grains should be soft and the bran layer tender, with just a suggestion of crunch. When done, turn off the heat and let the rice stand, covered, for 5 minutes. Drain off any unabsorbed liquid. Serve hot.

OVEN-BAKED: After bringing the rice and water to a boil, cover and set in the middle of an oven preheated to 350°F. Start checking for doneness after 35 minutes.

KEEPING AND REHEATING: See The Grain Bank, page 10.

cook's notes

■ Do not presoak or toast the rice. Both techniques cause the bran to separate from the starch during cooking, resulting in mushy rice that loses the glamorous sleek shape we love.

■ Do not add salt until some of the grains have butterflied, the poetic word for bursting open and curling. Adding salt from the start hardens the bran layer, retarding the absorption of water.

■ Avoid cooking wild rice like pasta, in a large pot of water, as some recipes suggest. To maximize flavor, use only slightly more water than needed, and then drain off the extra after the rice is tender.

■ If you find a batch of broken wild rice on a good sale, grab it. It makes a very pleasant couscous-like pilaf. Use a ratio of 2 parts liquid to 1 part broken rice and simmer, covered, until tender, 25 to 45 minutes. Drain off any unabsorbed liquid and season with butter, salt, and pepper.

compatible foods and flavors

■ Brown rice, oat groats, caramelized onions, carrots, chestnuts, squash, dried and fresh mushrooms, hazelnuts

cooking whole grains in a pressure cooker

With a pressure cooker, you can prepare whole grains on a whim. Brown rice is ready in 20 minutes and long-cooking grains like wheat berries are done in about 45. Some people find pressure-cooked grains more tender and digestible than grains cooked by standard stove-top steaming.

The user's guide that came with your cooker will acquaint you with the specifics of your model. For further information on pressure cooking, see my book *Pressure Perfect*.

In the following chart you'll find an alphabetical listing of the long-cooking grains that perform well under pressure. All of the timings are for *unsoaked* whole grains and assume that when the cooking time is up, you will quick-release the pressure as directed.

Grains with the same cooking time may be cooked together.

WHOLE GRAINS TIMING CHART

GRAIN	MINUTES UNDER HIGH PRESSURE
Barley, pearl	18
Barley, hulled and hull-less	18
Hominy	45
Job's tears	35
Oat groats (whole oats)	30
Rice, brown basmati, medium-, short-, and long-grain	15
Rice, red Colusari	15
Rice, red Wehani	15
Rice, black Japonica	15
Rice, whole-grain blends that call for 45 minutes cooking time	15
Rye berries	25
Sorghum, whole	28
Triticale kernels	30
Wheat berries	35
Wheat, Kamut	35
Wheat, spelt	35
Wild rice	25

basic pressure-cooked whole grains

The best way to cook grains in the pressure cooker is in lots of water—like pasta. Using this method, the grains cook evenly and there is no concern about scorching the bottom of the pot.

There are two important things to remember when cooking grains under pressure: (1) *You must add 1 tablespoon oil per cup of dry grain (2 tablespoons when cooking barley and oats)*. The oil is necessary to subdue the foam that rises as grains cook under pressure; it will be drained off with the water after cooking is completed. (2) *Do not fill the cooker more than halfway.* You can cook a maximum of 1½ cups of dry grain in a 4-quart cooker and 3 cups of dry grain in a 6-quart cooker.

For yields per cup, check the charts under individual grains.

CUPS GRAIN	CUPS WATER	TABLESPOONS OIL*	TEASPOONS SALT (OPTIONAL)
1	4	1	½
1½	5½	1½	¾
2	7	2	1
3	8	2	1

* Double the amount of oil when cooking barley and oats.

Place the grains and water in the cooker. Add the oil and salt (if using). Lock the lid in place, turn the heat to high, and bring the cooker up to high pressure. Reduce the heat just enough to maintain the pressure at high and cook for the time indicated in the Whole Grains Timing Chart (opposite).

Turn off the heat. Quick-release the pressure by setting the cooker in the sink and running cold water over the lid. Remove the lid and check the grains for doneness by cutting a few in half: they should be one color throughout. If the grains require more cooking, simmer them uncovered until done.

Drain. (You may reserve the broth for making soup.) Let the grains sit in the strainer for a few minutes before serving.

KEEPING AND REHEATING: See The Grain Bank, page 10.

stand-alone
soups

and
grain salads

soups

salads

SOUPS

amaranth, quinoa, and corn chowder

3 tablespoons unsalted butter

1½ cups finely chopped leeks (white and light green parts)

1 cup finely diced celery (remove "strings" by peeling celery before dicing)

½ cup finely diced red bell pepper

¼ teaspoon salt; plus more to taste

¼ cup amaranth

½ cup ivory quinoa, thoroughly rinsed (page 56)

¼ teaspoon dried thyme

4 cups fresh or thawed frozen corn kernels

1 cup whole milk

2 tablespoons minced fresh flat-leaf parsley

Ingredients indigenous to the New World, such as amaranth, quinoa, and corn, taste good together. In this soup, the amaranth and quinoa add substance and a subtle flavor that complements the more familiar taste of sweet corn.

SERVES 6

In a large, heavy pot, melt 2 tablespoons of the butter over medium-high heat. Stir in the leeks, celery, red bell pepper, and ¼ teaspoon salt. Cook, stirring frequently, until the vegetables are soft, about 5 minutes.

Stir in the amaranth and 3 cups of water. Bring to a boil over high heat. Stir in the quinoa and thyme. Return to a boil. Reduce the heat slightly and cook at a gentle boil, partially covered, for 10 minutes.

Meanwhile, in a blender or food processor, puree 3 cups of the corn kernels with 1 cup of water. When the quinoa has cooked for 10 minutes, stir the corn puree and the remaining corn kernels into the soup. Add salt to taste. Reduce the heat and simmer until the quinoa and amaranth are tender, 3 to 5 more minutes. When the quinoa is done, there will be no starchy white dot in the center of each grain, and some of the germs' "tails" may unfurl and float freely. On close inspection, the amaranth will look like tiny opaque bubbles floating on the surface.

Stir in the milk and remaining tablespoon of butter. Add more salt, if needed. Divide into portions and garnish each with a little parsley.

NOTE: The soup thickens on standing; thin as needed with additional milk, and add salt to taste.

VARIATIONS

• For dots of color, use 2 tablespoons of red quinoa and a scant ½ cup ivory quinoa. Add the red quinoa when you add the amaranth.

• Use half-and-half or heavy cream instead of milk.

• Use dried tarragon instead of thyme.

shrimp, corn, and quinoa soup

Instead of water, use 4 cups of fish or clam broth. Use oregano instead of the thyme. Once the quinoa is tender, add ½ pound peeled small shrimp. Cook until the shrimp turn pink, about 1 minute. Omit the milk.

barley, beef, and mushroom soup

¼ ounce (¼ cup) dried mushrooms
(porcini are divine but supermarket
dried mushrooms are fine)

1 pound beef chuck, cut into ½-inch
pieces

Salt and freshly ground pepper to
taste

1½ to 2½ tablespoons vegetable oil

1 tablespoon balsamic vinegar

3 cups chopped leeks (white and light
green parts)

1 cup finely diced carrots

½ pound cremini or button
mushrooms, some sliced, some
halved or quartered

¾ cup barley, preferably hull-less,
rinsed

¼ cup chopped fresh dill

Surely one of the best-known and most-loved grain soups is mushroom-barley. Typically it is made with pearl barley, so named because its bran layer has been rubbed or "pearled" off.

While you can make this soup with any type of barley, I encourage you to try it with hull-less barley. Unlike other forms of this much-loved grain, the hull-less variety has the courtesy to resist guzzling up every last drop of liquid if the soup sits a while.

SERVES 6

Set the dried mushrooms in a heatproof glass measuring cup or bowl and pour 2 cups of boiling water over them. Cover and set aside until the mushrooms are soft, 10 to 15 minutes.

Meanwhile, season the beef with salt and pepper. Heat 1½ tablespoons of the oil in a large, heavy pot over high heat. Brown the meat on all sides, 8 to 10 minutes. Stir in the balsamic vinegar and cook for an additional 30 seconds. Use a slotted spoon to transfer the meat to a plate.

If there is no fat left in the pot, add the remaining tablespoon of oil. Add the leeks, carrots, and fresh mushrooms. Season with a sprinkling of salt. Cook over medium-high heat, stirring occasionally, until the vegetables soften, about 5 minutes. Stir in the barley, browned beef, and 6 cups of water.

Remove the soaked mushrooms with a slotted spoon and add them to the soup. Pour in the soaking water, taking care to leave behind any grit that has settled to the bottom. Season the soup with salt and pepper to taste.

Bring the soup to a boil over high heat. Reduce the heat and simmer, partially covered, until the beef and barley are tender, 50 to 60 minutes. Stir in the dill and adjust the seasonings to taste. Serve hot.

GRAIN EXCHANGE
Use Kamut instead of barley.

vegetarian mushroom-barley soup
Omit the beef. Instead of adding 6 cups of water, use vegetable broth. Use 2 teaspoons Japanese soy sauce to replace some of the salt.

bulgur soup with lamb and chickpeas

1 tablespoon olive oil

1½ cups chopped leeks (white and
    light green parts)

1 pound ground lamb

¼ teaspoon salt, plus more to taste

2 teaspoons sweet paprika

1 teaspoon dried mint

1 teaspoon cumin seeds

¼ teaspoon ground cardamom

¼ to ½ teaspoon crushed red pepper
    flakes

⅛ teaspoon ground cinnamon

½ cup coarse bulgur

1 can (28 ounces) diced tomatoes,
    with liquid

1 can (15 to 19 ounces) chickpeas,
    drained and rinsed

¼ cup (tightly packed) chopped fresh
    cilantro

This quick rustic soup is infused with the scents and season-ings of North Africa, where bulgur is a favored grain. If possi-ble, make the soup a day ahead to give the flavors a chance to deepen.

SERVES 6 TO 8

Heat the oil in a large, heavy pot over medium-high heat. Add the leeks and cook until they soften slightly, about 3 minutes. Add the lamb and ¼ teaspoon salt. Reduce the heat slightly and cook until the lamb is no longer pink, breaking up the meat as you go.

Stir in the paprika, mint, cumin, cardamom, red pepper flakes, and cinnamon. Stir in 6 cups of water and the bulgur. Bring to a boil over high heat. Cover, reduce the heat, and simmer for 5 minutes.

Stir in the tomatoes, chickpeas, and salt to taste. Return to a boil. Reduce the heat and simmer, partially covered, until the bulgur is tender and the flavors have mingled, about 10 minutes more. Skim off the fat. (Alternatively, cool to room temperature, refrigerate, and remove the fat that congeals on top. Return to a boil.) Just before serving, stir in the cilantro.

VARIATION

Omit the dried mint and add 3 tablespoons chopped fresh mint with the cilantro.

GRAIN EXCHANGE

Reduce the water to 5 cups. Omit the bulgur. Instead, add 1½ cups cooked brown rice, farro, or wheat berries when you add the tomatoes.

hominy minestrone with basil pesto

1 tablespoon olive oil

1½ cups diced leeks (white and light green parts) or onion

2 teaspoons minced garlic

2 teaspoons balsamic vinegar

4 cups low-sodium chicken or vegetable broth

1 teaspoon dried oregano

Pinch of crushed red pepper flakes

1 medium carrot, halved lengthwise and cut into ¼-inch slices

1 medium bunch escarole (about 8 ounces), coarsely chopped

2 cups cooked Basic Hominy (page 36) or 1 can (19 ounces), drained

1 can (28 ounces) diced tomatoes, with liquid

1 can (15 ounces) chickpeas, drained and rinsed

Pinch of sugar (optional)

¼ cup grated Pecorino Romano or Parmesan cheese

Salt and freshly ground pepper

FOR THE BASIL PESTO

3 cups (tightly packed) fresh basil leaves

Generous ½ cup pine nuts or walnuts, toasted

½ cup grated Pecorino Romano or Parmesan cheese (or a combination), plus more to pass at the table

½ teaspoon salt, or to taste

4 to 6 tablespoons olive oil

Hominy adds a toothsome twist to this classic Italian soup, offering more robust flavor and texture than the traditional elbow pasta.

The pesto is essential for vibrant color and flavor. If basil is not in season or time is in short supply, use your favorite store-bought pesto.

SERVES 6 TO 8

Heat the oil in a large, heavy pot. Add the leeks and cook them over medium-high heat, stirring frequently, until they are wilted, about 5 minutes. Add the garlic and vinegar and continue cooking for another minute.

Stir in 2½ cups of water and the broth. Add the oregano, red pepper flakes, carrot, escarole, hominy, tomatoes, and chickpeas. Bring to a boil. Cover and cook over medium heat until the flavors have mingled and the escarole is tender, about 25 minutes. Add a generous pinch of sugar, if needed, to balance the acidity of the tomatoes.

While the soup is cooking, prepare the basil pesto. Place the basil and pine nuts in the bowl of a food processor and pulse a few times to chop coarsely. Add the cheese and salt. With the motor running, pour enough of the oil into the feed tube to create a thick paste. Add additional salt to taste.

When the soup is done, stir in the cheese. Season with salt and pepper. Ladle into soup bowls and top with a dollop of basil pesto.

VARIATIONS

• Substitute cannellini, kidney, or navy beans for the chickpeas.

• Add 1½ teaspoons fennel seeds when you add the garlic.

• Use flat-leaf parsley instead of basil in the pesto.

farro soup with kale and cannellini

1 cup farro, picked over and rinsed

2 tablespoons olive oil

1 large onion, diced

1 medium carrot, diced

2 stalks celery, diced

3 cloves garlic, minced

1 cup dried cannellini beans, soaked
   overnight in ample water to cover

1 can (15 ounces) diced tomatoes,
   with liquid

1 teaspoon salt, plus more to taste

1 bunch kale (about 14 ounces)

½ cup chopped fresh basil or parsley

¼ cup Parmesan cheese

Freshly ground pepper to taste

Chewy nubbins of farro give special appeal to a hearty Mediterranean vegetable-bean soup that's loaded with calcium-rich kale. If you don't have time to cook the beans from scratch, check out the Express Farro and Chickpea Soup variation, opposite.

SERVES 6 TO 8

Set the farro in a large bowl or spouted glass measuring cup and add ample cold water to cover. Set aside while you cook the beans.

Heat 1 tablespoon of the oil in a large, heavy pot over medium-high heat. Stir in the onion, carrot, and celery. Cook until the onion softens, about 3 minutes. Add the garlic and continue to cook until the onion is lightly browned, a few minutes more.

Drain the cannellini beans and add them to the pot. Add 8 cups of water. Bring the liquid to a boil, then cover the pot and simmer until the beans are almost tender, 40 to 60 minutes (depending on age and storage conditions).

Drain the farro. Add the farro, tomatoes, and salt. Return to a boil, then cover and simmer for 10 minutes.

Meanwhile, prepare the kale: Discard a few inches of the tough root ends. Thinly slice the stems and coarsely chop the leaves. Rinse well by dunking it in a large bowl or sink full of water. Drain well.

When the farro has simmered for 10 minutes, stir in the kale gradually, adding more as each batch wilts. Cover and continue cooking until the beans, farro, and kale are tender, usually 10 to 20 minutes more. Add the remaining tablespoon of oil, the basil, cheese, and salt and pepper to taste.

VARIATION

Use Great Northern or navy beans instead of cannellini beans.

GRAIN EXCHANGE

Substitute 1 cup uncooked Kamut for the farro. Add it when you add the soaked beans.
Increase the water to 9 cups.

express farro and chickpea soup

Soak the farro for 10 to 15 minutes. Instead of dried cannellini beans, substitute 1 can (16 or
19 ounces) chickpeas, drained and rinsed. Add them when you add the drained farro.

oat and turkey soup with tex-mex flavors

2 tablespoons olive oil

1 large onion, diced

1 stalk celery, diced

1 teaspoon salt

2 cans (10 ounces each) diced
   tomatoes with green chiles, with
   liquid

2 teaspoons chili powder

1 teaspoon dried oregano

1/8 teaspoon ground cinnamon

3 pounds bone-in turkey thighs,
   skinned

1/2 cup steel-cut oats

1 cup frozen corn kernels, rinsed under
   hot water

1 ripe avocado, halved, pitted, peeled,
   and cut into 1/2-inch cubes

3 to 4 tablespoons coarsely chopped
   fresh cilantro

2 to 3 tablespoons freshly squeezed
   lime juice

Freshly ground pepper to taste

Oats add a mellow texture and inviting sheen to this whole-some soup. Serve it with warm tortillas for dunking.

SERVES 5 TO 6

In a large, heavy pot, heat 1 tablespoon of the oil. Stir in the onion, celery, and 1/4 teaspoon of the salt. Cook over medium-high heat, stirring occasionally, until the onion is translucent, 3 to 4 minutes. Stir in the tomatoes, remaining salt, chili powder, oregano, and cinnamon.

Add 5 cups of water, and stir to scrape up any browned bits sticking to the bottom of the pot. Add the turkey thighs and bring to a boil. Reduce the heat to low. Cover and simmer for 15 minutes.

Stir in the oats. Cover and continue simmering until the turkey is tender and easily pulls away from the bone, 25 to 45 minutes longer, depending on the size of the thighs. Transfer the turkey to a cutting board. If the oats are not tender, continue simmering the soup, uncovered, until they are done. Otherwise turn off the heat. Skim off any fat that rises to the top of the soup.

When the turkey is cool enough to handle, remove the meat from the bones and shred it into bite-sized pieces. Stir the corn and shredded turkey into the soup. Reheat, if necessary.

Turn off the heat and stir in the avocado, the remaining tablespoon of olive oil, the cilantro, and lime juice to taste. Correct the seasoning with salt and pepper. Serve hot in large bowls.

VARIATION
Add 1 diced zucchini for the last 5 minutes of cooking.

GRAIN EXCHANGE
Use hull-less barley instead of steel-cut oats. Add the barley
with the turkey thighs.

thai chicken soup with chinese black rice

2 cups reduced-sodium chicken broth

1 can (15 ounces) unsweetened coconut milk

2 to 3 teaspoons Thai red or yellow curry paste

1 can (15 ounces) diced tomatoes, including liquid

1½ pounds bone-in, skinned chicken thighs or split breasts

4 scallions, thinly sliced (keep white and green parts separate)

¼ cup finely diced red bell pepper

1½ cups cooked Basic Chinese Black Rice (page 75)

¼ cup chopped fresh cilantro or basil

2 to 3 tablespoons freshly squeezed lime juice

Thai fish sauce or soy sauce (optional)

Lime wedges, to serve at the table

Thanks to the flavor-packed Thai curry paste available in most supermarkets, this soup has complex flavor but is quick and easy to prepare. A fine-quality Chinese black rice goes by the name Forbidden Black Rice and is sold in many supermarkets and specialty shops.

SERVES 4

In a 4-quart pot, blend the chicken broth, coconut milk, and curry paste to taste. Set the pot over medium heat. Add the tomatoes, chicken, scallion whites, and bell pepper. Bring to a simmer. Cover and simmer until the chicken is cooked, 20 to 30 minutes, depending upon size.

Remove the chicken. When it is cool enough to handle, shred or chop the meat and discard the bones. Return the chicken to the pot and stir in the rice. Add the cilantro, scallion greens, lime juice to taste, and fish sauce, if needed to perk up the flavors.

Before ladling out each portion, stir well to bring the rice up from the bottom. Serve with lime wedges.

VARIATIONS

• Add a handful of baby spinach or frozen peas along with the cilantro.

• Add a few tablespoons of chopped fresh mint in addition to the cilantro.

GRAIN EXCHANGE

Instead of black rice, use brown basmati, brown jasmine, or Thai black sticky rice.

rye berry soup with cabbage and dill sour cream

2 tablespoons unsalted butter

2 large onions, halved and thinly sliced

1 or 2 cloves garlic, minced

2 tablespoons tomato paste

2 tablespoons sweet paprika

1/2 teaspoon caraway seeds, chopped

8 cups (tightly packed) shredded
cabbage (1 3/4 pounds)

6 cups reduced-sodium chicken or
vegetable broth

2 teaspoons sugar

2 to 3 cups cooked Basic Whole Rye
Berries (page 80)

Salt and freshly ground pepper to
taste

2 to 3 tablespoons freshly squeezed
lemon juice

FOR THE DILL SOUR CREAM

1 cup sour cream

1/2 cup chopped fresh dill

1 teaspoon apple cider vinegar

Here is a comforting soup inspired by the flavors of Eastern Europe. I like to think of Boris Pasternak warming up with a bowlful when he was writing the snowy scenes in *Dr. Zhivago*.

The combination of tender cabbage and chewy rye berries is particularly appealing. For a double rye experience, serve the soup with a hearty rye bread.

SERVES 6

Heat the butter in a large, heavy pot over medium-high heat. Add the onions and cook, stirring frequently, until they soften, about 4 minutes. Stir in the garlic, tomato paste, paprika, and caraway and cook for another minute, stirring constantly. Lower the heat if the mixture threatens to burn.

Stir in 2 cups of water and the cabbage. Bring to a boil, cover, and lower the heat to medium. Cook until the cabbage wilts, stirring occasionally, 8 to 10 minutes. Add the broth, sugar, rye berries, and salt and pepper. Cook the soup until the cabbage is tender and the flavors have mingled, 15 to 20 additional minutes.

Meanwhile, prepare the dill sour cream. In a small bowl, blend the sour cream, dill, and vinegar.

When the soup is done, stir in lemon juice to taste, and adjust the seasonings.

To serve, ladle the soup into bowls and top each portion with a dollop of dill sour cream.

VARIATIONS

• Sprinkle a small pinch of finely chopped caraway seeds onto the dill topping.

• After adding the broth, stir in 1/2 pound potatoes, peeled and cut into 1/2-inch dice.

• Use 1/4 teaspoon ground juniper berries instead of the caraway seeds.

chilled cucumber-yogurt soup
with bulgur timbales

FOR THE SOUP

8 large cucumbers, peeled, halved
   lengthwise, and seeded

1 1/3 cups plain low-fat yogurt

3/4 cup 2% milk

1/3 cup freshly squeezed lemon juice

3 to 4 tablespoons fruity olive oil

Salt

FOR THE TIMBALES

1 1/3 cups cooked Coarse Bulgur
   (page 100)

1/3 cup finely diced seeded tomato

2 teaspoons olive oil

2 teaspoons freshly squeezed lemon
   juice

3 tablespoons coarsely chopped fresh
   mint, plus 4 small sprigs for garnish

1/4 teaspoon cumin seeds, toasted and
   finely chopped

Salt to taste

In this elegant soup, a refreshing cucumber-yogurt puree forms a moat around a mound of brightly seasoned bulgur. It's the perfect light lunch in the dog days of summer.

SERVES 4

Reserve half of one cucumber. Place the remaining cucumbers into a food processor with the yogurt, milk, lemon juice, and oil to taste. Puree. (Some of the cucumber pulp will remain evident in the puree.) Add salt to taste. Chill the puree and reserved cucumber separately.

Meanwhile, make the timbale mixture: Combine the bulgur, tomato, oil, lemon juice, chopped mint, cumin, and salt in a small bowl. Cover and set aside to marinate for 10 to 15 minutes.

To serve: Divide the cucumber puree among four wide, shallow soup bowls. Cut the reserved cucumber into fine dice and stir into the puree.

Press enough of the bulgur mixture into a 1/3-cup measuring cup to reach the top. Run a knife along the edges to loosen the timbale. Position it over the center of a soup bowl and turn it over. Tap the bottom to release the timbale into the puree. Repeat to make 3 more servings. Garnish each portion with a sprig of mint.

GRAIN EXCHANGE

Substitute quinoa or short-grain brown rice for the bulgur.

SALADS

barley tabbouleh

4 cups cooked Basic Hulled or
  Hull-less Barley (page 25)
2 cups (tightly packed) finely chopped
  fresh flat-leaf parsley leaves and
  tender stems (from 2 hefty
  bunches)
2 cups peeled, seeded, diced
  cucumbers
2 cups diced plum tomatoes
1/2 cup (tightly packed) finely chopped
  fresh mint
1/4 cup fruity olive oil
1/4 cup freshly squeezed lemon juice,
  plus more if needed
Salt to taste

Classic tabbouleh becomes an entirely new dish when sweet, chewy barley replaces the traditional fine bulgur. Because barley is more filling than bulgur, the salad falls squarely into the main dish category.

SERVES 4 TO 6

Combine all of the ingredients in a large bowl. Adjust the seasonings. Let sit for a few minutes before serving.

VARIATION
Use 1/3 cup chopped oil-packed sun-dried tomatoes instead of the fresh tomatoes.

GRAIN EXCHANGE
Use wheat berries, farro, sorghum, or Kamut—or a combination of grains—instead of the barley.

greek barley salad
Use fresh dill instead of mint. Add 1/2 to 1 cup crumbled feta and 1/4 cup chopped, pitted Alfonso or Kalamata olives. Add more olive oil, lemon juice, and salt if needed.

chinese black rice, orange, and avocado salad

2 cups cooked Basic Chinese Black
　　Rice (page 75)
2 cups diced peeled oranges
¼ cup freshly squeezed orange juice
¼ cup raw, unsalted pumpkin seeds,
　　toasted
1½ teaspoons grated orange zest
¼ teaspoon salt, plus more to taste
⅛ teaspoon ground chipotle
1 ripe Hass avocado, peeled, pitted,
　　and cut into ½-inch dice
4 large lettuce cups or leaves
Unpeeled orange wedges, for garnish
　　(optional)

China meets the Southwest in this unusual fusion salad. Glistening Chinese black rice—usually sold under the label Forbidden Black Rice—set off against bright orange segments and avocado's pale green gives the mixture striking visual appeal.

SERVES 4

In a bowl, combine the black rice, oranges, orange juice, pumpkin seeds, orange zest, salt, and chipotle. Gently mix in the avocado. Add more salt, if needed.

Place a lettuce cup on each plate and spoon the salad into the lettuce cups. Garnish with orange wedges, if you wish.

GRAIN EXCHANGE
Use Wehani or wild rice instead of the black rice.

brown rice salade niçoise

⅓ cup minced red onion

1½ teaspoons balsamic vinegar

1 can (about 6 ounces) tuna packed in olive oil, undrained

3 cups cooked Basic Short-Grain Brown Rice (page 66)

1 small red or yellow bell pepper, seeded and diced

⅓ cup pitted, chopped oil-cured black olives

2 tablespoons minced drained capers (chop if large)

1 to 3 tablespoons freshly squeezed lemon juice

1 to 2 tablespoons olive oil (optional)

2 tablespoons minced fresh flat-leaf parsley

Salt and freshly ground pepper

6 cups (loosely packed) shredded romaine

1 pound green beans, trimmed, steamed, and cooled

4 hard-boiled eggs, peeled and halved

Chewy, easy-to-love short-grain brown rice makes an appealing grain base for a salad containing many of the elements of a traditional salade niçoise. The tuna and its soaking oil become a major part of the dressing, coating each grain with the savor of the sea. It's important to use a good-tasting canned tuna; I have found that the best are imported from Italy and well worth the extra cost.

SERVES 4

In a small bowl, combine the red onion and vinegar. Set aside to soak for at least 10 minutes.

Empty the tuna and oil into a large bowl. Flake the tuna with a fork. Add the brown rice, bell pepper, olives, and capers. Stir in the onion and any unabsorbed vinegar. Add the lemon juice, olive oil (if using), parsley, and salt and pepper to taste.

To serve, place a bed of lettuce on each plate and spoon the salad on top. Arrange the green beans and eggs alongside.

VARIATIONS

• Add 1 teaspoon grated lemon zest.

• Add 2 teaspoons chopped fresh lemon thyme.

• Instead of parsley, add minced fresh tarragon to taste.

• Add shredded radicchio to the romaine.

GRAIN EXCHANGE

Substitute farro or any type of whole barley for the brown rice.

bulgur and chickpea salad with parsley dressing

FOR THE DRESSING

¼ cup olive oil

¼ cup freshly squeezed lemon juice

½ cup (tightly packed) fresh flat-leaf
parsley leaves and tender stems

2 tablespoons plain low-fat yogurt

1 teaspoon (packed) grated lemon
zest

1 teaspoon salt

¼ teaspoon harissa or pinch of
cayenne (optional)

FOR THE SALAD

1 can (15 to 19 ounces) chickpeas,
drained and rinsed

2½ cups cooked Coarse Bulgur
(page 100)

1½ cups diced seeded cucumber

1 cup diced radishes

¼ cup thinly sliced scallion greens

This refreshing grain salad has a Middle Eastern feel. Serve it with whole-wheat pita bread for a pleasing light lunch.

SERVES 4

In a food processor or blender, blend the oil, lemon juice, parsley, yogurt, lemon zest, salt, and harissa (if using).

In a large serving bowl, combine the chickpeas, bulgur, cucumbers, radishes, and scallion greens. Add the dressing and toss to coat. Let the salad sit for 5 minutes before serving.

VARIATIONS

• Substitute fresh dill or mint for the parsley.

• Substitute ⅓ cup diced pickled turnips for the radishes.

• Omit the radishes and substitute finely diced plum tomatoes.

GRAIN EXCHANGE

Instead of bulgur, use Kamut, wheat berries, or spelt.

farro salad with prosciutto and asparagus

FOR THE SALAD

12 spears asparagus, trimmed

4 cups cooked Basic Farro (page 96)

¼ pound thinly sliced prosciutto, coarsely chopped

2 tablespoons chopped fresh flat-leaf parsley

FOR THE DRESSING

3 tablespoons olive oil

2 to 3 tablespoons grated Parmesan cheese

2 to 3 tablespoons freshly squeezed lemon juice

1 teaspoon grated lemon zest

½ teaspoon Dijon mustard

Salt and freshly ground pepper to taste

Served warm or at room temperature, this Mediterranean-inspired salad makes a light and attractive meal. Think of it in spring, when slender asparagus makes its first appearance in the market.

SERVES 6

To prepare the salad: Steam the asparagus until tender but still crisp and bright green. Run it under cold water to stop the cooking process. Drain well. Cut the asparagus into ¼-inch slices.

In a large bowl, combine the farro, prosciutto, asparagus, and parsley.

To make the dressing: In a small bowl, blend the oil, 2 tablespoons each Parmesan and lemon juice, plus the lemon zest and mustard. Toss into the salad. Add salt and pepper to taste, plus additional Parmesan and lemon juice if needed.

GRAIN EXCHANGE

Use pearl barley or short-grain brown rice instead of farro.

kamut-chicken salad with romaine, olives, and sage

FOR THE SALAD

4 cups cooked Basic Whole Kamut
    Kernels (page 94)

2 to 3 cups diced roast chicken

½ cup chopped pitted ripe black
    olives

½ cup chopped pitted Mediterranean-
    style green olives

5 cups (tightly packed) shredded
    romaine

1 cup (tightly packed) shredded
    radicchio

12 to 16 fresh sage leaves, thinly
    sliced crosswise

FOR THE DRESSING

¼ cup olive oil

¼ cup freshly squeezed lemon juice

2 teaspoons (packed) grated lemon
    zest

½ teaspoon salt, plus more if needed

Because Kamut grains are large and dense, it's appealing to "aerate" them with buoyant leafy greens like shredded romaine. Add the greens and dressing just before serving so that the salad will be nice and crisp.

SERVES 6

In a large bowl, combine the Kamut, chicken, and olives.

Prepare the dressing by combining the oil, lemon juice, lemon zest, and salt.

Just before serving, add the lettuce, radicchio, and sage. Toss in the dressing. Add salt to taste.

VARIATIONS

• Use 1 to 2 teaspoons chopped fresh rosemary instead of the sage.

• Substitute roast turkey for the chicken.

GRAIN EXCHANGE

Use rye berries, spelt, triticale, or wheat berries instead of Kamut.

quinoa and calamari salad

FOR THE SALAD

1 small red onion, halved lengthwise
  and thinly sliced
1 tablespoon balsamic vinegar
1 pound squid, cleaned
3 cups cooked Basic Quinoa
  (page 58)
1 cup diced celery
½ cup chopped red bell pepper
¼ cup minced pitted oil-cured black
  olives
½ cup (tightly packed) chopped fresh
  flat-leaf parsley

FOR THE DRESSING

¼ cup olive oil
2 to 3 tablespoons freshly squeezed
  lemon juice
1 teaspoon salt
½ teaspoon dried oregano
½ teaspoon Dijon mustard
1 small clove garlic, minced
Freshly ground black pepper to taste

The versatility of quinoa amazes me. This salad is a case in point. Although a traditional calamari salad has "Mediterranean" stamped all over it, this grain of the highland Andes is right at home with the flavors of southern Italy.

The salad's taste improves after sitting for 30 minutes at room temperature or overnight in the refrigerator. Serve it at room temperature on a bed of greens mixed with slivers of radicchio to add some bright color. It makes an unusual addition to a summer buffet table.

SERVES 4

Bring a large pot of salted water to a boil. Prepare a large bowl of ice water.

In a small bowl, combine the onion and vinegar and set aside.

Rinse the squid. Cut long tentacles in half crosswise. Cut the bodies crosswise (including any flaps) into ¼-inch rings. Add the squid to the boiling water and cook uncovered until it turns opaque, 35 to 60 seconds. Immediately drain the squid and transfer it to the bowl of ice water to halt the cooking. When the squid is cool, drain it and pat dry.

Transfer the squid to a salad bowl. Toss in the quinoa, celery, red pepper, olives, and parsley.

Prepare the dressing: In a small bowl, whisk together the oil, 2 tablespoons lemon juice, salt, oregano, mustard, garlic, and black pepper.

Toss the dressing and onion along with any unabsorbed vinegar into the squid salad. Set it aside for 30 minutes or refrigerate overnight. Before serving the salad, add more lemon juice to perk up the flavors.

GRAIN EXCHANGE

Use farro, coarse bulgur, or wheat berries instead of quinoa.

quinoa and shrimp salad

Substitute 1 pound cooked, peeled shrimp for the calamari.

■ ■ ■

rye berry slaw with smoked trout and dill

FOR THE SLAW

4 cups cooked Basic Whole Rye Berries
   (page 80)
½ pound red cabbage, shredded
   (about 3 tightly packed cups)
6 ounces smoked trout or mackerel,
   flaked
1 medium carrot, coarsely grated
½ cup chopped fresh dill

FOR THE DRESSING

¼ cup freshly squeezed lemon juice
3 tablespoons canola or other neutral
   oil
1 tablespoon sweet paprika
1 teaspoon caraway seeds, chopped
½ to ¾ teaspoon salt

Dill, caraway, and paprika are principal seasonings in northern European kitchens, so it's no surprise that they work so beautifully with cabbage and smoked fish—other ingredients common to that part of the world. Rye usually appears in the form of bread, so it's a nice change to experience the chewy, faintly sour grain in a slaw.

Although slaws are commonly thought of as side dishes, this one is hearty enough to be served as an entrée. It also makes an unusual addition to a buffet table.

SERVES 6

In a large bowl, combine the rye berries, cabbage, trout, carrot, and dill.

To prepare the dressing: In a small bowl, blend the lemon juice, oil, paprika, caraway seeds, and ½ teaspoon salt.

Toss the dressing into the rye berry mixture. Add more salt, if needed. Let the salad sit for 15 minutes before serving. Serve at room temperature.

GRAIN EXCHANGE

Substitute 2 cups long-grain brown rice, wild rice, or Kamut for 2 cups of the rye berries.

wheat berry salad with apples and mint

½ cup freshly squeezed orange juice

2 tablespoons olive oil

1½ tablespoons apple cider vinegar

1 teaspoon salt, plus more to taste

¾ cup (tightly packed) fresh mint
   leaves

2 cups cooked Basic Wheat Berries
   (page 94)

2 teaspoons grated orange zest (from
   2 juice oranges)

1 small green apple

1 small red apple

½ cup hazelnuts, toasted and coarsely
   chopped

Chewy wheat berries develop a juicy "squish" when marinated briefly in dressing. A citrus dressing is a particularly good complement to the tart green apple and vibrant mint tossed into the mix.

The salad tastes best when freshly made; the wheat berries tend to harden when refrigerated. To improve the texture of any leftovers, loosely cover the bowl of salad with waxed paper, and microwave it for about 20 seconds. Perk up the taste with a little lemon juice.

Serve the salad on its own or with roast chicken or grilled meat.

SERVES 4 TO 6

Blend the orange juice, oil, vinegar, salt, and ½ cup of the mint in a food processor or blender.

Set the wheat berries in a medium bowl. Pour the dressing over them and toss to coat. Stir in the orange zest. Set aside for at least 15 minutes. Toss occasionally.

Meanwhile, core the unpeeled apples and cut them into ¼-inch dice. Stack the remaining mint leaves and roll them into a log. Slice them as thinly as you can. Toss them into the salad along with the apples and hazelnuts. Add more salt, if needed.

VARIATION

After blending the dressing, stir in 2 to 3 tablespoons finely chopped crystallized ginger.

GRAIN EXCHANGE

Use short-grain brown rice, triticale, spelt, or Kamut instead of wheat berries.

whole-grain bread salad with tomatoes and basil

2 pounds ripe tomatoes

½ teaspoon salt, plus more to taste

1 large clove garlic, halved

8 slices rustic whole-grain bread, preferably 1 to 2 days old

½ to ¾ cup (tightly packed) fresh basil leaves

¼ cup olive oil

2 tablespoons balsamic or red wine vinegar

⅓ cup Niçoise or other small, black Mediterranean olives

Whole-grain bread makes an outstanding panzanella, the traditional Italian salad that puts day-old bread to tasty use. Make it with a good-quality whole-grain bread—perhaps one that includes some seeds—for a rustic variation on the classic theme.

For a heartier meal, serve the salad with roasted vegetables and a few thin slices of smoked mozzarella.

SERVES 4 TO 6

Set the rack in the bottom third, and preheat the oven to 425°F.

Core the tomatoes and cut them in half crosswise (if small) or into quarters (if large). Set a strainer over a large bowl and use your fingers to remove the tomato seeds, allowing the seeds to fall into the strainer and the juices to drip through into the bowl. Use a spoon to press down on the seeds to release all of the tomato liquid. Discard the seeds. Dice the flesh and add it to the bowl. Toss in the salt.

Rub the garlic on both sides of the bread. Set the bread on a baking sheet and toast for 5 minutes. Flip it over and continue toasting until the bread is crisp, usually 2 to 3 minutes more. When the bread is cool enough to handle, tear it into bite-sized pieces and toss it into the bowl.

Let the mixture sit until the bread has absorbed most of the tomato liquid, about 15 minutes or longer. Just before serving, tear the basil leaves in half (if small) or quarters (if large) and toss them in. Stir in the oil, vinegar, olives, and salt to taste.

tuna and whole-grain bread salad

Toss in a can of undrained tuna packed in olive oil and reduce the olive oil in the recipe to 2 tablespoons.

wild rice and turkey salad with pear dressing

FOR THE PEAR DRESSING

1 large ripe Bartlett pear

2 tablespoons canola or peanut oil

1½ tablespoons sherry vinegar

1 teaspoon honey

1 teaspoon grated orange zest

½ teaspoon salt

⅛ teaspoon ground allspice

FOR THE SALAD

3 cups cooked Basic Wild Rice
  (page 110)

3 cups diced roast turkey

½ cup pecans, toasted and coarsely
  chopped

⅓ cup chopped dried cranberries

⅓ cup thinly sliced scallion greens

Here is a fetching main dish salad to prepare when your refrigerator overflows with holiday leftovers. It also makes a festive contribution to a potluck any time of year, prepared with store-bought roast turkey.

SERVES 4

Quarter the unpeeled pear and remove the core and seeds. Puree the pear in a mini food processor. Transfer it to a large bowl and blend in the oil, vinegar, honey, orange zest, salt, and allspice.

Stir in the wild rice, turkey, pecans, cranberries, and scallion greens. Adjust the seasonings to taste. Let the salad sit for 10 minutes before serving. Serve at room temperature.

VARIATION

Use roast chicken instead of turkey.

GRAIN EXCHANGE

Substitute Wehani rice for the wild rice.

main

courses

risottos, pilafs, and polentas

stir-fries and skillet dishes

braises, stews, casseroles, and savory pies

RISOTTOS, PILAFS, AND POLENTAS

farro risotto with butternut squash, ham, sage, and toasted walnuts

1½ tablespoons olive oil

1 cup chopped leeks or onions

4 cups low-sodium chicken or
  vegetable broth

1 cup semi-pearled farro

⅓ cup dry white wine or dry
  vermouth

3 tablespoons minced fresh sage
  or ½ teaspoon dried

2 cups grated butternut squash (about
  ½ pound)

2 cups diced country ham (4 to
  6 ounces)

¼ cup grated Parmesan or Romano
  cheese, plus more for garnish and to
  pass at the table

¼ cup chopped walnuts, toasted

Salt and freshly ground black pepper
  to taste

When Italians make risotto from farro, they call it *farrotto*. Farro has enough silken starch to make this an appealing variation of the classic risotto made with rice.

Ham adds substance, and the butternut squash melts into a sweet sauce that coats the grains an autumnal orange.

SERVES 4

Heat the olive oil over medium-high heat in a large, heavy saucepan. Add the leeks and cook, stirring occasionally, until they soften but do not brown, 4 to 5 minutes.

Meanwhile, bring the broth to a simmer in a separate saucepan. Stir the farro into the leeks and continue cooking until the farro is lightly toasted, 2 to 3 minutes. Stir in the wine and cook until it evaporates, about a minute.

Stir in 2 cups of the broth, 2 tablespoons of the fresh sage or ½ teaspoon dried, and the squash. Simmer, stirring from time to time, until the mixture becomes thick, about 10 minutes.

Gradually stir in the remaining broth, each time returning to a boil, then reducing to a simmer, until the mixture thickens.

After the farro has cooked for a total of 20 minutes, begin tasting for doneness. When it is tender but still chewy, stir in the ham.

Turn off the heat, and stir in the Parmesan, walnuts, and salt and pepper to taste. Ladle into shallow bowls. Garnish individual portions with the remaining fresh sage and a light dusting of Parmesan. Serve immediately.

WINE RECOMMENDATION: A full-bodied aromatic white, like a gewürztraminer or a pinot gris, will complement the sweetness of the squash and make a nice foil for the salty ham. Or try a fruity sparkling wine, like an Italian Prosecco, which will cut through the richness of the creamy starch and the cheese.

barley risotto with wild mushrooms

½ ounce (about ½ cup) dried porcini
or other dried mushrooms, rinsed

1 tablespoon olive oil

2 cups chopped leeks (white and light
green parts) or onions

1 teaspoon whole fennel seeds

1 cup pearl barley

2 tablespoons black barley (optional,
but nice for color)

⅓ cup dry sherry or red wine

3 cups low-sodium chicken broth

3 to 6 tablespoons grated Parmesan or
Romano cheese, to taste, plus more
for garnish and to pass at the table

3 tablespoons minced flat-leaf parsley

Salt and freshly ground black pepper
to taste

Risotto made with pearl barley is a delightfully chewy alternative to traditional risotto made with white Arborio rice. The barley's starch melts into a luscious sauce infused with the earthy flavor of wild mushrooms.

The most efficient way to prepare this risotto (and any other risotto, in my opinion) is in a pressure cooker. If you don't own one, check the standard stove-top instructions, opposite.

Most people will be content to eat this risotto as an entrée accompanied by a side salad or steamed green vegetable. It also makes a lovely side dish for roast meats or osso buco.

SERVES 4 TO 6

Place the mushrooms in a heatproof glass measuring cup and pour 2 cups of boiling water on top. Cover and set aside.

In a 4-quart or larger pressure cooker, heat the oil. Add the leeks and fennel seeds and cook over medium-high heat, stirring frequently, until the leeks are softened, about 4 minutes.

Stir in the barley, lightly coating it with oil. Add the sherry and continue cooking until it evaporates. Stir in the broth. Add the soaked mushrooms and soaking liquid, taking care to leave behind any grit that has settled to the bottom of the cup.

Lock the pressure cooker lid in place and bring the cooker up to high pressure over high heat. Reduce the heat to maintain the pressure at high and cook for 18 minutes. Release the pressure by placing the cooker under cold running water. Remove the lid, tilting it away from your face to avoid the escaping steam.

Set the uncovered cooker over high heat and cook, stirring frequently, until the barley is tender (it will still be slightly chewy) and the mixture has thickened to a porridge consistency, about 5 minutes. Stir in Parmesan to taste and the parsley. Add salt and pepper to taste.

Ladle the risotto into bowls or onto lipped plates. Dust it with a little more cheese, and serve the extra cheese in a small bowl.

WINE RECOMMENDATION: Risotto is at home in Piedmont, a region in Italy that offers red wines perfect for drinking with this dish. Try a barbera or dolcetto, which both have bright red fruit qualities and a pleasant earthiness that complements the mushrooms.

standard stove-top risotto

For best results, use a lightly pearled barley, such as the type available in the supermarket, and a heavy, 3-quart saucepan. Add only 2 cups of chicken broth once the sherry has evaporated, and reserve the remaining cup. After adding the mushrooms and salt, cover the pot and simmer until the barley is tender, 35 to 45 minutes. Uncover, raise the heat a little, and bring the mixture to a boil. Over a period of 5 to 10 minutes, gradually stir in the remaining cup of broth as the mixture thickens and develops the creamy consistency of a typical risotto.

brown rice salad and flank steak with asian flavors

FOR THE STEAK

1 medium onion, quartered

2 cloves garlic

2 tablespoons tomato paste

2 tablespoons Japanese soy sauce
(shoyu or tamari)

1-inch chunk fresh ginger, quartered

1 tablespoon honey

2 teaspoons toasted sesame oil

1½ pounds flank steak

Freshly ground black pepper to taste

FOR THE SALAD

3 cups cooked Basic Short-Grain
Brown Rice (page 66)

1 cucumber, peeled, seeded, and cut
into matchsticks (about 1½ cups)

1 cup (tightly packed) coarsely grated
carrots

1½ tablespoons sesame seeds,
preferably black

3 tablespoons peanut butter

2 tablespoons seasoned rice vinegar,
or plain rice vinegar plus
¼ teaspoon sugar

2 teaspoons Japanese soy sauce
(shoyu or tamari), plus more to
taste

1 teaspoon toasted sesame oil

1 small clove garlic, minced (optional)

Chili oil (optional)

Flank steak is a good choice for a worknight dinner, especially if you've marinated it the night before. Serve thin slices of the broiled steak fanned out over a bed of brown rice tossed with carrots, cucumber, and a peanut dressing. I've given instructions for broiling the meat, but it's also delicious cooked on an outdoor grill.

In some parts of the country, flank steak is called plank steak, London broil, and jiffy steak.

SERVES 4 TO 5

Marinate the flank steak: In a food processor, pulse the onion and garlic to chop. Add the tomato paste, soy sauce, ginger, honey, and sesame oil. Process to create a coarse paste. Transfer the sauce to a large zipper-top plastic bag.

Lightly score the flank steak on both sides, across the grain, about 6 times. Put the steak into the bag. Loosely seal the bag and massage to coat the meat. Close the bag and refrigerate the steak for at least 6 hours or overnight. Gently shake the bag occasionally to distribute the marinade.

Prepare the brown rice: Shortly before broiling the flank steak, rehydrate the rice in the microwave (see page 10), if it is not freshly cooked. In a bowl, combine the rice, cucumber, carrots, and sesame seeds. Prepare the sauce by blending the peanut butter, rice vinegar, 3 tablespoons of water, the soy sauce, sesame oil, garlic (if using), and a few drops of chili oil (if using) in a mini processor or a small bowl. Add a little more water if the mixture is thicker than a standard creamy dressing. Toss enough dressing into the rice to coat the ingredients. Adjust the seasonings to your taste.

Broil the flank steak: Place an oven rack 2 to 3 inches from the broiler. Turn on the broiler. Line a broiler pan with foil.

Remove the flank steak from the bag and scrape off most of the seasoning paste. Set the steak on the prepared pan. Season well with pepper. Broil the first side for 3 minutes (rare) or 4 minutes (medium). Turn it over and broil the steak for an additional 3 or 4 minutes.

Remove the steak from the broiler and transfer it to a cutting board. Let it rest for 5 minutes. Reserve any pan juices on the foil.

With a very sharp knife, slice the steak thinly on a sharp angle against the grain.

To serve: Place a mound of the brown rice salad on one side of the plate. Fan out slices of steak so that they lean partially against the rice. Drizzle pan juices on top. Serve any extra peanut sauce in a small bowl at the table.

GRAIN EXCHANGE

- Use Kamut or wheat berries instead of brown rice.
- Use half Wehani and half long-grain brown rice.

WINE RECOMMENDATION: A pinot noir from California has enough body to stand up to steak and a ripe fruit quality that complements the honeyed marinade well.

bulgur pilaf with moroccan roast chicken

FOR THE CHICKEN

One 4-pound chicken, rinsed and
　　patted dry

Salt and freshly ground pepper

2 tablespoons vegetable oil

1½ tablespoons grated fresh ginger

2 teaspoons ground cinnamon

½ teaspoon ground allspice

½ teaspoon ground cloves

½ teaspoon ground cardamom

¼ teaspoon cayenne

¾ cup (tightly packed) pitted prunes,
　　quartered

6 thin slices lemon, pitted, plus more
　　for garnish

2 tablespoons butter, melted
　　(optional)

FOR THE BULGUR PILAF

Generous pinch of saffron threads

1½ tablespoons butter

½ cup finely diced shallots or onion

1½ cups coarse bulgur

1 teaspoon salt

½ cup slivered almonds, toasted

¼ cup chopped fresh mint

I love the way Moroccan cooks use exotic spices with abandon and combine meat and fruit in the same dish. This culinary aesthetic reminds me of the recipes I examined in my doctoral dissertation, a transcription of *The Fourme of Cury,* a fourteenth-century English manuscript from the household of Richard II. In many of the recipes, fruit and meat are combined in much the same way, revealing that in those far-off days, the western European kitchen was very influenced by the Arabic cooking of North Africa.

SERVES 4

Set a rack in the center and preheat the oven to 350°F.

Season the chicken well, inside and out, with salt and pepper.

In a small bowl, blend the oil with the ginger, cinnamon, allspice, cloves, cardamom, and cayenne.

Starting at the neck opening, gently press your hand between the skin and the flesh all over the chicken to loosen the skin. Rub half of the the spice oil into the flesh under the skin.

Toss the prunes and lemon slices in the remaining spice oil. Stuff these into the cavity of the chicken. Secure the opening with skewers or toothpicks. For a very crisp skin, brush the chicken with the melted butter.

Set the chicken on a roasting rack in a roasting pan and bake until an instant-read thermometer inserted where the thigh meets the leg registers 165°F, 1 to 1½ hours. Remove from the oven, and let rest for 10 minutes before carving.

After the chicken has been roasting for about 35 minutes, begin preparing the bulgur pilaf: In a small bowl, stir the saffron into 1 tablespoon of warm water. Set aside.

Melt the butter in a heavy 2-quart saucepan. Add the shallots and cook over medium-high heat until they soften, about 3 minutes. Stir in the bulgur and continue cooking, stirring frequently, until the bulgur emits a faint toasted aroma, about 3 minutes. Add 3¼ cups of water plus the saffron and its soaking water. Bring to a boil. Stir in the salt. Cover, lower the heat, and simmer until the bulgur is tender, 20 to 25 minutes. If all of the water has been absorbed and the bulgur is not done, stir in ¼ cup hot water and cook over very low heat for a few more minutes. Turn off the heat, and let the bulgur steam for 10 minutes or until the chicken is done.

To serve: Remove the stuffing from the chicken. Discard the lemon slices. Stir the prunes, almonds, and mint into the bulgur. Add salt to taste. If you wish, skim the fat from the chicken pan juices and stir them in.

Carve the chicken and serve each portion with a large spoonful of the bulgur pilaf.

WINE RECOMMENDATION: A full-bodied, exotically scented gewürztraminer or pinot gris from Alsace stands up well to this assertively spiced chicken.

bulgur timbales and lamb chops with north african spices

FOR THE CHOPS

3 to 4 tablespoons olive oil

1 teaspoon minced garlic

1½ teaspoons salt

½ teaspoon ground cardamom

½ teaspoon ground cinnamon

A few twists of freshly ground black pepper

Generous pinch of cayenne

8 loin lamb chops (each about ¾-inch thick)

FOR THE BULGUR TIMBALES

1 tablespoon olive oil

1 small onion, finely chopped

1½ teaspoons ground coriander

¼ teaspoon ground cardamom

Generous ¼ teaspoon ground cinnamon

1 cup coarse bulgur

½ cup coarsely grated carrots

¾ teaspoon salt

4 thin slices lemon, pitted

⅓ cup coarsely chopped dried (moist) apricots

¼ cup pine nuts, toasted

Mint sprigs, for garnish

For an exotic dinner with more complex flavor than the short preparation time would suggest, pair quick-cooking bulgur with even quicker-cooking lamb chops coated in a lively seasoning paste. To get dinner on the table even faster, spread the seasoning paste on the chops a day ahead and refrigerate them overnight.

SERVES 4

To prepare the seasoning paste: In a small bowl, combine 2 tablespoon of the olive oil, the garlic, salt, cardamom, cinnamon, black pepper, and cayenne. Spread the paste on both sides of the lamb chops. Cover the chops, and set them aside while you prepare the bulgur.

To prepare the bulgur: Heat the oil in a heavy 2-quart saucepan. Add the onion and cook over medium-high heat until translucent, about 3 minutes. Stir in the coriander, cardamom, and cinnamon, and cook for another minute. Stir in the bulgur and coat it with the oil. Continue cooking, stirring frequently, to toast the bulgur, about 3 minutes. Stir in the carrots, 2¼ cups of water, the salt, and lemon slices.

Bring the bulgur to a boil. Cover, lower the heat, and cook it over medium-low heat until the bulgur is tender, 20 to 25 minutes. If all of the water has been absorbed and the bulgur is not done, stir in ¼ cup hot water and cook over very low heat for a few more minutes. Remove from the heat and let the bulgur steam for 10 minutes, or until the chops are ready.

Meanwhile, cook the lamb chops: Heat 1 tablespoon of the oil in a large skillet. Add as many chops as will fit in one layer without crowding. Cook them uncovered for 4 minutes. Turn them over and cook the second side until an instant-read thermometer inserted in the thickest part registers 125° to 130°F, 3 to 5 more minutes. Reserve the cooked chops in a warm place. Cook any remaining chops, adding more oil if needed.

To finish the timbales: If there is any unabsorbed liquid, drain it off. Discard the lemon slices. Stir in the apricots and pine nuts. Adjust the seasonings. Press the bulgur into a 1-cup ramekin or coffee cup, and invert a portion onto a plate. Repeat to make three more timbales. Lean two chops against each timbale. Garnish each plate with a few sprigs of mint.

VARIATION

To quickly make a few tablespoons of sauce, after frying the chops pour 1/4 cup of orange juice and 1 tablespoon of balsamic vinegar into the skillet and boil until syrupy, scraping up any browned bits sticking to the bottom of the skillet. Drizzle the sauce on the chops.

GRAIN EXCHANGE

Use kalijira brown or Chinese black rice instead of the bulgur. Reduce the water to 2 cups.

WINE RECOMMENDATION: A full-bodied, spicy, smoky red wine from southern Italy pairs well with this North African–inspired dish — try an inky aglianico or negroamaro from Campania or Puglia.

quinoa and chili-scented pork chops with roasted red pepper dressing

FOR THE SALAD

1 cup beige quinoa

2 tablespoons red or black quinoa
(optional, but nice for color)

1 cup fresh or frozen corn kernels

1 large red bell pepper, roasted,
seeded, and quartered

3 tablespoons olive oil

2 to 3 tablespoons freshly squeezed
lime juice

¾ teaspoon salt, plus more for the
tomatoes

½ cup (tightly packed) chopped
cilantro

1 jalapeño pepper, seeded and diced

1 generous cup cherry tomatoes,
halved or quartered

FOR THE CHOPS

1 tablespoon olive oil

2 teaspoons chili powder

¾ teaspoon granulated garlic

⅛ teaspoon ground cinnamon

½ teaspoon salt

4 loin pork chops, each about
1-inch thick

Vegetable oil, for frying

There's a natural affinity between quinoa and other New World foods such as corn, bell peppers, and jalapeño peppers, and this warm quinoa salad is a case in point. I've added chili powder to the seasoning paste for the pork chops so that they have a matching flavor profile.

SERVES 4

To prepare the quinoa: Bring a large pot of water to a boil. Add the quinoa and cook for 10 minutes. Add the corn and continue cooking until the quinoa is translucent and there is no tiny dot of uncooked starch in the center, 1 to 3 more minutes. Pour the quinoa and corn through a fine-meshed strainer. Run cold water over the mixture to stop the cooking process. Drain well and transfer the mixture to a large bowl.

To make the dressing: In a mini chopper or food processor, blend the red pepper, 2 tablespoons of the olive oil, 2 tablespoons lime juice, and the salt. Toss the dressing, cilantro, and jalapeño into the quinoa. Add more lime juice and salt to taste. In a small bowl, toss the cherry tomatoes with the remaining tablespoon of olive oil and sprinkle lightly with salt. Set aside.

To prepare the pork chops: In a small bowl, make a paste by stirring together the olive oil, chili powder, granulated garlic, cinnamon, and salt. Spread a thin layer of the paste on both sides of the chops.

Brush a large skillet or grill pan lightly with vegetable oil and heat until sizzling hot. Cook the chops over high heat until browned on the bottom, about 1½ minutes. Turn them over and brown the second side. Reduce the heat to low, cover the pan, and cook the chops for 4 minutes (if boneless) or 5 minutes (if bone-in). Turn the chops over. Cover the pan and cook until chops are cooked to taste, usually 4 to 5 additional minutes. Test for doneness by slicing into the thickest part of the chop.

To serve: Add more lime juice to the quinoa salad, if needed. Make a bed of the quinoa salad on each of four dinner plates. Set a chop on top. Spoon the cherry tomatoes on the side.

WINE RECOMMENDATION: Dry rosé from southern France, a versatile food wine, has the body to stand up to the pork and the spice and acidity to match the lime and tomatoes.

■　■　■

quinoa and turkey cutlets with fusion flavors

FOR THE TURKEY CUTLETS

¼ cup orange juice

1 tablespoon freshly squeezed lime juice

1 tablespoon toasted sesame oil

1 tablespoon Japanese soy sauce (shoyu or tamari)

1 teaspoon chopped chipotle chile in adobo sauce or ⅛ teaspoon cayenne pepper

4 turkey cutlets (each ½-inch thick, about 1 pound total)

Olive oil, for frying

FOR THE QUINOA

4 cups cooked Basic Quinoa (page 58)

½ cup diced red bell pepper

⅓ cup chopped cilantro, plus 2 tablespoons for garnish

1 large jalapeño pepper, seeded and minced

3 to 4 tablespoons freshly squeezed lime juice

2 tablespoons olive oil

1 teaspoon grated orange zest

1 teaspoon salt

¼ cup hulled, raw, unsalted pumpkin seeds, toasted, for garnish

Orange slices, for garnish

Marinating turkey cutlets guarantees a moist result. Including soy sauce in the marinade colors the quickly pan-fried cutlets a rich brown. This is a city girl's recipe, but if you have a grill, toss the cutlets on it, and use the unabsorbed marinade for basting.

While the marinade is Asian-inspired, the accompanying quinoa has the flavor stamp of the Southwest. Because they are both seasoned with orange and lime, the cutlets and quinoa makes a good match. Serve the quinoa warm or at room temperature.

SERVES 4

In a zipper-top plastic bag, combine the orange and lime juices, sesame oil, soy sauce, and chipotle. Add the cutlets, seal the bag, and massage to coat. Refrigerate the cutlets for 1 hour to a maximum of 4 hours. Shake the bag occasionally to distribute the marinade.

To prepare the quinoa: In a large bowl, combine the quinoa, red pepper, ⅓ cup cilantro, and jalapeño pepper. In a small bowl, combine 3 tablespoons lime juice, the olive oil, orange zest, and salt. Pour the dressing over the quinoa and toss. Add extra lime juice, if needed.

To cook the cutlets: Heat a thin slick of olive oil in a large skillet over high heat. Remove the cutlets from the bag, leaving any unabsorbed marinade behind. Fry (in batches, if necessary) until well browned on one side, 2 to 3 minutes. Flip over and cook on the second side until they are nicely browned and the center is no longer pink, another 2 to 3 minutes.

To serve: Mound a generous cup of the quinoa on one side of each dinner plate. Lean a cutlet against the quinoa. Sprinkle the pumpkin seeds and extra cilantro over the quinoa and cutlet. Garnish each plate with a few orange slices.

VARIATION

Dice the cooked cutlets and toss them into the quinoa.

GRAIN EXCHANGE

Use coarse bulgur or brown basmati rice instead of quinoa.

WINE RECOMMENDATION: A wine with slight sweetness pairs well with this salty, citrusy dish. Try an off-dry riesling from Washington State, Australia, or the Pfalz region of Germany.

corn polenta with sausage and peppers

FOR THE SAUSAGE AND PEPPERS

1 tablespoon olive oil

1 large onion, halved and thinly sliced

2 cloves garlic, minced

½ pound fresh Italian sausages

4 large bell peppers, cored and cut
into ½-inch strips

4 large plum tomatoes, diced, or
1 can (15 ounces) diced tomatoes,
with liquid

¼ teaspoon crushed red pepper flakes
(optional; use if sausages aren't
spicy)

⅓ cup (tightly packed) chopped fresh
basil

1 tablespoon chopped fresh mint or
extra basil

1 to 3 teaspoons balsamic vinegar

Salt and freshly ground pepper
to taste

Grated Parmesan or Romano cheese,
for garnish and to pass at the table

FOR THE POLENTA

2 cups coarse yellow cornmeal,
preferably stone-ground

1½ teaspoons salt

Cook the sausage and peppers while the polenta is simmering for an easy weeknight supper, made especially pretty if you use a combination of red, yellow, and green bell peppers.

A salad of radicchio, endive, and watercress tossed with a simple vinaigrette makes a nice accompaniment.

SERVES 6

To prepare the sausage and peppers: Heat the oil in a large, deep skillet. Add the onion and cook over medium heat, stirring from time to time, until lightly browned, 10 to 15 minutes. Add the garlic and cook for another minute.

Squeeze the sausages from their casings and add to the skillet. Break up the sausage and cook until it is browned. Toss in the peppers and tomatoes. Bring to a boil. Reduce the heat, cover, and simmer until the peppers are collapsed and tender, about 20 minutes.

While the peppers are simmering, prepare the polenta: In a bowl, blend the polenta with 3 cups of cold water. In a heavy 3-quart pot, bring 2 cups of water and the salt to a rolling boil. Lower the heat slightly. Gradually stir in the polenta mixture. Return to a boil.

Cook uncovered, adjusting the heat so that the polenta simmers, with big bubbles puffing up here and there on the surface. As the mixture thickens, use a large spoon to stir every few minutes, taking care to scrape up grains sticking to the bottom of the pot. The polenta will be done when it becomes thick and creamy, and the cornmeal is soft with no hint of grittiness, 15 to 20 minutes. Stir in a bit more boiling water if the polenta becomes very thick before the cornmeal tastes cooked.

To serve: Stir the basil and mint into the peppers. Season to taste with vinegar, salt, and pepper. Spoon the polenta onto individual plates. Top with the pepper mixture. Garnish with cheese and pass extra cheese at the table.

VARIATION
Use ¼ cup chopped fresh flat-leaf parsley instead of the basil.

WINE RECOMMENDATION: An earthy, cherry-inflected barbera from Italy's Piedmont region is a nice choice for this rustic, Italian-inspired dish.

wild and brown rice with sesame-soy glazed salmon

FOR THE RICE

½ cup wild rice

¾ ounce (about 20 medium) dried shiitake caps

3 scallions, thinly sliced (keep white and green parts separate)

1 cup short-grain brown rice

2 to 3 teaspoons Japanese soy sauce (shoyu or tamari)

½ to 1 teaspoon toasted sesame oil

1 tablespoon black sesame seeds

FOR THE SALMON

2-inch chunk fresh ginger, peeled and cut into eighths

2 large cloves garlic

2 tablespoons Japanese soy sauce (shoyu or tamari), plus more to pass at the table

1 tablespoon toasted sesame oil

1 teaspoon molasses

Peanut oil, for frying

4 salmon steaks or skinned fillets (each about 1-inch thick)

2 tablespoons rice vinegar

1 large lemon, cut into 8 wedges, for serving

Pan-fry salmon with a gingered sesame-soy glaze and serve it with a simple Asian-inspired pilaf for an elegant dinner.

SERVES 4

To prepare the rice: Bring 3 cups of water to a boil in a medium pot. Add the wild rice and cook at a gentle boil, uncovered, until the rice is tender and some of the grains have burst open and curled, 45 to 60 minutes. Drain well and set aside.

While the wild rice is cooking, bring 2 cups of water to a boil in a heavy 2-quart saucepan. Press the dried shiitake into the water. Cover and let sit until the shiitake are soft, about 15 minutes. Cut the caps into strips about ¼-inch thick and return them to the soaking water.

Return the water and shiitake to a boil. Stir in the scallion whites and brown rice. Return to a boil, cover, and reduce the heat. Simmer until the rice is tender, 35 to 40 minutes. It's fine if there is some unabsorbed liquid. Stir in the wild rice, soy sauce, sesame oil to taste, and most of the scallion greens. (Save a few for garnish.) Turn off the heat, cover, and let the rice sit for 10 minutes, or until the fish is ready.

To prepare the salmon: In a processor, finely chop the ginger and garlic. Add the soy sauce, sesame oil, and molasses, and blend well to create the glaze.

Heat a thin slick of peanut oil in a large skillet over high heat until sizzling. Spread some glaze onto one side of each steak. Set the steak, glazed-side down, in the skillet. Reduce the heat to medium-high and cook uncovered for 1½ minutes. Spread glaze on the top side of each steak, and flip over. Turn the heat to medium-low and continue cooking until the fish flakes easily and is almost opaque in the thickest section, 3 to 4 minutes longer. Remove to a platter and lightly tent with foil to keep warm. (The fish will finish cooking in the residual heat.) Stir the rice vinegar and any remaining glaze into the pan and cook over medium-high heat, stirring constantly, until the sauce develops a sheen, a minute or so.

If there is any liquid left in the rice, bring it to a boil and cook while stirring until the liquid evaporates. Stir in the black sesame seeds.

To serve: Divide the rice among four plates and set a salmon steak on top. Drizzle a little of the sauce onto the salmon and garnish with the remaining scallion greens. Set 2 lemon wedges alongside. Pass a small pitcher of soy sauce at the table.

VARIATION
Tear ½ sheet toasted sushi nori (sea vegetable wrapper for sushi) into tiny bits, and stir it into the hot rice.

WINE RECOMMENDATION: Richly-flavored salmon and pinot noir are natural partners. Since the glaze is slightly sweet, choose a pinot noir that shows lots of ripe fruit, like one from California.

teff polenta with ethiopian chicken stew

FOR THE CHICKEN STEW

1 tablespoon sweet paprika

3/4 teaspoon ground ginger

1/2 teaspoon ground cinnamon

1/2 teaspoon ground cardamom or
   4 cardamom pods, crushed to reveal
   the seeds

1/8 teaspoon ground cloves

1/8 teaspoon cayenne, or more to taste

1/8 teaspoon freshly ground black
   pepper, plus more for seasoning the
   chicken

3 pounds bone-in chicken parts

Salt

2 to 3 tablespoons olive or peanut oil

1 large onion, coarsely chopped

2 large cloves garlic, minced

About 1 cup reduced-sodium chicken
   broth

FOR THE TEFF POLENTA

1 1/2 cups teff grains (not flour)

1 teaspoon salt, plus more to taste

Freshly ground black pepper

I've created a streamlined and mild version of the traditional Ethiopian chicken *wot*, a fiery stew seasoned with chiles and a mix of mostly sweet spices called *berbere*. Like most stews, this one tastes even better the next day.

Teff is the essential grain of the Ethiopian kitchen, and when cooked into a soft chocolate-brown polenta, it makes an ideal base for the stew's flavorful sauce. Prepare the teff polenta just before serving.

SERVES 4

To prepare the chicken: In a small bowl, combine the paprika, ginger, cinnamon, cardamom, cloves, cayenne, and pepper. Set aside.

Season the chicken with salt and pepper. Heat 2 tablespoons of the oil in a heavy Dutch oven or saucepan wide enough to hold the chicken in one layer. Brown the chicken, skin side down, over high heat in two batches. Set the chicken aside.

Reduce the heat to medium-high. Stir in the onion, adding 1 tablespoon of oil, if needed. Cook over medium-high heat until the onion begins to soften, about 3 minutes. Stir in the garlic and cook for 1 minute. Stir in the ground spices and cook, stirring frequently, for 20 seconds.

Stir in the chicken broth, taking care to release any browned bits sticking to the bottom of the pot. Bring to a boil. Lower the heat to a simmer, and return the chicken to the pot, browned side up. Cover and simmer until the chicken is tender and registers 165°F on an instant-read thermometer in the thickest part, 25 to 45 minutes, depending upon the size of the pieces. Add more broth or some water if the mixture becomes dry. Skim off the fat.

Prepare the teff polenta: While the chicken is cooking, bring some water to boil in a kettle; you'll need 4^1/$_2$ cups. Set a heavy 3-quart saucepan over medium heat. Add the teff and toast it, stirring frequently, until the grains emit a mild toasty aroma and begin to pop, 3 to 6 minutes. (You will notice little white dots of popped grain but may not hear the popping.)

Turn off the heat. Stand back to avoid getting splattered, and gradually stir in 4^1/$_2$ cups boiling water and the salt. Stir well. Reduce the heat, cover, and cook at a gentle boil until the grains are tender and the mixture develops a porridge-like consistency, 15 to 20 minutes. Stir every few minutes to prevent the grains from sticking to the bottom of the pot. Break up lumps by smashing them against the side of the pot. Add more salt, if needed, and pepper to taste.

To serve: Mound the teff polenta on four plates, and ladle the chicken stew on top.

GRAIN EXCHANGE
Serve over corn polenta instead of teff polenta.

WINE RECOMMENDATION: This sweetly spiced stew calls for an intensely flavored white, like a pinot gris or a gewürztraminer from France's Alsace region.

STIR-FRIES AND SKILLET DISHES

barley and sesame chicken stir-fry

FOR THE SAUCE

⅓ cup dry sherry

3 tablespoons Japanese soy sauce
  (shoyu or tamari), plus more if
  needed

2 tablespoons seasoned rice vinegar,
  or 2 tablespoons plain rice vinegar
  plus ½ teaspoon white sugar

1 tablespoon Dijon mustard
  (whole-grain is nice)

1 tablespoon grated fresh ginger

2 large cloves garlic, minced

1 tablespoon toasted sesame oil

1 teaspoon molasses or dark brown
  sugar

½ teaspoon crushed red pepper flakes

FOR THE STIR-FRY

1½ pounds boneless, skinless chicken
  thighs or breasts

1 bunch broccoli

1 tablespoon peanut or canola oil

1 can (8 ounces) sliced water
  chestnuts, drained

4 cups cooked Basic Barley (any type;
  page 25)

1 tablespoon sesame seeds, toasted

3 tablespoons sliced scallion greens

Stir-fries are ideal for quick meals, especially when you have leftover cooked barley—or any other sturdy grain—in The Grain Bank (see page 10). To make prep quicker still, purchase the chicken already sliced for stir-fry.

SERVES 4

First make the sauce: In a bowl, combine the sherry, soy sauce, vinegar, mustard, ginger, garlic, sesame oil, molasses, and red pepper flakes.

Slice the chicken into thin strips along the grain and place them in a small bowl. Add 3 tablespoons of the sauce and toss the chicken to coat. Set aside.

Cut the broccoli florets from the stalks. Reserve the stalks for another purpose. Cut the florets into small pieces about 1½ inches across the top.

Heat a large wok or skillet over high heat. Add the peanut oil and swirl to coat the surface. Add the broccoli and stir-fry for 30 seconds.

Stir in the chicken, water chestnuts, barley, and remaining sauce. Cook uncovered, stirring frequently, until the chicken is cooked, 3 to 4 minutes. Stir in the sesame seeds and scallion greens. Add more soy sauce, if needed.

VARIATIONS

• Add ¼ teaspoon ground star anise or Chinese 5-spice powder to the sauce.

• Instead of water chestnuts, use canned baby corn.

GRAIN EXCHANGE

Instead of barley, use short-grain brown rice, Chinese black rice, Colusari red rice, or a combination of cooked grains.

WINE RECOMMENDATION: A soft, fruity chenin blanc, like many from Vouvray in France and from South Africa, complements the salty-sweet flavors in this dish.

vegetarian brown rice and tofu stir-fry

Instead of chicken, use 1 pound Asian-style baked tofu, cut into cubes. Cook for only 1 minute before adding the sesame seeds.

brown rice with stir-fried beef and vegetables

1 pound beef chuck, cut into cubes, partially frozen

2 tablespoons Japanese soy sauce (shoyu or tamari)

1 tablespoon minced fresh ginger

1 to 2 teaspoons minced garlic

2 tablespoons peanut or canola oil, plus more if needed

4 scallions, thinly sliced (keep white and green parts separate)

2 medium carrots, cut into long matchsticks

1 large rib celery, very thinly sliced on the diagonal

1 teaspoon toasted sesame oil

4 cups cooked Basic Short-Grain Brown Rice (page 66)

½ cup roasted, salted peanuts

Chuck is a cut of beef usually reserved for stew because it is considered tough. However, if you cut it extremely thinly and toss it into a very hot pan, you can use it successfully (and economically) for making a stir-fry. When selecting the meat, make sure that it has some marbling. Very lean meat will indeed be tough, no matter how thinly you slice it. Partially freeze the chuck for easier slicing.

SERVES 4

With a very sharp knife, cut the beef into very thin slices across the grain.

Place the beef in a bowl. Drizzle 1 tablespoon of the soy sauce on top. Add the ginger and garlic and stir to distribute. Set aside for at least 15 minutes, or cover and refrigerate overnight.

Set a large wok or skillet over high heat. When hot, swirl in 1 tablespoon of the peanut oil. When the oil is sizzling hot, add the beef and scallion whites. Stir constantly until the beef is no longer pink on the outside, 3 to 4 minutes. Avoid overcooking, which may toughen the beef. Transfer the beef and scallions to a bowl.

Add the remaining tablespoon of peanut oil to the wok. Stir in the carrots and celery. Stir continuously until the vegetables are tender-crisp, 3 to 4 minutes. Transfer to the bowl containing the beef.

Reduce the heat to medium. Mix 2 tablespoons of water, the remaining tablespoon of soy sauce, and the sesame oil in a small bowl. Pour into the wok. Scrape up any browned bits sticking to the bottom and sides of the wok. Stir in the rice. (If the rice is cold and hard, cover, reduce the heat to low, and cook until it is moist and heated, 1 to 2 minutes.) Stir in a bit more water, if needed.

Stir in the vegetables and beef, and cook just long enough to reheat the beef. Stir in the peanuts and serve immediately with the scallion greens as garnish.

VARIATION

When you marinate the beef, add ¼ teaspoon crushed red pepper flakes.

GRAIN EXCHANGE

Use Chinese black rice, wild rice, barley, or Job's tears instead of brown rice.

WINE RECOMMENDATION: A salty stir-fry with beef takes well to a fruity red wine. Try a Beaujolais, or if you prefer something fuller, a California pinot noir.

corn grits with collard greens and andouille

FOR THE GRITS

1 cup corn grits (fine or coarse),
 preferably stone-ground

½ teaspoon salt, plus more to taste

1 tablespoon olive oil

½ cup grated Romano cheese

FOR THE COLLARDS

1 large bunch collard greens
 (about 1½ pounds)

1 tablespoon olive oil

1 large onion, chopped

1 large red bell pepper, seeded
 and diced

4 fully cooked andouille sausages
 (¾ pound)

2 teaspoons minced garlic

1 teaspoon dried oregano

Salt and freshly ground pepper to
 taste

1 cup canned crushed tomatoes with
 added puree

Hot pepper sauce or crushed red
 pepper flakes to taste

Most people associate collards with long-, slow-simmered soups and stews, but finely chopped collards are delicious when cooked quickly until just tender and still bright green. In this recipe, the collards pick up some heat from spicy andouille sausage.

I've allowed for a scant cup of cooked grits for each person because they are very filling. Increase the amount (see grits cooking chart, page 35) to serve larger portions, or to ensure that you have leftovers for another meal.

SERVES 3 TO 4

Place the grits in a bowl and cover them with water. Skim off any chaff that rises to the surface. Drain them in a fine-meshed strainer.

Bring 4 cups of water and the salt to a boil in a heavy 3-quart pot. Gradually stir in the grits. Reduce the heat to medium-low and simmer uncovered, stirring frequently at first to avoid lumping, then occasionally to prevent the grits from sticking to the bottom of the pot, until the mixture thickens, 5 to 10 minutes.

Lower the heat, and continue cooking uncovered until the grits are tender (the texture remains slightly gritty, as the name suggests) and the mixture is thick and creamy, 30 to 40 minutes for fine to medium grits, 45 to 60 minutes for coarse grits. Add more water during this time if the mixture becomes very dry before the grits are fully cooked. Turn off the heat and stir in the oil and cheese. Add salt to taste. Cover the grits and set them aside until the collards are ready.

While the grits are cooking, prepare the collards: Trim off the root ends. Stack the leaves, roll them into a log, and cut the stems and leaves into very thin slices. Rinse them thoroughly in a sink full of water. Drain them in a colander.

Heat the oil in a wide, heavy saucepan. Add the onion and bell pepper and cook them over medium-high heat, stirring frequently, until the onion is lightly browned, about 4 minutes. Meanwhile, finely dice one of the sausages. Add the diced sausage, garlic, and oregano and cook for another minute.

Add 1 cup of water and bring the mixture to a boil. Stir in the collards. Sprinkle them lightly with salt and pepper. Cover and cook over medium-high heat until the collards are tender, 5 to 15 minutes (depending on age and condition). Add more water if the mixture becomes dry.

While the collards are cooking, slice the remaining sausages on the diagonal. If you wish, brown the slices in a nonstick skillet. When the collards are tender, stir in the sliced sausage and tomatoes. Simmer the mixture uncovered until the flavors mingle and the sausage is hot, about 5 minutes. Adjust the seasonings and add hot pepper sauce to taste, or pass the hot pepper sauce at the table.

To serve, place a mound of grits on each plate. Top the grits with a generous portion of the collard mixture.

VARIATION
Use chicken or turkey andouille instead of pork.

GRAIN EXCHANGE
Instead of grits, serve Basic Soft Polenta (page 38).

WINE RECOMMENDATION: A slightly chilled Beaujolais will cut through the richness of the sausage and grits. Dry rosé is also a pleasing choice for this rustic dish.

any-grain scrambled eggs with salami

1 tablespoon olive oil

1 large onion, coarsely chopped

1 clove garlic, minced

1 cup diced salami or other cured
   sausage

1 cup cooked chewy whole grains
   (any type; pages 16–111)

4 large eggs, lightly beaten

1 teaspoon chopped fresh thyme
   or ¼ teaspoon dried

Salt and freshly ground pepper
   to taste

2 tablespoons chopped fresh flat-leaf
   parsley or basil

Toss cooked grains into a skillet with salami and eggs for a casual high-protein meal. The scramble works best with dense, chewy grains such as short-grain brown rice, whole oats, or hull-less barley, which contrast with the eggs' softness. Avoid small grains, such as amaranth, quinoa, and teff, which wouldn't work well in this context.

SERVES 2

Heat the oil in a large skillet. Add the onion and cook over medium-high heat, stirring frequently, until soft and lightly browned, about 8 minutes. Stir in the garlic and salami and cook, stirring frequently, until the salami starts to brown, another few minutes.

If the grains have been refrigerated and are dried out, add ¼ cup of water and stir in the grains. Cover the skillet and steam until they absorb the water and become moist, 30 to 60 seconds. If the grains are freshly cooked, simply stir them in without adding water.

Stir in the eggs and thyme. Season to taste with salt and pepper. Cook over medium heat, stirring constantly, until the eggs are scrambled, about 2 minutes. Stir in the parsley and serve immediately.

WINE RECOMMENDATION: Try a medium-bodied, fruity chardonnay without oak.

farro with fresh tomato sauce and basil

3 tablespoons olive oil

1 large clove garlic, minced

6 large plum tomatoes, finely chopped

1 tablespoon balsamic vinegar

1/2 teaspoon dried oregano

4 cups cooked Basic Farro (page 96)

Salt and freshly ground black pepper

1/2 cup (tightly packed) coarsely
   chopped fresh basil

Grated Parmesan or Romano cheese
   (or a combination), for garnish and
   to pass at the table

When tomatoes come into season, make this quick fresh sauce and toss in some cooked farro. It's one of those simple dishes that makes you think you're in a small town in Tuscany.

SERVES 4

Heat the oil in a large skillet over medium-high heat. Add the garlic and cook, stirring, for about 30 seconds. Stir in the tomatoes, vinegar, and oregano, and cook, stirring frequently, until the tomatoes soften slightly, 4 to 5 minutes.

   Stir in the farro. Season to taste with salt and pepper. When the farro is hot, turn off the heat and stir in the basil.

   Serve in pasta bowls, with a light dusting of cheese on top. Serve additional cheese in a bowl at the table.

GRAIN EXCHANGE
Use barley instead of farro.

WINE RECOMMENDATION: A Chianti or other Italian wine based on the sangiovese grape has pleasing cherry flavors and is zippy enough to stand up to the acidic tomatoes.

popcorn-crusted catfish

4 catfish fillets (¼ pound each), about
   ¼-inch thick (see Note)
Salt
Freshly ground pepper to taste
2 cups popped Basic Popcorn
   (page 40)
⅓ cup whole-wheat pastry flour
1 large egg
⅛ teaspoon ground chipotle or
   cayenne pepper
Peanut oil for shallow pan-frying

With its subtle sweetness and familiar crunch, ground popcorn makes an irresistibly crisp crust for catfish. If you (like me) have never had a special fondness for catfish, try it this way and let me know if you change your mind. Or try the popcorn crust with any other type of fish fillet.

Serve the catfish with coleslaw and buttermilk cornbread.

SERVES 4

Season the fillets with salt and pepper to taste. Set aside.

In a spice grinder or mini chopper, grind the popcorn in batches to a medium-fine meal. You should have about 1⅓ cups. Stir in ¾ teaspoon salt. (If using salted store-bought popcorn, do not add salt.) Spread the popcorn meal on a plate.

Spread the flour on another plate.

Beat the egg in a shallow bowl with a fork. Blend in the chipotle.

Press each fillet into the flour to coat both sides. Gently shake off excess flour. Dip into the egg mixture, then coat both sides thoroughly with the ground popcorn. Set the coated fillets on a platter.

Pour a thin slick of oil into a large nonstick skillet and heat over high heat until smoking. Cook the fillets in two batches until the coating is brown and crisp and the inside flakes easily at the thickest part, about 2 minutes per side. Serve immediately.

NOTE: If the fillets are thicker than ¼-inch, preheat the oven to 375°F. After browning both sides, pop the fillets into the oven until the inside flakes easily at the thickest part.

GRAIN EXCHANGE
Use blue cornmeal instead of whole-wheat pastry flour.

WINE RECOMMENDATION: Popcorn has an inherent sweetness, so a fruity but not oaked white wine is in order. Try a dry chenin blanc from Vouvray in France.

kamut, broccoli rabe, and sausage medley

1 bunch broccoli rabe

1 tablespoon olive oil

3 fully cooked Italian-style chicken or
turkey sausages, diced

⅓ cup chopped oil-packed sun-dried
tomatoes

2 cups cooked Basic Whole Kamut
Kernels (page 94)

Pinch of crushed red pepper flakes
(optional)

2 teaspoons balsamic vinegar

Salt to taste

Grated Romano cheese, for garnish

If you're a fan of broccoli rabe, this combination will appeal to you for a casual, lusty supper. Kamut, with its mild, buttery taste, makes a good foil for the intense flavors of sausage and broccoli rabe.

SERVES 3 TO 4

Holding the broccoli rabe in a bunch, trim off and discard the root ends. Cut the stems into ¾-inch pieces. Chop the leaves coarsely, attempting to keep the florets whole.

Heat the olive oil in a wide saucepan. Stir in the sausage and cook over medium-high heat, stirring frequently, until it is lightly browned, about 3 minutes.

Add ¾ cup of water, the tomatoes, Kamut, and red pepper flakes (if using). Set half of the broccoli rabe on top, cover, and cook over high heat for 1 minute, or until it wilts. Add the remaining broccoli rabe, cover, and continue cooking until the broccoli rabe is tender, 4 to 7 minutes more. If the mixture becomes dry, add more water.

Stir in the vinegar and salt to taste. Pass the cheese in a bowl at the table for garnish.

VARIATION
Use kale instead of broccoli rabe.

GRAIN EXCHANGE
. Substitute hominy for the Kamut.
. Omit the Kamut and serve the stew over soft polenta.

WINE RECOMMENDATION: Salty, garlicky sausages pair nicely with bright, berry-inflected reds like Beaujolais from France and dolcetto from Italy.

hominy with shredded chicken and peppers

2 tablespoons olive oil

1 large onion, thinly sliced

1 large green bell pepper, seeded and
cut into ½-inch strips

1 large red bell pepper, seeded and cut
into ½-inch strips

¼ teaspoon salt, plus more to taste

2 large cloves garlic, minced

1 jalapeño, seeded and minced

2 teaspoons dried oregano

½ teaspoon whole cumin seeds

2 to 2½ cups cooked Basic Hominy
(page 36)

1 cup reduced-sodium chicken broth

1 cup seeded, diced fresh plum
tomatoes

1½ to 2 cups shredded roast chicken

Hot pepper sauce (optional)

2 tablespoons chopped fresh cilantro,
for garnish

2 limes, cut into wedges

Hominy marries well with the flavors of the Southwest—no surprise since this large-kernel dried corn is native to that region. Hominy is so filling that a modest amount of shredded chicken turns the stew into a main dish.

Although eating freshly cooked hominy is a special treat, this is a particularly easy dish to prepare if you use canned hominy and store-bought rotisserie chicken. Be sure to accompany it with lime wedges. A last-minute squirt of the juice really brightens the flavors.

SERVES 4

Heat the oil in a large skillet over medium-high heat. Add the onion, bell peppers, and salt. Cook, stirring frequently, for 3 minutes. Add the garlic, jalapeño, oregano, and cumin, and continue cooking until the onion is lightly browned and the peppers are beginning to soften, a few minutes longer.

Stir in the hominy. Add the chicken broth and tomatoes, and bring to a boil. Lower the heat slightly and continue cooking, stir-ring frequently, until the flavors meld and some of the liquid has evaporated, 2 to 5 minutes. Stir in the chicken and cook until heated through. Season to taste with hot pepper sauce (if using) and more salt, if needed. Ladle into bowls. Garnish each portion with cilantro and serve lime wedges alongside.

VARIATIONS

• Substitute roast turkey for the chicken.

• Add 1 cup frozen corn when you add the chicken.

• Instead of hot pepper sauce, add 1 mashed chipotle in adobo when you add the jalapeño to the onions.

• Omit the chicken broth and fresh plum tomatoes and substi-tute 1 can (15 ounces) diced tomatoes, including liquid.

• Garnish with 1 diced ripe avocado along with the cilantro.

GRAIN EXCHANGE

• Substitute 1 can (15 to 19 ounces) white or yellow hominy, drained and rinsed, for the cooked Basic Hominy.

• Use Job's tears instead of hominy.

WINE RECOMMENDATION: Cabernet franc, with its herbal aromatics and Bing cherry fruit, is an interesting choice for this peppery dish. The best cabernet francs come from the Loire Valley region of France, but New York State is also having some success with this grape. If you decide to make the stew quite spicy, opt for beer instead—the wine's tannins will exaggerate the heat on your palate.

quinoa-beef picadillo

1 tablespoon olive oil

1 large onion, diced

1 large green bell pepper, seeded
   and diced

2 teaspoons minced garlic

1 teaspoon cumin seeds

1 pound lean ground beef

½ teaspoon salt

1 teaspoon dried oregano

½ teaspoon chili powder

⅛ teaspoon ground cinnamon

1 can (28 ounces) diced tomatoes
   with green chiles, with liquid

⅓ cup pimiento-stuffed olives, cut
   into thirds crosswise

¼ cup raisins

2 tablespoons drained capers

3 cups cooked Basic Quinoa
   (page 58)

Freshly ground pepper to taste

Lime wedges, for serving

Picadillo, a zesty ground beef stew of Spanish origin, was welcomed enthusiastically into the kitchens of many Caribbean and Latin American cooks during the Colonial period. Variations abound, but I favor the ones that achieve a balance of sweet and salty by including raisins and pimiento-stuffed olives.

Though picadillo is traditionally served over rice, by mixing high-protein quinoa right into the stew, you can go easy on the meat and still have a very satisfying meal.

SERVES 4 TO 6

Heat the oil over high heat in a large, deep skillet. Add the onion and green pepper and cook, stirring frequently, until the onion is translucent, about 3 minutes. Stir in the garlic and cumin seeds and cook 1 minute more. Add the beef and salt. Break the meat up into bits. Continue cooking until the beef is brown and crumbly, 3 or 4 minutes. Pour off any rendered fat.

Stir in the oregano, chili powder, cinnamon, tomatoes, olives, raisins, and capers. Bring to a boil. Reduce the heat, cover, and simmer the mixture until the flavors have mingled, about 15 minutes. Stir in the quinoa and adjust the seasonings, adding pepper to taste. Cook until the mixture is hot, about 1 minute more.

Serve in large, shallow bowls. Accompany with a bowl of lime wedges.

VARIATION

Use ground turkey or pork or meatloaf mix instead of beef.

GRAIN EXCHANGE

Use hull-less barley or brown rice instead of quinoa.

WINE RECOMMENDATION: Dry rosé is often the choice when seeking a suitable match for dishes with a mélange of flavors—briny olives and capers, sweet raisins, spicy cinnamon, and acidic tomatoes. Try a grenache-based rosé from Spain or southern France.

BRAISES, STEWS, CASSEROLES, AND SAVORY PIES

saffron-basmati rice with chicken in garam masala sauce

¼ teaspoon saffron threads

FOR THE CHICKEN

1½ pounds chicken tenders

Salt

3 tablespoons unsalted butter

1 large onion, finely diced

1 teaspoon garam masala, plus more
   to taste

1 can (15 ounces) diced tomatoes,
   with liquid

½ cup low-sodium chicken broth

3 cups cooked Basic Brown Basmati
   Rice (page 63)

½ cup roasted pistachio nuts, finely
   chopped

¾ cup well-stirred canned
   unsweetened coconut milk

1½ teaspoons grated fresh ginger

2 tablespoons chopped fresh cilantro,
   for garnish

This is an elegant-but-easy Indian-inspired dish created by my talented assistant Jenn Iserloh. Using a blend like garam masala and mixing it into coconut milk creates complex flavor in a flash.

SERVES 4

Break the saffron threads into a small bowl by rubbing them between your fingers. Stir in 1 tablespoon of warm water and set aside for at least 10 minutes.

Meanwhile, prepare the chicken: With kitchen scissors, cut away and discard the white tendon that runs down the top of each tender. Season the tenders with salt. Set aside.

In a large, shallow saucepan, heat 1 tablespoon of the butter over medium-high heat until it foams. Stir in the onion and cook, stirring occasionally, until soft and translucent, 4 to 5 minutes. Stir in the garam masala and cook for an additional minute, stirring constantly to avoid burning the spices.

Increase the heat to high. Add the chicken and stir until it is coated with the spices. Stir in the tomatoes and chicken broth. Add more garam masala, if needed. Cover and lower the heat to medium. Cook until the chicken is no longer pink inside, 8 to 12 minutes.

While the chicken is cooking, melt the remaining 2 tablespoons butter in a large skillet over medium heat. Stir in the saffron and any unabsorbed water. Stir in the rice and continue stirring until the rice is uniformly colored with the saffron, hot, and moist, a minute or two. (If necessary add a little more water to rehydrate the rice.) Turn off the heat and stir in the pistachios. Cover until needed.

When the chicken is done, stir in the coconut milk, ginger, and salt to taste. Cook only until the sauce is hot to avoid overcooking the chicken. Adjust the seasonings.

Spoon the rice onto plates, and set the chicken to the side. Drizzle some of the sauce on top of the rice. Garnish with the cilantro.

VARIATIONS

• Substitute chicken or turkey breast cutlets or boneless chicken thighs.

• Use your favorite curry blend to taste instead of garam masala.

GRAIN EXCHANGE

Use jasmine or long-grain brown rice instead of brown basmati.

WINE RECOMMENDATION: Something straightforward is in order here for this complex dish. An Italian white, like Soave or tocai friulano, will have the acidity to take on the tomatoes and will let the fragrant spices shine through.

brown basmati rice and thai coconut shrimp

1 can (14 ounces) unsweetened
　　coconut milk (light is fine, if you
　　prefer)
½ tablespoon Thai red curry paste,
　　plus more to taste
Thai fish sauce or salt (optional)
1 small red bell pepper, seeded
　　and diced
1 cup frozen peas
3 cups cooked Basic Brown Basmati
　　Rice (page 63)
1 pound medium shrimp, peeled and
　　cleaned
2 tablespoons thinly sliced scallion
　　greens
12 large fresh basil leaves (or
　　equivalent), stacked, rolled, and
　　thinly sliced
Lime wedges, for serving

By blending a good-quality Thai curry paste into coconut milk, it's easy to create a sophisticated Thai curry sauce in minutes. Stir in some shrimp, brown rice, and peas, and this one-pot dinner is on the table in a matter of minutes.

SERVES 3 TO 4

In a large skillet, blend the coconut milk and curry paste to taste. Add Thai fish sauce or salt, if more flavor is needed. Add the red bell pepper. Bring to a gentle boil over medium-high heat. Stir in the peas and rice.

When the mixture returns to a gentle boil, add the shrimp. Continue cooking and stirring until the rice is hot and the shrimp turn pink, about 2 minutes. Stir in the scallions and basil. Serve in shallow bowls, accompanied with a bowl of lime wedges.

VARIATION
Use cooked green beans, cut into 1-inch pieces, instead of the peas.

GRAIN EXCHANGE
Instead of basmati, use short-grain or long-grain brown rice or Kamut.

WINE RECOMMENDATION: Wines with a bit of sweetness help tame the heat of curries. Off-dry rieslings are wonderful with Thai curries because the grape's exotic floral quality is especially lovely with coconut milk.

thai salmon with brown basmati rice
Instead of shrimp, use 1 pound thin salmon fillets. When the mixture returns to a gentle boil, set the fillets on top of the rice, cover the skillet, and cook until the fish flakes, 3 to 5 minutes. Break the fillets into large chunks and stir into the rice.

kamut with mussels in tomato broth

1 tablespoon olive oil

½ cup finely diced shallots

2 teaspoons minced garlic

1 teaspoon fennel seeds

½ cup dry vermouth, red wine, or
white wine

1 can (28 ounces) diced tomatoes,
with liquid

Pinch of crushed red pepper flakes

4 pounds mussels, beards removed

3 cups cooked Basic Whole Kamut
Kernels (page 94)

3 tablespoons chopped fresh flat-leaf
parsley

Salt and freshly ground pepper

Freshly squeezed lemon juice
(optional)

As they steam open, mussels create an intensely briny broth, as good as the best fish stock I know. Add a little wine and tomatoes, and you have a sophisticated pool in which to float golden, buttery Kamut.

SERVES 4

In a large pot, heat the oil over high heat. Add the shallots and cook, stirring frequently, until they soften, about 3 minutes. Add the garlic and fennel seeds and continue cooking for another 2 minutes.

Add the wine, tomatoes, red pepper flakes, and ¼ cup of water and bring to a boil. Add half the mussels, cover, and steam over high heat until they open, 3 to 5 minutes. Transfer the mussels with a slotted spoon to a large serving bowl or four large individual soup bowls. Tent with foil to keep warm. Add the remaining mussels to the pot and steam them open. Transfer these to the bowl(s).

Stir the Kamut into the tomato broth in the pot and cook until heated. Stir in the parsley and salt and pepper to taste. Add lemon juice, if needed, to sharpen the flavors. Ladle the Kamut and broth over the mussels. Serve immediately.

GRAIN EXCHANGE

Use short-grain brown rice or Chinese black rice instead of Kamut.

WINE RECOMMENDATION: Tomatoes often call for a high-acid red wine, but shellfish can make red wine taste metallic. A full-bodied, dry rosé from southern France or Spain will make both ingredients happy.

kamut with mussels in thai-flavored tomato broth

Omit the fennel seeds and blend in ½ to 1 tablespoon Thai green curry paste when you add the tomatoes. Use fresh cilantro or basil instead of parsley.

wild rice medley with braised chicken in balsamic-fig sauce

FOR THE RICE MEDLEY

¾ cup wild rice

¾ cup short-grain brown rice

¼ cup red or beige quinoa

⅓ cup hazelnuts, toasted and coarsely
   chopped

1 tablespoon hazelnut or olive oil

Salt and freshly ground black pepper
   to taste

FOR THE CHICKEN

4 chicken breast halves

Salt and freshly ground black pepper

1 tablespoon vegetable oil, for frying

1 medium onion, diced

¼ cup balsamic vinegar

1½ cups reduced-sodium chicken
   broth, plus more if needed

12 dried Mission figs, halved
   lengthwise

2 teaspoons chopped fresh rosemary,
   plus rosemary sprigs for garnish

Wild rice can be intense on its own, so I often combine it with other grains. Unless you cook all of the grains separately and combine them afterwards, you need to be a daredevil because the cooking time of wild rice is wildly unpredictable.

Since I'm an impatient cook with daredevil tendencies, I offer you a medley of grains cooked together. However, I have chosen the companion grains carefully, so success is close to guaranteed.

The festive grain medley of wild rice, brown rice, and quinoa is especially delicious when robed with the rich fig sauce.

SERVES 4

Bring 14 cups (3½ quarts) of water to a boil in a large pot. Add the wild rice and boil over high heat, uncovered, for 10 minutes. Reduce the heat slightly. Stir in the brown rice and continue boiling uncovered for 35 minutes, stirring occasionally to prevent the grains from sticking to the bottom of the pot. At this point, if any of the wild rice has split open, stir in the quinoa. Otherwise wait until that point to add the quinoa. Cook until all of the grains are tender, usually 10 to 12 minutes longer. Drain. Return the grains to the hot pot, cover, and let sit.

While the rice is cooking, rinse the chicken breasts and pat them dry. Trim off any fat. Season both sides well with salt and pepper.

Heat the oil in a large saucepan until smoking. Over high heat, brown the breasts well, two at a time, skin-side down, about 4 minutes. Transfer them to a platter. (It is not necessary to brown the second side.)

Pour off and discard all but a thin slick of fat. Add the onion and cook over medium-high heat until lightly browned, about 3 minutes. Pour in the vinegar, taking care to scrape up any browned bits stuck to the bottom of the pan. Cook over high heat until most of the vinegar has evaporated, about 1 minute.

Stir in the broth and the figs. Bring to a boil. Add the chicken, browned side up. Lower the heat, cover, and simmer until the chicken is tender and registers 165°F on an instant-read thermometer in the thickest part, 25 to 45 minutes, depending on the size of the breasts. Add more broth, if needed.

When the chicken is done, transfer the pieces to the center of a large platter and tent it with foil. Skim any fat off the top of the sauce or sop it up with a paper towel. Use an immersion blender to create a coarse puree. Stir in the fresh rosemary. Season the sauce to taste. Simmer uncovered to thicken, if you wish.

To serve, transfer the hot grains to a bowl. Toss in the hazelnuts and hazelnut oil, and season to taste with salt and pepper. Spoon the wild rice medley around the chicken. Spoon the sauce over the chicken and a little over the rice. Garnish the platter with rosemary sprigs.

GRAIN EXCHANGE

• Use Wehani rice instead of wild rice.

• Use Colusari red rice instead of brown.

WINE RECOMMENDATION: A red wine is in order here, to complement the boldly flavored sauce. The secret is to try one that is not so dry that it will clash with the sweet figs. A fruity but spicy red like primitivo from southern Italy or a zinfandel from the United States would be just right.

barley and turkey chili with jalapeño sour cream and amaranth crunch

FOR THE JALAPEÑO SOUR CREAM

2 jalapeños, seeded (reserve some
seeds for added heat if desired)

¾ cup sour cream

1 tablespoon freshly squeezed lime
juice

1 teaspoon sweet paprika

¼ teaspoon salt

FOR THE CHILI

1 tablespoon olive oil

1 large onion, diced

1 medium green bell pepper, seeded
and diced

2 large cloves garlic, minced

1 pound ground turkey

2½ teaspoons chili powder

1 teaspoon unsweetened cocoa
powder (optional)

⅛ teaspoon ground cinnamon

1 can (28 ounces) diced tomatoes
(preferably fire roasted), with liquid

1 teaspoon salt

2 cups cooked Basic Hulled, Hull-less,
or Pearl Barley (page 25)

Popped Amaranth Crunch (page 21)

This robust chili has two unusual toppings: a smooth jalapeño-laced sour cream and amaranth crunch, a crisp seasoning made of popped amaranth and toasted pumpkin seeds.

SERVES 4 TO 6

To prepare the jalapeño sour cream: In a mini chopper or food processor, puree the jalapeños, sour cream, lime juice, paprika, and salt. Set aside or refrigerate overnight.

To make the chili: Heat the oil in a 3-quart saucepan. Stir in the onion and green pepper and cook over medium-high heat for 2 minutes. Stir in the garlic and cook while stirring for another minute. Add the turkey. Turn the heat to high. Break up the turkey into small bits and stir in the chili powder, cocoa powder (if using), and cinnamon.

Stir in the tomatoes, ½ cup of water, and salt. Cover and simmer for 5 minutes. Stir in the barley, cover, and simmer until the barley becomes infused with flavor and the turkey is cooked, about 5 minutes more.

Serve in bowls with a dollop of jalapeño sour cream and a sprinkling of amaranth crunch on top. Pass the remaining jalapeño sour cream and amaranth crunch in bowls at the table.

GRAIN EXCHANGE

Use short-grain brown rice, hominy, or Job's tears instead of barley.

WINE RECOMMENDATION: A brown ale is a great choice for this chili flavored with sweet cinnamon. A rich but soft red wine, like a merlot or a zinfandel, pairs nicely as well.

barley-chorizo skillet pie

8 large eggs

¼ cup chopped fresh cilantro

½ to ¾ teaspoon salt (use lower amount if chorizo is quite salty)

2 tablespoons olive oil

1 large onion, finely diced

1 medium green bell pepper, seeded and finely diced

3 to 4 ounces Spanish cured chorizo, diced (about 1 cup)

2 teaspoons minced garlic

1½ to 2 cups cooked Basic Hulled or Hull-less Barley (page 25)

½ cup grated manchego or Monterey Jack cheese (about 2 ounces)

This recipe is a riff on a traditional Spanish skillet cake made with thinly sliced potatoes and eggs. I've substituted barley for the potato and added chorizo and peppers to transform a tapa into an entrée.

The skillet pie is started on top of the stove and finished under the broiler. It's a good choice for brunch or a light supper with mixed greens tossed in a sherry vinaigrette. Or cut it into smaller wedges and serve among other tapas.

SERVES 6

In a bowl, whisk together the eggs, cilantro, and salt. Set aside.

Heat 1 tablespoon of the oil in a 10- or 12-inch well-seasoned cast-iron or nonstick ovenproof skillet. Add the onion, bell pepper, and chorizo and cook over medium-high heat, stirring frequently, until the pepper is tender, about 5 minutes. Add the garlic and continue cooking for 1 minute more. Stir in the barley and the remaining 1 tablespoon oil.

Pour the eggs evenly over the vegetable-grain mixture. Reduce the heat to medium. Use a spatula to push the cooked egg at the edges of the skillet towards the center, allowing the uncooked egg to seep to the bottom. Cook over medium-low heat uncovered until the edges are set and the bottom is nicely browned, 10 to 12 minutes.

Meanwhile, preheat the broiler.

Sprinkle the cheese on top. Broil the pie until the cheese is browned and bubbly, about 2 minutes. Serve from the pan, or slide whole onto a large platter or cutting board. Let rest for 5 minutes before slicing into wedges. Serve hot, warm, or at room temperature.

italian farro pie with salami

Substitute flat-leaf parsley for the cilantro, salami for the chorizo, farro for the barley, and ⅓ cup grated Romano cheese for the manchego.

posole with pork and chipotle

2 cups dried whole hominy

1 pound pork shoulder, trimmed and
   cut into 1½-inch cubes

Salt and freshly ground pepper

2 tablespoons olive oil

1 large onion, diced

2 large cloves garlic, minced

1 tablespoon tomato paste

1½ teaspoons dried oregano

2 large bay leaves

1 pork bone (optional)

2 cups crushed tomatoes in tomato
   puree

1 to 2 chipotles in adobo, membranes
   and seeds removed, finely minced,
   plus ½ teaspoon adobo sauce

¼ cup chopped fresh cilantro, for
   garnish (optional)

Whole trimmed radishes, for serving
   (optional)

Here is a savory project for a winter afternoon. Posole (also spelled pozole) is the Mexican name for a pork stew as well as the name of dried large-kernel field corn. Many regions of Mexico have their own versions, but essentially posole is a hearty stew that is soulful in its simplicity.

Once you've soaked the dried hominy overnight, the stew takes about 3 hours to cook—but there is relatively little prep and the cooking requires only occasional attention. Posole is the type of dish that develops more intense flavor the longer it sits, so you can even prepare it a day or two before you plan to serve it.

SERVES 6

Soak the hominy overnight in 12 cups (3 quarts) of water. Drain the hominy, reserving the liquid.

Season the pork well with salt and pepper. Heat the oil in a heavy 4-quart pot over high heat. Brown the pork well in three to four batches (making sure not to crowd the pot), 2 to 3 minutes on each side. As you finish each batch, transfer it to a platter and set aside.

Reduce the heat to medium-high. If there is fat in the pan, spoon off all but 1 tablespoon. Add the onion and cook, stirring frequently, until lightly browned, about 4 minutes. Add the garlic and tomato paste and cook, stirring constantly, for an additional minute.

Stir in 8 cups (2 quarts) of the hominy soaking liquid, the soaked hominy, oregano, bay leaves, and ½ teaspoon salt. Add the pork bone (if using). Over high heat, bring the mixture almost to a boil. Reduce the heat to low, cover, and simmer for 1 hour. Stir in the tomatoes, chipotle and adobo sauce, and the browned pork, along with any juices accumulated on the platter. Set the cover slightly off center and continue simmering until the pork is fork-tender and the hominy is done (it will be chewy, but the center should be soft and somewhat creamy), an additional 45 minutes to 1 1/2 hours. Skim off any fat that rises to the surface. Add more hominy soaking liquid or water if the mixture becomes too thick and threatens to stick to the bottom of the pot.

Remove the pork bone and bay leaves. Adjust the seasoning. Serve in large soup bowls. Garnish individual portions with cilantro (if using), and serve a bowl of radishes for accompaniment, if you wish.

WINE RECOMMENDATION: Cold beer is probably the best match for this stew because it tames the chipotles' heat so well. But a lightly chilled red wine with no tannins is also a good choice—try a frothy, gulpable lambrusco from Italy.

express hominy stew

Follow the instructions above, except use 4 cups of water instead of 8 cups of soaking liquid, and 2 cans (15 to 19 ounces each) of hominy, drained and rinsed, instead of homemade hominy. Stir in the canned hominy 30 minutes after adding the pork.

■ ■ ■

bulgur and lamb kibbe

2 teaspoons olive oil, pus extra for
  greasing dish

3/4 to 1 teaspoon salt

1 cup fine bulgur

1 large onion, quartered

1/4 cup (tightly packed) combination
  of fresh flat-leaf parsley and mint

1/2 teaspoon ground cinnamon

1/2 teaspoon ground cumin

1/4 teaspoon ground allspice

1/4 teaspoon cayenne (optional)

1 pound ground lamb

Pistachio nuts (preferably salted),
  coarsely chopped, for garnish

Kibbe—bulgur in combination with ground lamb or beef—is commonly used in the Middle East to make meatballs and loaves of all shapes and sizes. Not only does this approach stretch the meat (and lower the cholesterol of the dish), it creates a pleasingly soft and light texture that is very comforting.

For ease, in this recipe I spread the lamb-bulgur mixture out in a rectangular pan, bake it, and then slice it into squares.

SERVES 6 TO 8

Set the rack in the middle and preheat the oven to 375°F. Lightly brush a rectangular baking dish, about 12 by 8 inches, with oil.

Bring 1 cup plus 1 tablespoon of water and 1/2 teaspoon of the salt to a boil in a heavy 2-quart saucepan. Stir in the bulgur. Cover and let sit off the heat for 10 minutes or until needed.

Puree the onion in a food processor. Add the fresh herbs, cinnamon, cumin, allspice, cayenne, and remaining 1/4 to 1/2 teaspoon salt (depending upon how salty you like your food). Process to blend. Add the bulgur and process until well blended.

Transfer the mixture to a large bowl and use your hands to mix in the lamb. (At this point, if you wish, fry up a tiny patty of the mixture to check the seasoning and make adjustments.) Pat the mixture evenly into the prepared pan. Drizzle the olive oil on top.

Bake until the center is cooked and no longer pink, 30 to 45 minutes. Let sit for 5 minutes before cutting into squares. Sprinkle pistachio nuts on top of each portion.

VARIATION

Use ground beef or a combination of beef and pork instead of lamb.

WINE RECOMMENDATION: A fruit-driven American syrah would complement this herbal and spicy lamb dish well.

bulgur burgers

Shape the mixture into hamburger-size patties and broil or grill.

bulgur meatballs

Shape the mixture into balls. Brown them in oil, then simmer in tomato sauce until cooked through.

stuffed pita

Cut the cooked mixture into cubes and stuff them into pita with shredded lettuce and diced tomato. Drizzle with a sauce made from tahini paste thinned with water and seasoned with salt and lemon juice.

hearty grain casserole

1 tablespoon olive oil, plus extra for greasing pan

3 cups cooked whole grains (defrost if frozen)

2 cooked Italian-style chicken or turkey sausages, diced

1 cup (tightly packed) grated provolone cheese (about 5 ounces)

1 can (15 ounces) diced tomatoes, with liquid

1 large red bell pepper, seeded and diced

⅓ cup (tightly packed) chopped fresh flat-leaf parsley or basil, plus more for garnish

¼ cup pine nuts

¼ cup grated Romano cheese

1 teaspoon minced garlic or ½ teaspoon granulated garlic

1 teaspoon dried oregano

¼ to ½ teaspoon crushed red pepper flakes

Salt and freshly ground black pepper to taste

I often make this casserole when I have a batch of leftover cooked grains in The Grain Bank (page 10). Like most casseroles, it's even tastier the second day. Serve it with a crisp green salad.

SERVES 4 TO 6

Place the rack in the center and preheat the oven to 375°F. Oil an 8-inch square baking pan.

In a large bowl, combine the grains, sausages, ¾ cup of the provolone, the tomatoes, bell pepper, parsley, pine nuts, Romano, oil, garlic, oregano, red pepper flakes, and salt and black pepper.

Transfer the mixture to the prepared pan. Cover with aluminum foil and bake until hot throughout, 30 to 35 minutes. Uncover. Sprinkle on the remaining ¼ cup cheese. Continue baking until the cheese is melted and the casserole is bubbly, 3 to 5 minutes. Scoop out individual portions and garnish with parsley.

VARIATIONS

• Use ⅓ cup chopped walnuts or hazelnuts instead of pine nuts.

• Try smoked mozzarella or a mixture of cheeses instead of provolone.

WINE RECOMMENDATION: A simple, everyday Italian red, like a dolcetto or a montepulciano d'Abruzzo, is a nice choice for this rustic casserole.

southwest rice casserole

Use jalapeño Jack instead of provolone, cilantro instead of parsley, and ground chipotle instead of red pepper flakes. Omit the Romano cheese.

millet pie with spinach and feta

1 tablespoon olive oil, plus more
    for greasing pie plate
1 medium onion, diced
1 teaspoon dried oregano
1 cup hulled millet, rinsed
12 ounces baby spinach
5 ounces crumbled feta (about 1 cup)
1 red bell pepper, roasted, seeded, and
    diced
2 tablespoons chopped fresh flat-leaf
    parsley, plus sprigs for garnish
Salt and freshly ground pepper
    to taste

When cooked in a generous amount of liquid, millet becomes porridgy and sets up like grits as it cools: soft with a toothsome texture. Think of this quick-cooking dish when vegetarians are coming to town. Bright patches of spinach and roasted red pepper give the pie a festive air.

SERVES 4

Lightly oil a 9-inch pie plate. Set aside.

Heat the oil in a medium saucepan. Add the onion and cook over medium-high heat until lightly browned, about 3 minutes. Stir in the oregano. Add 3½ cups of water and bring it to a boil.

Stir in the millet. Reduce the heat to medium, cover the pot, and cook the millet for 10 minutes. Uncover and boil the mixture over medium-high heat, stirring occasionally, until most of the remaining water evaporates, 5 to 8 minutes.

Continue cooking over very low heat until the millet becomes very soft and the mixture is thick and porridgy, usually about 5 minutes more. A minute or so before the millet is tender, stir in the spinach, a large handful at a time. If the mixture becomes dry before the millet is tender, add boiling water, about ¼ cup at a time.

Turn off the heat and stir in the feta, red pepper, parsley, and salt and pepper. Pour the mixture into the prepared pie plate. Set aside to cool until set, about 1 hour.

To serve, cut into wedges and serve at room temperature. Alternatively, reheat in the microwave. Set a sprig or two of parsley alongside individual portions.

WINE RECOMMENDATION: A dry, crisp Italian white, like verdicchio or vermentino, has the zesty acidity to cut through the cheese and a bitter green edge that will match well with the spinach.

masa harina–beef casserole

FOR THE FILLING

1 tablespoon olive oil

1 medium onion, coarsely chopped

1 medium green bell pepper, seeded
   and diced

1½ pounds ground chuck

2 cloves garlic, minced

1 teaspoon dried oregano

1 teaspoon whole cumin seeds
   or ½ teaspoon ground

¾ teaspoon salt

Freshly ground black pepper

1 can (15 ounces) diced tomatoes
   with green chiles, with liquid

FOR THE MASA TOPPING

1¼ cups masa harina

1½ teaspoons salt

1 teaspoon chili powder

1 large egg

½ cup sour cream

¼ teaspoon baking soda

1 cup fresh or frozen corn kernels

The flour called masa harina has a very distinctive corn flavor. It is traditionally used in making tamales, but for cooks who want the flavor without the fuss, try using masa harina as a topping for well-seasoned ground beef, as I have done here.

SERVES 6

Place the rack in the bottom third and preheat the oven to 350°F. Have ready a rectangular baking dish, about 11 by 7 inches. Line a large rimmed baking sheet with foil to set under the pan in case of bubble-overs.

To prepare the filling: Heat the oil in a large skillet. Add the onion and green pepper and cook over medium-high heat, stirring occasionally, until the onion is soft, about 5 minutes.

Stir in the chuck, garlic, oregano, cumin, salt, and pepper to taste. Cook the meat over medium-high heat, breaking it up into small bits as you go. When the meat turns brown, stir in the tomatoes and bring to a boil. Lower the heat, and simmer uncovered while you prepare the masa topping.

To prepare the topping: Pour 4 cups of cold water into a heavy 3-quart pot. Gradually whisk the masa harina into the water until it's thoroughly blended. Stir in the salt and chili powder. Bring the mixture to a boil over high heat. Reduce the heat and cook at a gentle boil, stirring frequently, until the mixture thickens to the consistency of a batter, 3 to 5 minutes. Remove from the heat.

In a small bowl, lightly beat the egg. Stir in the sour cream and 1 cup of the hot masa batter. Stir the egg mixture and the baking soda into the pot containing the remaining masa mixture.

Taste the meat and adjust the seasonings. Lift the meat mixture with a slotted spoon and transfer it into the baking dish, leaving any liquid behind. Pour the masa batter over the meat and smooth off the top. Scatter the corn kernels on the batter.

Place the baking dish on the baking sheet to catch any spills. Bake until the casserole is bubbly and the top is brown, 40 to 45 minutes. Remove from the oven and let sit for 10 minutes before serving. To serve, scoop out portions with a large spoon.

VARIATIONS

• Instead of tomatoes with green chiles, use 1 can plain diced tomatoes and 1 to 2 teaspoons mashed chipotles in adobo.

• Sprinkle 1 cup grated Monterey Jack cheese on top of the masa batter before adding the corn.

GRAIN EXCHANGE

Use fine cornmeal instead of masa harina.

WINE RECOMMENDATION: Mexican-inspired recipes can be tough for wine pairings, because they often combine rich meaty flavors with heat from chiles. A light, lager-style beer is a refreshing choice for this hearty dish, but you could also try a red wine with minimal tannins, like a soft merlot or a jammy red zinfandel.

oat and amaranth–crusted ham and cheese quiche

FOR THE CRUST

½ cup old-fashioned rolled oats

½ cup beige amaranth

½ teaspoon salt

3 tablespoons unsalted butter, melted, plus more for preparing the pie dish

2 to 4 tablespoons ice-cold water

1 large egg white, lightly beaten (save the yolk for the filling)

FOR THE FILLING

2 large eggs

1 large egg yolk

1 cup 2% milk

1 teaspoon Dijon mustard

1 teaspoon chopped fresh rosemary

⅛ teaspoon salt

1 cup (loosely packed) grated Gruyère

1 cup chopped country ham

This unusual cracker-like, protein-rich crust offers oats' pleasing sweetness and amaranth's hint of corn.

SERVES 4 TO 6

Place the rack in the center and preheat the oven to 350°F. Butter a 9-inch pie plate. Set aside.

To make the crust: Grind the oats into a fine flour in a spice grinder. Transfer to a medium bowl.

Heat a large skillet. Add the amaranth and stir constantly until the seeds begin to pop and smell toasty, about 3 minutes. Remove from the heat and pour into a small bowl to cool. Transfer half of the amaranth seeds to a spice grinder and grind them into a fairly fine flour. (The amaranth flour may be slightly coarser than the oat flour.) Transfer the flour to the bowl with the oat flour, and then grind the second batch of popped amaranth.

Add the second batch of amaranth flour and the salt to the bowl. While stirring, gradually add the melted butter. Stir in 2 tablespoons of the cold water. Add more water, if needed, to create a dough that holds its shape when pressed together.

Press the dough evenly, about ¼-inch thick, onto the bottom and up the sides of the pie plate. Bake for 15 minutes. Liberally coat the pie crust with the egg white, taking care to fill in any cracks. Return to the oven for 1 minute. Set on a cooling rack. Keep the oven on.

To prepare the filling: In a bowl, mix the eggs, yolk, milk, mustard, rosemary, and salt.

Distribute the cheese and ham on the pie crust. Pour the egg mixture on top. Bake until the top is browned and the center is set, 30 to 40 minutes. Let cool on a rack for 5 to 10 minutes before slicing into portions.

VARIATION

Use olive, corn, or peanut oil instead of melted butter for the crust.

WINE RECOMMENDATION: A dry riesling from France's Alsace region has the acidity to cut through the salty flavors and the richness to stand up to the hearty quiche.

vegetarian quiche

Omit the ham and add 3 tablespoons chopped sun-dried tomatoes and/or pitted olives.

on the

side

pilafs

casseroles

grain and vegetable combos

polentas, grits, and griddle cakes

PILAFS

bhutanese red rice pilaf

1 cup Bhutanese red rice
1 tablespoon unsalted butter
½ cup finely diced shallots
½ cup finely diced carrots
2 tablespoons dried currants
½ teaspoon salt
1 bay leaf
¼ teaspoon dried thyme
2 tablespoons pine nuts, toasted
1 tablespoon chopped fresh dill
Grated zest of 1 small lemon

Bhutanese rice is a colorful grain grown at high altitudes in the Himalayas. As it cooks, the bran's red color leaches into the water and is absorbed by the grain, dyeing the interior starch red. Since Bhutanese red rice cooks in under a half hour, it's a good grain to keep on hand for times when you need to get dinner on the table quickly.

SERVES 4

Rinse the rice and set aside to drain. In a heavy 2-quart Dutch oven or saucepan, melt the butter. Add the shallots and carrots and cook over medium-high heat until the shallots are translucent, 3 to 4 minutes.

Add the rice and stir until it is coated with butter. Add 2 cups of water, the currants, salt, bay leaf, and thyme, and stir. Bring to a boil.

Cover, reduce the heat, and simmer until the rice is tender, 20 to 25 minutes. When properly cooked, the rice will be one color throughout when cut in half crosswise.

Turn off the heat. Remove the bay leaf. Stir in the pine nuts, dill, and lemon zest. Fluff up and serve.

VARIATION
Substitute ⅓ cup finely chopped red onion for the shallots.

GRAIN EXCHANGE
Use Chinese black rice instead of Bhutanese.

brown rice pilaf with walnuts and dried cranberries

3 tablespoons unsalted butter

¾ teaspoon salt

¼ teaspoon pumpkin pie spice, or
   ⅛ teaspoon ground cinnamon and
   a pinch each of allspice and freshly
   grated nutmeg

½ cup walnut halves

3 cups cooked Basic Long-Grain Brown
   Rice (page 63)

3 tablespoons Marsala or sweet sherry

2 tablespoons dried cranberries

¾ teaspoon grated orange zest

Freshly ground black pepper (optional)

This is a slightly sweet, elegant pilaf that goes well with roast lamb, chicken, and duck.

SERVES 4

Heat the butter in a large skillet over medium heat. When it starts to foam, add the salt, pumpkin pie spice, and walnuts. Stir frequently until the walnuts are lightly toasted, 2 to 3 minutes.

Stir in the rice, then add the Marsala and cranberries. Cover and cook until the rice is moist and heated through. If the rice begins to stick or seems dry, stir in a few tablespoons of water, cover, and cook for another minute or two over low heat.

Turn off the heat, and stir in the orange zest. Adjust the seasonings, adding black pepper, if you wish.

VARIATIONS

- Coarsely chop the walnuts.
- Use chopped dried apple or currants instead of cranberries.
- Press portions into ramekins and unmold onto plates to serve.

GRAIN EXCHANGE

Substitute brown basmati, jasmine, or short-grain rice for the long-grain brown rice.

roasted brown rice pilaf scented with leeks

1 tablespoon unsalted butter

½ cup chopped leeks (white and light green parts)

1 cup long- or short-grain brown rice

¼ teaspoon dried thyme

½ teaspoon salt, or to taste

Oven-roasting rice and then steaming it produces a nutty, puffed-open grain that more than triples in volume and is light and bouncy. This technique works equally well with long- and short-grain brown rice. In fact, they are virtually indistinguishable after cooking.

SERVES 4

Place the rack in the bottom third of the oven and preheat the oven to 400°F. Bring water to a boil in a kettle. You'll need 2 cups.

Heat the butter in a heavy 2-quart Dutch oven over medium heat until it foams. Add the leeks and cook until they begin to wilt and soften, about 5 minutes. Turn off the heat.

Meanwhile, spread the rice out on a large rimmed baking sheet and set in the oven. Stir every few minutes for even browning, and continue roasting until the grains have darkened a few shades and smell toasty, 6 to 10 minutes total. Watch closely to avoid burning.

Stir the roasted rice into the leeks. Stand back and add 2 cups boiling water, the thyme, and salt. Cover, reduce the heat, and simmer until the rice is tender, or just short of tender, about 35 minutes. Turn off the heat and let stand, covered, for 10 minutes. Fluff up and serve.

baked roasted brown rice pilaf

Use an ovenproof pot. After roasting the rice, reduce the oven heat to 350°F and move the rack to the center. After adding the roasted rice, water, salt, and thyme to the leeks, cover the pot and bake for 35 minutes. Remove from the oven and let stand for 10 minutes. Fluff up and serve.

curried kalijira rice pilaf with cashews and peas

1 teaspoon whole fennel seeds

½ teaspoon whole cumin seeds

2 tablespoons unsalted butter

1 tablespoon grapeseed or other
neutral oil

2 teaspoons mild curry powder, plus
more to taste

½ teaspoon salt, plus more to taste

4 cups cooked Basic Kalijira Brown
Rice (page 65)

1 cup frozen peas

Pinch of cayenne (optional)

½ cup coarsely chopped roasted
unsalted cashews

2 tablespoons chopped fresh cilantro

Here is a quick pilaf to serve with Indian foods. Vary it by using different curry blends. A personal favorite is Sun Brand's mild Madras curry powder. Another good choice is Penzeys Maharajah blend, available by mail-order.

I like to enhance any commercial blend by adding toasted whole spices for hits of intense flavor.

SERVES 4

Set a large nonstick skillet over medium heat. Add the fennel and cumin seeds and toast, stirring almost constantly, until the spices become aromatic, 2 to 3 minutes.

Stir the butter and oil into the spices. When the butter has melted, reduce the heat to medium-low and stir in the curry powder and salt. (Add salt at this time only if your curry blend doesn't already contain it; check the label.) Continue cooking and stirring for 1 minute.

Stir in the rice. Set the peas in a strainer and run some hot water over them to partially thaw. Drain well and stir into the rice. Season with cayenne (if using) and more curry powder and salt, if needed. When the peas are tender, turn off the heat and stir in the nuts and cilantro.

VARIATIONS

• Use chopped pistachios or toasted almonds instead of cashews.

• Add 2 tablespoons dried currants or chopped dried mango when you add the rice.

• Press the cooked pilaf into timbales and unmold in the middle of each plate.

GRAIN EXCHANGE

Use brown basmati rice instead of kalijira.

oat pilaf with carrots and thyme

1 tablespoon unsalted butter
   or olive oil
1 cup finely diced onions
1 cup finely diced carrots
½ cup finely diced celery
1½ cups whole oat groats, rinsed
2 teaspoons chopped fresh thyme or
   ½ teaspoon dried
¾ teaspoon salt, plus more to taste
1½ teaspoons grated lemon zest
Freshly ground pepper

Oats have a natural sweetness and a silken texture similar to that of barley, making them a good candidate for a pilaf with a moist, stuffing-like consistency. Baking the pilaf is a gentle way to cook the oats and prevents them from sticking to the bottom of the pan. This side dish is quite versatile, but pairs especially nicely with meatloaf and roast chicken.

SERVES 6 TO 8

Place a rack in the center of the oven and preheat the oven to 350°F. Bring some water to a boil in a kettle. You will need 2 cups.

Melt the butter in a heavy 2-quart Dutch oven or ovenproof saucepan over medium heat. Add the onions, carrots, and celery, and cook, stirring occasionally, until the onion softens, 3 to 5 minutes.

Add the oats and stir until they are coated with butter. If using dried thyme, add it now. Turn off the heat. Stir in 2 cups of boiling water and the salt. Cover and set in the oven.

After 35 minutes, taste the oats. If they are tender, remove them from the oven and let sit for 5 minutes. If the oats are not done and all of the water has been absorbed, pour on ¼ to ⅓ cup more boiling water. Continue baking until the oats are tender, which should not take more than 10 minutes longer, then let rest for 5 minutes. Stir in the fresh thyme, if using, and lemon zest. Season with salt and pepper to taste.

VARIATION

Use low-sodium chicken broth instead of water. Do not add salt to taste until after cooking.

GRAIN EXCHANGE

Use pearl or hull-less barley instead of oats. Increase the water to 4 cups. If there is unabsorbed water after cooking, lift out the mixture with a slotted spoon to serve.

CASSEROLES

any-grain and honeyed squash casserole with hazelnuts

FOR THE SQUASH MIXTURE

2 pounds butternut squash, peeled, seeded, and grated (about 7 cups)

3 tablespoons honey

½ teaspoon minced fresh rosemary

3 tablespoons dried currants

3 tablespoons Marsala or dry sherry

¼ teaspoon salt

Freshly ground pepper to taste

FOR THE TOPPING

3 cups cooked whole grains (any type; pages 16–111)

1 teaspoon salt

3 tablespoons unsalted butter, melted

1 tablespoon honey

¾ cup hazelnuts, roughly chopped

Is it because they are both such ancient, biblical foods that grains and honey seem to be made for each other? To create the topping for this vegetable crumble, the grains are sweetened, scattered on top of the squash, and baked in a casserole dish. Opt for chewy grains like barley, wheat berries, or short-grain brown rice. Use one grain or a combination.

Grating the squash dramatically speeds up cooking time. Honey enhances the squash's natural sweetness, making this casserole a festive way to celebrate the arrival of fall.

SERVES 4 TO 6

Set a rack in the center of the oven and preheat the oven to 400°F.

In a large bowl, combine the squash, honey, rosemary, currants, Marsala, salt, and pepper. Transfer the mixture to a 2-quart gratin dish or a 7 x 11-inch rectangular baking dish.

In the same bowl, stir together the grains, salt, butter, and honey until the grains are well coated. Distribute the grains over the squash in an even layer. Cover the dish with aluminum foil and bake until the squash is tender, 20 to 25 minutes.

Remove the foil and sprinkle with the hazelnuts. Continue baking until the hazelnuts are lightly browned, 4 to 5 minutes longer.

barley-carrot kugel with honey glaze

Butter, for greasing the pan

3 large eggs

3 tablespoons honey

2 tablespoons unsalted butter, melted

1½ tablespoons chopped fresh
  tarragon or 1 teaspoon dried

½ teaspoon salt

2 cups cooked Basic Hulled, Hull-less,
  or Pearl Barley (page 25)

1 pound carrots, coarsely grated
  (4 cups)

⅓ cup dried currants

½ cup walnuts, toasted and chopped

Using cooked barley as the base for this casserole is a chewy change from the traditional Jewish potato kugel. I've added carrots to accentuate the barley's natural sweetness and provide some lively color.

The kugel goes well with roast chicken, brisket, or pot roast. Or serve large portions as a vegetarian entrée. It also makes a great 4 o'clock snack, accompanied by a cup of tea.

SERVES 6 TO 8

Set a rack in the middle of the oven and preheat the oven to 375°F. Lightly grease an 8-inch square baking dish. Set aside.

In a large bowl, lightly beat the eggs. Blend in 2 tablespoons of the honey, the butter, tarragon, and salt. Stir in the barley, carrots, currants, and walnuts.

Pour the mixture into the prepared pan. Drizzle the remaining tablespoon of honey on top. Bake uncovered until the kugel is firm in the center and the top is lightly browned, 45 to 50 minutes. If the top browns before the center feels firm, cover lightly with foil and continue cooking until done.

Set the pan on a rack and cool for 5 minutes. Either scoop up with a serving spoon, or run a knife along the edges, cut into squares, and lift out with a spatula.

VARIATION

Substitute 3 tablespoons fresh dill or 1½ teaspoons dried for the tarragon.

GRAIN EXCHANGE

Use coarse bulgur or short-grain brown rice instead of the barley.

brown and wehani rice casserole with tomatoes and feta

1 pound plum tomatoes, coarsely
    chopped, or 1 can (15 ounces) diced
    tomatoes, with liquid

3 tablespoons olive oil

1 teaspoon dried oregano

½ teaspoon salt, plus more to taste

1½ cups cooked Basic Short-Grain
    Brown Rice (page 66)

1½ cups cooked Basic Wehani Rice
    (page 73)

⅓ cup chopped fresh flat-leaf parsley

⅓ cup niçoise or other small black
    olives (pitting optional)

1 cup crumbled feta (6 to 7 ounces)

Salt and freshly ground pepper

Although I call for a combination of brown and Wehani rices, you can use most any grain to make this versatile Mediterranean dish. Dense wheat or rye berries work well in the winter, while quinoa and coarse bulgur result in a lighter dish, appealing in mild weather.

Serve the casserole as a side dish or a vegetarian entrée.

SERVES 4 TO 6

Place a rack in the middle of the oven and preheat the oven to 375°F.

In a food processor or blender, puree 1 cup of the chopped tomatoes with the olive oil, oregano, and salt. (If using canned tomatoes, use the drained liquid plus enough diced tomatoes to equal 1 cup.) Set aside.

In a large bowl, combine the remaining diced tomatoes with the grains, parsley, olives, ½ cup of the feta, and the pureed tomatoes. Add salt and pepper to taste.

Transfer to a 2-quart baking dish. Cover with foil and bake for 20 minutes.

Remove the dish from the oven and preheat the broiler. Lift off the foil, stir the grains, and sprinkle the remaining feta on top. Set the dish under the broiler until the feta is melted, about 3 minutes.

Let the casserole rest for 5 minutes before serving.

VARIATION

Use grated sharp Cheddar instead of feta.

cornmeal spoonbread

1 cup fine yellow or white cornmeal, preferably stone-ground, plus 1 tablespoon for coating the pan

1⅛ teaspoons salt

1 teaspoon sugar

4 tablespoons (½ stick) unsalted butter, cut into bits, plus more for coating the pan

½ cup well-shaken buttermilk

3 large eggs, separated

3 tablespoons fresh or frozen corn kernels

1½ teaspoons sesame seeds

There are as many spoonbread recipes as there are Southern cooks. And after tasting this homemade dish, this Yankee understands why.

Spoonbread is an elegant soufflé that goes down very easily. (It also falls very quickly once you've removed it from the oven.) It has a delicate taste of corn and makes a welcome accompaniment to a holiday roast ham. I've also happily eaten a mound for lunch with nothing more than a crisp salad.

The topping of corn kernels and sesame seeds is my own invention. It's pretty and adds a nice textural dimension.

SERVES 4 TO 6

Set the rack in the center of the oven and preheat the oven to 375°F. Lightly butter a 1½- or 2-quart soufflé dish or an 8-inch square baking pan. Use 1 tablespoon of the cornmeal to coat the bottom and sides of pan. Set aside.

Pour 2½ cups of water into a heavy 2-quart Dutch oven or saucepan. Whisk in the cup of cornmeal until well blended. Set over high heat and bring to a boil. Stir in the salt and sugar. Reduce the heat and cook uncovered at a gentle boil, stirring frequently to prevent sticking and lumping, until the mixture resembles a thick porridge, 5 to 6 minutes.

Transfer the cornmeal mixture to a large bowl. Add the butter and stir until it melts. Stir in the buttermilk and then the egg yolks.

In a mixing bowl, whip the egg whites to soft peaks. Fold half the whipped whites into the cornmeal mixture until just incorporated. Then gently fold in the remaining whites. Do not overmix. (It's okay to have a few unincorporated streaks of white.) Pour the mixture into the prepared pan, and sprinkle the corn and sesame seeds on top.

Place the pan in the oven and bake until the spoonbread puffs up and the edges are golden brown, 30 to 40 minutes. The soufflé will remain somewhat jiggly, especially in the center. Serve immediately.

VARIATIONS

• Add 2 tablespoons crispy bacon bits along with the egg yolks.

• Substitute finely diced red bell pepper for the corn.

• Reduce the salt to $3/4$ teaspoon. Add $1/3$ cup grated Parmesan cheese when you stir in the butter.

• A few minutes before the spoonbread is done, distribute 3 tablespoons finely grated sharp Cheddar cheese on top.

wild rice and chestnut stuffing

1 ounce (about 1 cup loosely packed)
   dried porcini or other dried
   mushrooms

1 cup wild rice, rinsed

30 fresh chestnuts

1 tablespoon olive oil

1 tablespoon unsalted butter

1½ cups chopped leeks (white and
   light green parts)

1 cup finely diced celery

1 to 2 tablespoons finely chopped
   fresh sage, plus more for garnish
   (or use ½ to ¾ teaspoon dried
   rubbed sage)

1 tablespoon dry sherry

1 tablespoon balsamic vinegar

¼ cup dried cranberries

Salt and freshly ground black pepper
   to taste

Here is a beautiful holiday stove-top stuffing dotted with ruby red cranberries. Good-quality wild rice (see page 108) triples in volume as it absorbs a rich wild mushroom broth, offering an elegant contrast to the puffy nuggets of chestnut.

To reduce prep time, you can use bottled or vacuum-packed cooked chestnuts, but truth be told, they don't taste as good as freshly roasted.

SERVES 6 TO 8

Soak the mushrooms in 3½ cups of hot water until they are soft, 15 minutes or longer. Strain and reserve the mushroom liquid. Coarsely chop any large pieces of mushroom. Set aside.

In a heavy 2-quart Dutch oven or saucepan, bring the mushroom liquid and wild rice to a boil. Cover, reduce the heat, and cook at a gentle boil, stirring occasionally, until some of the grains have "butterflied" open and curled up, and the rice tastes tender, 45 to 65 minutes (depending upon storage conditions and age).

While the rice is cooking, roast the chestnuts: Set a rack in the center and preheat the oven to 400°F.

With the tip of a paring knife, cut an X on the flat side of each chestnut. Set, cut side up, on a rimmed baking sheet. Roast the chestnuts until the X puffs open, 20 to 25 minutes. Wrap the chestnuts in a kitchen towel for a few minutes. When they are cool enough to handle, remove the shells and use the towel to rub off the thin brown skins. Discard any chestnuts that are moldy.

Heat the oil and butter in a large, deep skillet or saucepan. Add the leeks, celery, and dried sage (if using) and cook over low heat, stirring occasionally, until the vegetables are soft, 15 to 20 minutes. Stir in the sherry, balsamic vinegar, and cranberries, and cook uncovered for a few minutes. Stir in the chestnuts and soaked mushrooms. Cover and set aside until the rice is done.

Stir the rice (including any unabsorbed cooking liquid) and fresh sage (if using) to taste into the leek mixture. Season with salt and pepper. Cover and simmer until the celery and leeks are tender and the flavors have mingled, about 5 minutes. Add a little water during this time if the mixture becomes dry. Garnish with additional sage, if using fresh.

GRAIN EXCHANGE

Substitute Wehani rice for wild.

buckwheat and cottage cheese casserole

1/3 cup rye flakes (rolled whole rye
    berries) or old-fashioned rolled oats

1 1/2 cups buckwheat groats

1 1/2 teaspoons dried dill

1 teaspoon salt

1/4 teaspoon freshly ground black
    pepper

1 tablespoon unsalted butter, plus
    more for preparing the pan

1 1/2 cups low-fat cottage cheese

2 large eggs, lightly beaten

3/4 cup sour cream

About 1/8 teaspoon sweet paprika

The savory combination of buckwheat and cottage cheese shows up in many traditional Russian cookbooks, and creates the kind of dense, comforting pudding that we yearn for when there's frost on the windows. Use toasted buckwheat (kasha) for a robust flavor, and untoasted buckwheat for a subtler dish.

Serve the casserole as an accompaniment to brisket, pot roast, or short ribs. Vegetarians will enjoy it as an entrée.

SERVES 8

Set a rack in the center and preheat the oven to 350°F.

Butter an 8-inch square baking dish. Coat the bottom and halfway up the sides with the rye flakes. Set aside.

In a heavy 2-quart Dutch oven or saucepan, combine 2 3/4 cups of water with the buckwheat, dill, 1/2 teaspoon of the salt, and the pepper. Bring to a boil over high heat. Stir in the butter. Cover, reduce the heat to low, and simmer until the buckwheat is tender, about 10 minutes. Stir in another 1/4 cup of water if the mixture gets dry before the buckwheat is tender.

Transfer the cooked buckwheat to a medium bowl. Stir in the cottage cheese, followed by the eggs and the remaining 1/2 teaspoon salt.

Pour the mixture into the prepared baking pan. With a rubber spatula, spread the sour cream in a layer on top. Dust with the paprika. Bake until the edges are firm and the center is set, 45 to 50 minutes.

Remove from the oven and let cool for 5 minutes. Run a knife along the edges and cut into 8 portions. Use a spatula to remove the pieces from the pan.

VARIATIONS

• Use 1/4 cup chopped fresh dill instead of dried.

• Blend 2 tablespoons sugar or honey into the beaten eggs.

GRAIN AND VEGETABLE COMBOS

kamut with saffron-scented mushrooms and leeks

Generous pinch of saffron threads

2 tablespoons unsalted butter

3 cups sliced leeks (white and light green parts)

1½ pounds cremini or button mushrooms, trimmed and quartered

¼ teaspoon salt, plus more to taste

1 cup low-sodium chicken or vegetable broth

1 teaspoon minced fresh ginger

3 cups cooked Basic Whole Kamut Kernels (page 94)

Freshly ground pepper

In a cookery manuscript from the household of Richard II dated 1390, there is a recipe for mushrooms and leeks scented with golden saffron. I've added Kamut, an ancient variety of wheat that is larger and tastier than the commonly available wheat berries. You can use either freshly cooked or frozen grains.

SERVES 4 TO 6

Sprinkle the saffron into 1 tablespoon of warm water and set aside.

Heat the butter in a large, deep skillet over medium-high heat until it foams. Add the leeks and cook, stirring frequently, until they soften, 4 to 5 minutes. Add the mushrooms and sprinkle on the salt. Continue cooking until the mushrooms release their liquid and are just short of tender, 7 to 10 minutes.

Stir in the broth, ginger, saffron (with steeping liquid), Kamut, and salt and pepper to taste. Cook uncovered over medium heat until some of the liquid has evaporated and the flavors mingle, about 5 minutes.

Serve in small bowls with some of the broth.

GRAIN EXCHANGE

Use Job's tears or brown rice instead of the Kamut.

bulgur with swiss chard and toasted hazelnuts

1½ pounds Swiss chard

½ teaspoon salt, plus more to taste

3 cups cooked Coarse Bulgur
(page 100)

2 to 3 tablespoons olive oil

1 to 2 tablespoons balsamic syrup
(see Note)

Generous ¼ cup hazelnuts, toasted
and coarsely chopped

This quick and easy recipe combines bulgur with steamed Swiss chard, but you can use it as a formula for most any grains and greens dish.

SERVES 6 TO 8

Holding the greens in a bunch, trim off any thick, fibrous portions of the stems. Thinly slice the remaining stems and leaves. Rinse well.

Heat ½ cup of water in a 6-quart pot. Add the sliced greens and sprinkle salt on top. (You may need to add half the greens, cover, and let them wilt before you have room to add the remaining greens.) Cover and cook over high heat, stirring occasionally, until the greens are soft and close to tender, about 5 minutes. If the mixture becomes dry and begins sticking to the bottom of the pot, stir in 3 to 4 tablespoons of water, or more as needed.

Stir in the bulgur. Cover and continue cooking until the grains are plump and heated throughout, and the greens are tender, 1 to 2 minutes more. Turn off the heat. If there is liquid on the bottom of the pot, drain it off.

Stir in the oil and balsamic syrup to taste. Season with salt, if needed. Stir in the hazelnuts.

NOTE: To make balsamic syrup, open the kitchen windows and turn on the exhaust fan to dissipate the pungent aroma. Boil 1 cup balsamic vinegar in a small, heavy saucepan until it is thick and syrupy and reduced to approximately ⅓ cup, about 12 minutes. Cool. Pour into a jar, cover, and store at room temperature. Lasts indefinitely.

VARIATION

Instead of olive oil, use 1 tablespoon each hazelnut oil and butter.

GRAIN EXCHANGE

Use farro, Job's tears, or barley instead of the bulgur.

farro with portobellos and thyme

3 large portobellos (about 1½ pounds)

3 tablespoons olive oil

2 cloves garlic, smashed

½ cup sliced shallots

¼ teaspoon salt, plus more to taste

⅓ cup Marsala

1 to 2 teaspoons chopped fresh thyme
   or ½ teaspoon dried

3 cups cooked Basic Farro (page 96)

This is one of those simple recipes that really delivers, probably because the main ingredients—earthy portobellos and farro—each bring so much personality to the dish.

SERVES 4

If the portobellos have stems, pry them out. Trim and finely chop the stems. Cut the portobello caps in half and cut each half into slices about ¼-inch thick.

Heat the oil in a large skillet. Add the garlic and shallots and cook over medium heat, stirring frequently, until the shallots begin to soften, 1 to 2 minutes. Add the mushrooms and sprinkle on ¼ teaspoon of the salt. Cook over medium-high heat, stirring frequently, until the mushrooms give up their liquid and brown, 4 to 5 minutes. Remove the garlic cloves.

Stir in the Marsala and dried thyme (if using), and cook until the Marsala has almost evaporated. Add the farro and cook until the grains are moist and thoroughly heated, a minute or two. If the grains taste dry or are sticking to the bottom of the pan, stir in ¼ cup of water, cover, and simmer for a few minutes. Add the fresh thyme (if using) and salt to taste.

VARIATION

Instead of portobellos, use 1½ pounds cremini or button mushrooms, sliced.

GRAIN EXCHANGE

Use brown rice, Job's tears, or barley instead of farro.

millet with gingered beets and orange

½ cup freshly squeezed orange juice

1 tablespoon unsalted butter

1 tablespoon grated fresh ginger

Salt to taste (optional)

2 cups diced peeled beets

2 cups cooked Basic Hulled Millet
  (page 48)

½ teaspoon grated orange zest

2 tablespoons pine nuts, toasted,
  for garnish

Cooking beets in orange juice gives them an added flavor dimension and accentuates their sweetness. Millet stirred into the beets turns a festive neon pink, ready for a party.

SERVES 4

Bring 1 cup of water and the orange juice to a boil in a 2-quart Dutch oven or saucepan. Stir in the butter, ginger, and salt (if using). Add the beets, cover, and cook over medium heat until they are tender, about 20 minutes.

Stir in the millet, cover, and cook over low heat until the millet is hot and the grains become uniformly moist, 3 to 5 minutes. Turn off the heat and stir in the orange zest and salt to taste. Garnish individual portions with the pine nuts.

GRAIN EXCHANGE

Use coarse bulgur or short-grain brown rice instead of millet.

oats with roasted beets and anise

1 pound beets (about 3 medium)

2 tablespoons olive oil

1 to 2 tablespoons freshly squeezed lemon juice

1 to 2 teaspoons raspberry vinegar

1 teaspoon grated lemon zest

1/2 teaspoon Dijon mustard

1/2 teaspoon anise seeds, finely chopped

1/4 teaspoon salt, plus more to taste

3 cups cooked Basic Whole Oats (page 54)

1/2 cup (loosely packed) chopped fresh dill

1/2 cup coarsely chopped walnuts, toasted

2 tablespoons thinly sliced scallion greens

Roasting beets intensifies their flavor. Including just a hint of anise and raspberry vinegar in the dressing for this warm salad accentuates the sweetness of both the beets and the chewy oats. Choose a light-tasting extra virgin olive oil, one that will not distract from the other flavors.

SERVES 4

Set the rack in the bottom third and preheat the oven to 375°F.

Trim off any beet greens, leaving 1/2 inch of the stems intact. Rinse the beets. Wrap each beet individually in a tightly sealed aluminum foil packet.

Set the beets on a foil-lined baking pan (to catch any leaks) and bake them until they are easily pierced—right through the foil— with a skewer or cake tester, 60 to 90 minutes.

While the beets are roasting, prepare the dressing: In a small bowl, whisk together the oil, 1 tablespoon lemon juice, 1 teaspoon vinegar, the lemon zest, mustard, anise seeds, and salt. Set aside.

When the beets are tender, carefully open the packets just enough to allow steam to escape. When the packets are cool enough to handle, rub the foil against the beets to loosen the skins. Slip off the skins and discard them, along with the foil.

Trim off the root and stem ends of the beets. Cut the beets into 1/4-inch dice. (If the oats aren't freshly cooked, put them in a bowl, set a paper towel on top, and heat them in the microwave.) Set the oats in a bowl and add the beets, dill, walnuts, and scallions. Stir the dressing well and toss it into the beet-oat mixture. Adjust the seasonings, adding more lemon juice, vinegar, and salt, if needed.

GRAIN EXCHANGE

Instead of the oats, use farro or Roasted Brown Rice Pilaf Scented with Leeks (page 204).

quinoa with summer squash and basil

1 tablespoon balsamic vinegar

2 teaspoons mashed oil-packed
   anchovies

2 tablespoons olive oil

1 clove garlic, minced

1 pound (3 medium) yellow summer
   squash, coarsely grated

3 cups cooked Basic Quinoa
   (page 58)

Salt (optional)

¼ cup (tightly packed) chopped
   fresh basil

This perky combo—bright yellow squash tossed with bouncy quinoa—goes well with grilled chicken or fish. Anchovies act as a flavor enhancer, but you won't actually taste them. You can serve this versatile side dish hot, warm, or at room temperature. It makes a very popular addition to a buffet table.

SERVES 4

In a small bowl, blend the vinegar and anchovies.

Heat 1 tablespoon of the oil in a large skillet over medium-high heat. Add the garlic and cook it for 30 seconds, stirring constantly. Add the squash and the anchovy mixture. Cook uncovered, stirring frequently, until the squash is tender, about 4 minutes.

Stir in the quinoa and the remaining tablespoon of oil. If serving hot, cook until the quinoa is heated. Add salt, if needed. Stir in the basil just before serving.

GRAIN EXCHANGE

Use farro, Kamut, or coarse bulgur instead of quinoa.

sorghum with cherry tomatoes and corn

3 tablespoons hulled, raw, unsalted
pumpkin seeds

1 tablespoon olive oil

1 clove garlic, minced

2 teaspoons balsamic vinegar

2 cups cooked Basic Sorghum
(page 84)

Salt and freshly ground pepper

1½ cups cherry tomatoes, halved or
quartered

1 cup fresh or frozen corn kernels

¼ cup chopped fresh flat-leaf parsley

Sorghum is a dense grain that benefits from the companion-ship of juicy ingredients like tomatoes and corn. As a bonus, you have your starch and veggies in one side dish that goes well with grilled or pan-fried fish.

You can easily use refrigerated or frozen cooked sorghum for this recipe because the grains are rehydrated just before the tomatoes and corn are added.

SERVES 4

Over medium heat, preheat a large skillet that has a lid. Add the pumpkin seeds and toast them, stirring constantly, until they begin to puff up, under a minute. Reduce the heat to medium-low, and stir in the oil and garlic. Cook until the garlic just begins to take on some color, about a minute.

Add 3 tablespoons of water to the skillet if the sorghum is freshly cooked, or ⅓ cup of water if the grains have been refrigerated or frozen. Stir in the balsamic vinegar and sorghum. Cover and simmer until the grains have a soft, moist interior, 2 to 5 minutes, adding more water if needed. Season with salt and pepper to taste.

Stir in the cherry tomatoes and corn. Cook until the corn is tender, 1 to 2 minutes. Remove from the heat. Stir in the parsley, adjust the seasonings, and serve.

GRAIN EXCHANGE

Instead of sorghum, use any dense grain such as hominy, Job's tears, or Kamut.

wild rice with gingered squash

1 medium kabocha or butternut
  squash (about 2 pounds)

Salt to taste

1- to 2-inch piece of ginger, peeled
  and coarsely chopped (1/8 to 1/4 cup)

2 to 3 teaspoons honey

2 cups cooked Basic Wild Rice
  (page 110)

1 tablespoon unsalted butter

1 1/2 teaspoons grated orange zest

Kabocha, with its rich texture and intense taste, is my favorite winter squash. The challenge of cutting up kabocha is considerably reduced by giving it a quick turn in the microwave. This starts the cooking process and softens the skin.

Some of the squash melts down and creates its own sauce as it steams in ginger-flecked water. Use the smaller amount of ginger if you prefer a subtler presence of its singular flavor. Honey-sweetened cooked wild rice creates an unusual topping for the squash. Serve with roast chicken or turkey.

SERVES 6 TO 8

If using kabocha squash, there is no need to peel it. Pierce the squash in five or six places with a fork. Microwave on high for 4 minutes. Let the squash sit undisturbed in the microwave for 5 minutes. Slice the squash in half through the stem end and remove the seeds. Chop the squash into 2-inch chunks. If using a butternut squash, omit the microwave step. Just peel, seed, and cut it into chunks.

Pour 1 cup of water into a large, heavy saucepan. Add the salt and bring to a boil. Stir in half of the ginger. Add the squash and distribute the remaining ginger on top. Cover and cook over medium-high heat until the squash is tender, 5 to 8 minutes (or about 12 minutes if you haven't microwaved it first). Check every few minutes and add boiling water, if needed, to maintain the water level.

Use a slotted spoon to transfer the squash to a serving platter, and tent it with foil. Stir 2 teaspoons of the honey into the cooking liquid, and boil over high heat until reduced and slightly syrupy, about 5 minutes. Stir in the wild rice, butter, and orange zest, plus more honey, if desired. Lower the heat and simmer for another minute. Pour the mixture over the squash and serve immediately.

GRAIN EXCHANGE

Substitute Wehani, Colusari red, or Chinese black rice for the wild rice.

POLENTAS, GRITS, AND GRIDDLE CAKES

amaranth polenta with wild mushrooms

½ ounce (½ cup loosely packed) dried porcini or other dried mushrooms

1 tablespoon unsalted butter or olive oil

¼ cup finely chopped shallots

1 cup amaranth

¼ teaspoon salt

Freshly ground pepper to taste

1 teaspoon chopped fresh thyme, plus more for garnish

Amaranth cooked with dried mushrooms develops a deep, earthy flavor. Serve puddles of this soft polenta with roasted fowl or braised game.

SERVES 3 TO 4

Bring water to a boil in a kettle, and pour 1¾ cups boiling water into a large heatproof glass measuring cup. Stir in the dried mushrooms. Cover and set aside until the mushrooms are soft, about 10 minutes. Chop any large pieces.

Meanwhile, heat the butter in a heavy 2-quart saucepan. Add the shallots and cook for 1 minute. Stir in the amaranth. Add the soaked mushrooms and soaking liquid, taking care to leave any grit on the bottom of the cup. Bring to a boil. Reduce the heat, cover, and simmer for 15 minutes. Stir in the salt, pepper, and thyme.

Continue simmering, covered, until the mixture is porridgy and the amaranth is tender, 10 to 15 more minutes. (Tender amaranth will still be crunchy, but shouldn't taste hard or gritty.) Stir in a bit more boiling water if the mixture becomes too thick before the amaranth is done.

Serve in small bowls with a sprinkle of thyme on top.

buckwheat polenta

1 cup buckwheat grits or coarse
   granulated buckwheat
¾ teaspoon salt
¼ teaspoon ground turmeric
   (necessary to improve color)
¼ cup grated Parmesan cheese
2 tablespoons unsalted butter or
   olive oil
Freshly ground pepper

Buckwheat grits make an excellent, quickly cooked polenta. You can use toasted buckwheat (kasha) for a hearty flavor or untoasted buckwheat for a mild polenta. Either purchase coarse granulated buckwheat or grind your own—done easily in a spice grinder.

Serve the polenta with braised veal, osso buco, or a venison stew.

SERVES 4

If using whole buckwheat groats, pulse them in several batches in a spice grinder to create a coarse meal (like grits).

Bring 4 cups of water and the salt to a boil in a heavy 2-quart Dutch oven or saucepan. Whisk in the buckwheat and turmeric.

Cook uncovered at a gentle boil, stirring occasionally, until the mixture develops a porridge-like consistency and the buckwheat tastes cooked, 10 to 12 minutes.

Turn off the heat. Stir in the Parmesan cheese and butter. Adjust the seasonings, adding pepper to taste.

VARIATIONS
• Add ¼ cup chopped sun-dried tomatoes or black olives along with the Parmesan cheese.
• Stir in 2 tablespoons of chopped fresh parsley or 1 teapsoon chopped fresh oregano just before serving.

grain griddle cakes with asian flavors

1 large egg

2 tablespoons 2% milk or water

2 tablespoons whole-wheat pastry
  flour

1½ teaspoons Japanese soy sauce
  (shoyu or tamari)

1 teaspoon rice vinegar

⅛ teaspoon baking soda

1 cup any cooked grain (one type or
  a mixture)

2 tablespoons minced red bell pepper

1½ tablespoons thinly sliced scallion
  greens

1 teaspoon grated fresh ginger

1 teaspoon toasted sesame oil

¼ teaspoon finely chopped fermented
  black beans (optional)

Oil for greasing the griddle, if
  necessary

Duck sauce and hot Chinese mustard,
  for serving (optional)

Grain cakes—savory pancakes containing cooked whole grains—make an unusual accompaniment to a vegetable stir-fry or grilled pork chops. They can be prepared with any cooked grain, so consider making them when you have leftovers.

Allow three griddle cakes per person. Double the recipe to serve four, or if you'd like to have extra cakes, which make good snacks.

MAKES EIGHT 2-INCH CAKES

In a food processor, combine the egg, milk, flour, soy sauce, rice vinegar, baking soda, and ½ cup of the grains. Process until the grains are coarsely chopped. Stir in the remaining grains, bell pepper, scallion greens, ginger, sesame oil, and fermented black beans (if using). Let the batter sit for 5 minutes so that the grains can soften and absorb the flavors.

Preheat a griddle or large nonstick skillet over medium heat. Brush it lightly with oil, if necessary, to prevent sticking. Pour a heaping tablespoon of batter per pancake onto the griddle. Gently flatten each pancake with a spatula, and push errant grains at the edges towards the center. Cook until the bottoms are firm and lightly browned, 3 to 5 minutes. Flip over, and reduce the heat to low. Cook until the second side is lightly browned and the pancake feels firm in the center, 2 to 3 minutes more.

Serve with duck sauce and mustard in small bowls on the side, if you wish.

southwest griddle cakes

Omit the soy sauce, ginger, sesame oil, and fermented black beans. Instead use ¼ teaspoon salt, ½ teaspoon dried oregano, ¼ to ½ teaspoon chili powder, and freshly ground pepper to taste. Top each pancake with a teaspoon or two of salsa.

millet with buttermilk and chives

2 tablespoons unsalted butter

4 cups cooked Basic Hulled Millet
(page 48)

1½ to 2 cups well-shaken buttermilk

1 heaping tablespoon scissor-snipped
fresh chives

Salt and freshly ground pepper

Millet marries surprisingly well with tangy buttermilk, creating a comforting side dish vaguely reminiscent of mashed potatoes. Serve with grilled or broiled steak, meatloaf, or a soupy stew.

SERVES 4

In a large skillet, melt the butter over medium heat. Stir in the millet and enough buttermilk to soften this very thirsty grain and to give the mixture a slightly creamy consistency and a nice tang. Stir in the chives, and season to taste with plenty of salt and pepper. When the mixture is hot, cover the skillet. Turn off the heat and let stand for 2 minutes. Serve immediately.

VARIATIONS

• Press into coffee cups or ramekins and unmold to serve.

• Instead of chives, substitute thinly sliced scallion greens.

• Stir in grated Cheddar cheese to taste.

polenta corn pancakes

1 cup fine yellow cornmeal, preferably
    stone-ground

3 tablespoons corn oil, plus additional
    for the griddle (if necessary)

1 cup fresh or frozen corn kernels
    (no need to thaw)

1/4 cup well-shaken buttermilk, plus
    more if needed

3 large eggs

1/4 cup finely chopped red bell pepper

2 tablespoons seeded, finely chopped
    jalapeño pepper

1 tablespoon finely chopped fresh
    sage or 1/2 teaspoon dried rubbed

2 teaspoons baking powder

1/2 teaspoon salt

1/4 teaspoon baking soda

1/4 teaspoon ground chipotle, or more
    to taste (optional)

These savory, soufflé-like pancakes studded with corn kernels are an elegant alternative to a mound of polenta. They pair well with anything from a stew to grilled sausages.

The idea for this recipe was inspired by Dorie Greenspan's imaginative *Pancakes from Morning to Midnight*. Figure on four to five pancakes per person. Vegetarians will enjoy them for dinner, with a steamed vegetable alongside.

MAKES TWENTY-FOUR 2 1/2-INCH PANCAKES

If you plan to hold the pancakes to serve all at once, preheat the oven to 200°F.

In a heavy 2-quart Dutch oven or saucepan, blend the cornmeal and 1 1/2 cups of water. Stir in the oil and bring the mixture to a boil over high heat. Reduce the heat to medium and cook at a gentle boil, stirring frequently, until the mixture becomes thick and porridgy, about 2 minutes.

Transfer the cornmeal mixture to a mixing bowl, and stir in the corn kernels and buttermilk. Set aside to cool for 5 minutes.

Meanwhile, in another large mixing bowl, lightly beat the eggs. Stir in the red bell pepper, jalapeño pepper, sage, baking powder, salt, baking soda, and chipotle (if using). Add the cornmeal mixture and stir to blend. The batter should be thick but pourable, like pancake batter; if necessary, thin by stirring in additional buttermilk.

Preheat a nonstick griddle or large skillet over medium heat. Brush the griddle lightly with oil, if necessary, to prevent sticking. Pour 2 tablespoons (1/8 cup) of batter per pancake onto the griddle, allowing space in between for the pancakes to spread. Cook until the bottoms are set and lightly browned, about 2 minutes.

Flip the pancakes. Reduce the heat to low, and cook until the second side is browned, 1 to 2 minutes. Continue with the remaining batter. Serve immediately or, to keep warm while you cook additional pancakes, place them in a single layer on a rack in the oven.

quinoa-plantain griddle cakes

1 ripe (black-skinned) plantain
   (8 to 9 ounces)

2 to 4 teaspoons sugar

3 large eggs

Generous ½ teaspoon salt

¼ teaspoon ground chipotle or
   crushed red pepper flakes

1½ cups cooked Basic Quinoa
   (page 58)

1 tablespoon whole-wheat pastry
   flour, plus more if needed

1 tablespoon milk, plus more if needed

Olive oil, for frying (if necessary)

Lime wedges, for serving

Quinoa gives these unusual pancakes a light, cakelike texture with a delicate crunch. The ripe plantain makes them fruity and sweet. Look for a plantain about the size of a large banana— or use two smaller ones. If you can find only green (unripened) plantains, let them sit on the counter until they turn yellow and then blacken, which takes about 5 days.

Try these griddle cakes with posole or grilled pork chops. Or make smaller fritters and serve them as finger food. And don't forget the lime wedges. A squeeze of juice at the last minute really heightens their flavor. Allow 3 or 4 cakes per person as a starchy side dish. They are as irresistible at room temperature as they are hot off the griddle.

MAKES ABOUT SIXTEEN 3-INCH CAKES

Slice off both ends of the plantain and halve it crosswise. Slit the peel lengthwise and gently unwrap it from the flesh (as if you were peeling off a candy wrapper). Cut each piece in half and place in a food processor. Pulse to coarsely chop.

Taste a tiny bit of plantain to judge its sweetness. Scrape down the bowl. Add 2 teaspoons of the sugar if the plantain is quite sweet; otherwise add 3 or 4 teaspoons. Add the eggs, salt, and chipotle. Process the mixture until well blended and fluffy, about 30 seconds.

Transfer to a large bowl and stir in the quinoa, flour, and milk. The mixture should have the consistency of a lumpy pancake batter. If it is too thin, add a bit more flour. If too thick, add enough milk so that it will easily spread into a pancake.

Preheat a well-seasoned or nonstick griddle or large skillet over medium heat. (Brush lightly with oil, if necessary, to prevent sticking.) When the griddle is hot enough for a drop of water to sizzle on it, pour a heaping tablespoon of the batter per pancake onto the griddle.

When the bottoms are speckled golden brown—this can happen quickly—flip them over. (If the cakes are fragile at this point, facilitate flipping by shoving the spatula under each cake and positioning a second spatula or a chef's knife on the other side of the cake to keep it from sliding.) Lower the heat, and cook until the second side is browned and the inside is cooked. If the pancakes are not browning quickly enough, raise the heat slightly.

Brush more oil on the griddle, if needed. Raise the heat, and repeat the process with the remaining batter. If the batter becomes thick on standing, thin it with a little more milk.

Serve the cakes hot or at room temperature, accompanied by lime wedges.

VARIATIONS

• Stir 1 minced, seeded jalapeño pepper into the batter when you add the quinoa.

• Add a pinch of ground cinnamon to the batter.

rye grits with bacon and potatoes

2 strips bacon, chopped

1 cup rye grits (also called cracked rye)

1 clove garlic, finely chopped

½ pound Yukon gold or red-skinned potatoes, coarsely grated (peeling optional)

6 juniper berries, crushed, or ¼ teaspoon ground allspice (optional)

½ teaspoon salt, plus more to taste

Freshly ground black pepper

Sour cream and scissor-snipped chives, for serving (optional)

Cracked rye cooks much more quickly than the whole kernel. The cooked grits are moist and, when combined with potatoes, especially comforting. Try rye grits with a grilled steak, or serve them with eggs as a "breakfast for supper."

SERVES 4

Set a kettle of water over high heat. You'll need 2¼ cups.

Put the bacon in a heavy 2½-quart pot. Turn the heat to medium-low and cook, stirring occasionally, until the bacon renders its fat and becomes crisp, about 6 minutes. Transfer the bacon to a paper towel to drain.

Heat the bacon fat over high heat. Stir in the rye grits, lower the heat to medium, and toast, stirring frequently, for 1 minute. Stir in the garlic and cook for an additional 30 seconds.

Turn off the heat and stand back to avoid spattering. Pour in 2 cups of boiling water, taking care to scrape up any browned bits stuck to the bottom of the pot. Stir in the potatoes, juniper berries (if using), and salt. Over high heat, return the mixture to a boil. Cover, reduce the heat, and simmer, stirring occasionally, until the rye grits and potatoes are tender or just short of tender, 10 to 15 minutes. If all of the water has been absorbed and the rye grits are not done, stir in ¼ cup additional boiling water. (Avoid stirring too much, which will make the mixture gummy.) Add more salt, if needed. Turn off the heat. Cover and steam for an additional 10 minutes, or until serving.

Just before serving, stir in the crisped bacon. Adjust the seasonings, adding pepper to taste. Divide among plates and garnish with sour cream and chives, if you wish.

GRAIN EXCHANGE

Use cracked wheat instead of cracked rye.

teff polenta triangles with caramelized apples

3 cups Basic Teff Polenta (page 88),
  chilled until firm

2 tablespoons olive oil

Salt and freshly ground pepper

2 tablespoons unsalted butter

3 large red apples, quartered, cored,
  and thinly sliced

2 large green apples, quartered, cored,
  and thinly sliced

2 tablespoons (packed) dark brown
  sugar

⅛ teaspoon ground cloves

1 tablespoon balsamic vinegar

Grated zest of 1 small lemon

Teff cooked in abundant water sets up just like corn polenta. Brushed with a little olive oil and baked in a hot oven, the polenta becomes a pleasingly crisp base for caramelized apples. Leave the apple peel intact for attractive dots of red and green.

The festive combination makes an ideal side dish for roast pork, chicken, or turkey.

SERVES 6

Set a rack in the bottom third of the oven and preheat the oven to 425°F. Line a baking sheet with parchment. Set aside.

Cut the slab of polenta into thirds and remove from the pan. If the slabs feel moist, pat them dry with paper towels. Brush lightly with oil on one side of each piece and season well with salt and pepper. Set each slab, oiled side down, on the parchment. Brush the tops with oil and season with salt and pepper. Set aside.

In a large skillet, heat 1 tablespoon of the butter and the remaining olive oil over medium-high heat. Add the apple slices, cover, and cook over medium heat, stirring occasionally, until the apples are fairly soft, 10 to 12 minutes. (If all of the apples won't fit, add half and wait for them to shrink before adding the rest.) Add the remaining tablespoon of butter. Sprinkle on the brown sugar and cloves. Cook over high heat, stirring constantly, until some of the slices are lightly browned, 5 to 6 minutes. Drizzle on the balsamic vinegar and cook for another minute, stirring constantly but gently so as not to break up the apples. Turn off the heat, partially cover, and set aside.

Set the teff in the oven and bake until the bottom feels dry and slightly crisp, about 5 minutes. Turn over and bake until the second side feels crisp, 3 to 5 more minutes. Remove from the oven and cut into 2-inch squares. Cut each square into triangles.

Divide the triangles among six plates. Top with the apples and a bit of lemon zest.

breakfast

and
brunch

pancakes and waffles

porridge, hash, and granola

PANCAKES AND WAFFLES

whole-grain pancake mix

½ cup old-fashioned rolled oats

3¼ cups whole-wheat pastry flour

¼ cup sugar

4 teaspoons baking powder

2 teaspoons baking soda

2 teaspoons salt

Homemade pancakes are a special treat. With this mix on hand, you can easily enjoy the treat more often. Since it's made of whole-grain flour, store it in your refrigerator or freezer to maintain freshness. The mix makes four packets, enough for four batches of pancakes (see next page).

MAKES 4 BATCHES OF PANCAKE MIX, 1 ⅓ CUPS EACH

Place the oats in a spice grinder or mini processor and process to the consistency of flour. Transfer to a bowl. Mix in the pastry flour, sugar, baking powder, baking soda, and salt. Place 1⅓ cups of the mix into each of four zipper-topped plastic bags. Refrigerate or freeze for up to 3 months.

VARIATIONS

• Add 1 teaspoon ground cinnamon.

• Add ⅓ cup sunflower seeds and/or ¼ cup dried currants.

GRAIN EXCHANGE

• Instead of rolled oats, used other rolled grains (sometimes labeled "flakes") such as rye, Kamut, or spelt.

• Instead of rolled oats, use ⅓ cup whole-grain flour, such as oat, spelt, Kamut, rye, or buckwheat.

whole-grain pancakes

2 large eggs

1¼ cups well-shaken buttermilk, plus more if needed

2 tablespoons butter, melted

½ teaspoon vanilla extract

1 packet (1⅓ cups) Whole-Grain Pancake Mix (opposite)

Safflower or canola oil, for greasing the griddle

MAKES TWELVE 3-INCH PANCAKES

If you plan to hold the pancakes to serve all at once, preheat the oven to 200°F.

In a large bowl, lightly beat the eggs. Blend in the buttermilk, butter, and vanilla. Add the pancake mix, and stir just until the mixture forms a lumpy batter. Avoid overmixing, which makes the pancakes gummy.

Heat a large griddle or skillet over medium heat. Use a silicone brush or paper towel to coat it lightly with oil. When a drop of water thrown on the griddle sizzles, pour on a scant ¼ cup of batter for each pancake, leaving space in between for the pancakes to spread. If the batter is too thick to pour easily, stir in a few more tablespoons of buttermilk.

When the pancakes become slightly dry around the edges and little bubbles appear on the surface, 2 to 3 minutes, flip them. Cook until brown on the second side, 1 to 2 additional minutes. Lower the heat if the pancakes are browning too quickly, leaving the interiors undercooked.

Serve immediately, or to keep warm while you cook additional pancakes, place them in a single layer on a rack in the oven.

pear-almond pancakes

Add 3 tablespoons additional sugar to 1 package of the pancake mix. Add ½ teaspoon almond extract to the liquid ingredients. After pouring the batter onto the griddle, gently press two ⅛-inch-thin slices of unpeeled pear into the top of each pancake.

whole-grain waffles

Increase the melted butter to 4 tablespoons. Mix the batter as for pancakes. Cook in a preheated waffle iron according to the manufacturer's instructions. Makes four 7-inch round waffles.

buckwheat pancakes with smoked salmon and dilled yogurt cheese

FOR THE YOGURT CHEESE

2 cups plain low-fat yogurt

2 tablespoons scissor-snipped fresh
   chives or minced red onion

2 tablespoons chopped fresh dill

FOR THE PANCAKES

1/2 cup toasted (kasha) or untoasted
   buckwheat groats, or 1/3 cup
   buckwheat flour

1 1/2 cups whole-wheat pastry flour

1/4 cup scissor-snipped fresh chives or
   thinly sliced scallion greens

2 tablespoons chopped fresh dill

2 teaspoons baking powder

1/2 teaspoon baking soda

1/2 teaspoon salt

2 large eggs

1 cup well-shaken buttermilk

1/2 to 3/4 cup 2% milk

4 tablespoons (1/2 stick) butter,
   melted and cooled

Safflower or canola oil, for greasing
   the griddle

6 to 8 ounces thinly sliced smoked
   salmon, cut into 2-inch pieces

Store-bought buckwheat flour is ground from toasted buckwheat—often called kasha—and is quite dark, with a pronounced earthy, grassy flavor. Use this for the full buckwheat experience, or grind flour from untoasted whole groats, which results in a much more delicate buckwheat flavor.

Allow at least 1 hour to drain the yogurt for cheese.

MAKES EIGHTEEN 3-INCH PANCAKES

To make the yogurt cheese: Spoon the yogurt into a fine-meshed strainer set over a bowl. Set aside for 1 to 4 hours to drain. (The longer you drain the yogurt, the thicker it will become.) Transfer the drained yogurt to a bowl and blend in the chives and dill. Cover and refrigerate until needed.

To make the pancakes: If using groats, grind them to a fine flour in a spice grinder. In a large bowl, combine the buckwheat flour with the whole-wheat flour, chives, dill, baking powder, baking soda, and salt.

In another bowl, lightly beat the eggs. Blend in the buttermilk, 1/2 cup milk, and butter.

Make a large well in the center of the dry ingredients. Pour in the buttermilk mixture. Use a spatula to gently fold the wet ingredients into the dry to create a slightly lumpy batter. Avoid overmixing, which can make the pancakes gummy.

If you plan to hold the pancakes to serve all at once, preheat the oven to 200°F.

Heat a large griddle or skillet over medium heat. Use a silicone brush or paper towel to lightly coat the griddle with oil. When a drop of water thrown on the griddle sizzles, pour 1/4 cup batter onto the griddle for each pancake, leaving space in between for the pancakes to spread. If the batter is too thick to pour easily, stir in a few more tablespoons of milk.

When the pancakes become slightly dry around the edges, 2 to 3 minutes, flip them. Cook until brown on the second side, 1 to 2 additional minutes. Lower the heat if the pancakes are browning too quickly, leaving the inside raw or doughy.

To keep the pancakes warm, place them in a single layer on a rack in the oven. To serve, set a piece of salmon on top of each pancake and top with a dollop of yogurt cheese. Serve immediately.

PANCAKE AND WAFFLE WISDOM

WHEN I was a kid, we made waffles every Sunday in a General Electric waffler. I wish I'd saved that shiny stainless steel beauty. Not only was it gorgeous to behold, but it produced crisp, golden waffles large enough to feed two hungry kids.

Homemade waffles and pancakes are so easy to make, I wonder why so many of us have fallen out of the habit. Hopefully the recipes in this section will restore both to your regular repertoire. Electric wafflers tend to be smaller these days, and they are not expensive. Using a nonstick one takes any potential stress out of waffle making.

If you love homemade pancakes as much as I do, treat yourself to a good, heavy cast-iron griddle. Consider purchasing the type that is flat on one side and ridged on the other so that you can fry on one side and grill on the other. Failing that, a large nonstick skillet will do.

Having the right spatula for easy flipping makes all the difference. I recommend a broad, flexible spatula with a very fine front edge that easily slips under the whole pancake with a gentle shove. OXO makes one with this convenient design.

Both pancakes and waffles freeze well. After they've cooled to room temperature, separate them with a sheet of waxed paper, stack, and enclose them in an airtight container. Thaw in the refrigerator or at room temperature, and reheat in a toaster oven or standard oven at 350°F. (Thawing pancakes and waffles in the microwave makes them soggy.)

blue cornmeal pancakes with pumpkin seeds and sage

1½ cups whole-wheat pastry flour

½ cup blue cornmeal

½ cup hulled, raw, unsalted pumpkin seeds

2 teaspoons baking powder

1 teaspoon baking soda

1 teaspoon salt

2 large eggs

1 cup well-shaken buttermilk

½ to ¾ cup 2% milk

¼ cup corn or canola oil, plus more for greasing the griddle

2 tablespoons finely chopped fresh sage or 1½ teaspoons crumbled dried sage leaves or ¼ teaspoon ground dried sage

Safflower or canola oil, for greasing the griddle

Pancakes made with blue cornmeal have a striking grayish blue color. Since blue corn plays a major role in the Hopi kitchen, I added other ingredients common to the Southwest: pumpkin seeds and sage. The pancakes are particularly special when made with fresh sage, but the dried herb will do in a pinch.

Blue cornmeal is readily available in any well-stocked health food store. Serve the pancakes with a few strips of bacon and warmed maple syrup or honey.

MAKES EIGHTEEN TO TWENTY 3-INCH PANCAKES

If you plan to hold the pancakes to serve all at once, preheat the oven to 200°F.

In a large bowl, combine the flour, cornmeal, pumpkin seeds, baking powder, baking soda, and salt. In a medium bowl, beat the eggs, and blend in the buttermilk, ½ cup milk, and oil. Stir the egg mixture and sage into the dry ingredients just until the mixture forms a lumpy batter. Avoid overmixing, which makes the pancakes gummy.

Heat a large griddle or skillet over medium heat. Use a silicone brush or paper towel to lightly coat the griddle with oil. When a drop of water thrown on the griddle sizzles, pour ⅛ cup (2 tablespoons) batter onto the griddle for each pancake, leaving space in between for the pancakes to spread. If the batter is too thick to pour easily, stir in a few more tablespoons of milk.

When the pancakes become slightly dry around the edges and little bubbles appear on the surface, 2 to 3 minutes, flip them over. Cook until brown on the second side, 1 to 2 additional minutes. Lower the heat if the pancakes brown too quickly while the interiors are still runny.

Serve immediately, or to keep the pancakes warm, place them in a single layer on a rack in the oven.

wheat and oat pancakes with bacon

4 strips bacon

⅓ cup old-fashioned rolled oats

1 cup whole-wheat pastry flour

2 tablespoons chopped fresh rosemary

1¼ teaspoons baking powder

¼ teaspoon baking soda

½ teaspoon salt

1¼ cups well-shaken buttermilk,
   plus more if needed

2 large eggs, beaten

Safflower or canola oil, for greasing
   the griddle

Warm maple syrup or honey,
   for serving

I got the idea for this delicious pancake from *Irish Traditional Food*, by the late Theodora Fitzgibbon. The traditional recipe, which is made entirely of rolled oats and includes all of the fatty bacon, was too rich and heavy for my taste. So I lightened up the pancake by grinding the oatmeal into flour (simply done in a spice grinder) and including whole-wheat pastry flour and leavening. I also cut back on the bacon fat.

MAKES ABOUT TEN 3-INCH PANCAKES

If you plan to hold the pancakes to serve all at once, preheat the oven to 200°F.

In a small skillet, fry the bacon until crisp. Drain on paper towels and let cool. Chop the bacon into tiny bits.

Meanwhile, grind the oats into flour in a spice grinder or mini processor. Transfer to a bowl and stir in the whole-wheat flour, bacon bits, rosemary, baking powder, baking soda, and salt.

In a small bowl, combine the buttermilk and eggs. Stir the wet ingredients into the dry ingredients just until barely blended. Avoid overmixing, which can result in gummy pancakes. The batter should be thick but pourable. Stir in more buttermilk, if needed.

Heat a large griddle or skillet over medium heat. With a silicone brush or paper towel, coat it lightly with oil. When a drop of water thrown on the griddle sizzles, ladle on ⅛ cup (2 tablespoons) of batter per pancake, leaving space in between for the pancakes to spread.

Flip the pancakes when they look dry around the edges (they will not bubble) and the bottoms are lightly browned, about 3 minutes. Cook until browned on the second side, 1 to 2 additional minutes. Lower the heat if the pancakes are browning too quickly, leaving the inside raw or doughy.

Serve immediately, or to keep the pancakes warm, place them in a single layer on a rack in the oven. Pass maple syrup at the table.

savory southwestern corn waffles
with black bean salsa

FOR THE SALSA

1½ cups cooked black beans or 1 can
(15 ounces), drained

1 small red bell pepper, seeded and
finely diced

1 small red onion, finely diced

3 tablespoons chopped fresh cilantro

1 jalapeño, seeded and finely chopped

2 tablespoons freshly squeezed lime
juice, plus more to taste

1 tablespoon olive oil

Salt

FOR THE WAFFLES

1½ cups whole-wheat pastry flour

½ cup yellow cornmeal, preferably
stone-ground

2 teaspoons baking powder

½ teaspoon baking soda

½ teaspoon salt

⅓ cup frozen corn kernels, rinsed
under hot water

¼ cup oil-packed sun-dried tomatoes,
minced

1 small jalapeño, seeded and diced

½ teaspoon dried oregano

2 large eggs

2 cups well-shaken buttermilk

¼ cup olive oil

Savory waffles with a substantial topping like black bean salsa make a nice change for brunch and provide an entertaining option for a casual supper.

MAKES SIX 7-INCH WAFFLES

To prepare the salsa: In a bowl, combine the beans, bell pepper, onion, cilantro, jalapeño, lime juice, olive oil, and salt to taste. Set aside to marinate while you prepare the waffles.

To prepare the waffles: In a large bowl, combine the flour, cornmeal, baking powder, baking soda, salt, corn, tomatoes, jalapeño, and oregano.

In a small bowl, beat the eggs. Blend in the buttermilk and olive oil. Whisk the wet ingredients into the dry just until combined. Do not overmix.

If you plan to serve the waffles all at once, preheat the oven to 200°F.

Heat a waffle iron according to the manufacturer's instructions. When a drop of water sizzles on the waffle iron, spoon on enough batter to cover about three quarters of the surface. Close the lid and bake until the waffle is golden brown and the edges are crisp. (Time varies from one waffle iron to the next.)

Serve immediately with a few spoonfuls of salsa on top. Or, to keep the waffles warm, place them in a single layer on a rack in the oven.

VARIATIONS

• Sprinkle crumbled queso fresco or goat cheese on top of the salsa.

• Set a fried egg on the waffle and scatter the salsa over it.

• Omit the salsa and serve each waffle with a slice of country smoked ham and grated Cheddar cheese.

whole-wheat–yogurt waffles with blueberries

2 cups whole-wheat pastry flour

2 tablespoons sugar

1½ teaspoons baking powder

½ teaspoon baking soda

¼ teaspoon salt

¼ teaspoon ground allspice

2 large eggs

1 cup plain low-fat yogurt

1 cup 2% milk

4 tablespoons (½ stick) unsalted
   butter, melted and slightly cooled

2 tablespoons honey

2 teaspoons grated lemon zest

1½ cups fresh or frozen (unthawed)
   blueberries

These waffles have a moist, tangy interior thanks to the yogurt and juicy blueberries. Try them with maple syrup or honey for breakfast. Top the waffles with ice cream for brunch or for an unusual dessert.

MAKES SIX 7-INCH WAFFLES

If you plan to serve the waffles all at once, preheat the oven to 200°F.

In a large bowl, combine the flour, sugar, baking powder, baking soda, salt, and allspice.

In a medium bowl, beat the eggs. Blend in the yogurt, milk, butter, honey, and lemon zest. Stir the wet ingredients and blueberries into the dry ingredients just until blended. Do not overmix or the waffles may become heavy.

Heat a waffle iron according to the manufacturer's instructions. When a drop of water thrown on the waffle iron sizzles, spoon on enough batter to cover three quarters of the surface. Close the lid and bake until the waffle is golden brown and the edges are crisp.

Serve immediately, or to keep the waffles warm, place them in a single layer on a rack in the oven.

VARIATION

Add 2 tablespoons poppy seeds to the dry ingredients.

GRAIN EXCHANGE

Use 1½ cups whole-wheat pastry flour and ½ cup cornmeal.
Increase the baking powder to 2 teaspoons.

teff waffles with caramelized bananas

FOR THE CARAMELIZED BANANAS

3 large ripe but still firm bananas

3 tablespoons unsalted butter

3 tablespoons (packed) dark brown
  sugar

FOR THE WAFFLES

1⅓ cups plus 1 tablespoon teff grains,
  preferably brown, or 1½ cups teff
  flour

2½ teaspoons baking powder

1 tablespoon white sugar

½ teaspoon salt

¼ teaspoon baking soda

½ teaspoon ground cinnamon

2 large eggs

1¼ to 1½ cups well-shaken
  buttermilk

6 tablespoons (¾ stick) unsalted
  butter, melted

1 teaspoon molasses

Fresh raspberries, for garnish
  (optional)

Maple syrup or honey, for serving

If you use brown teff—the most commonly available type—these waffles will be deep and chocolaty, with a texture so light that no one will believe they are made of whole grains.

MAKES FOUR 6-INCH WAFFLES

To caramelize the bananas: Peel the bananas and cut them in thirds crosswise. Cut each piece in half lengthwise. Melt the butter in a large nonstick skillet over medium heat. Blend in the brown sugar. Turn the heat to medium-high. Add the bananas, cut-side down, and fry until the bottoms are golden, 2 to 3 minutes. Flip them over and cook until the second side is golden, about 2 additional minutes. Turn off the heat and set the skillet aside.

To make the waffles: If using whole teff, place a large skillet over medium heat. Add the grains and toast, stirring constantly, until they emit a toasty aroma and begin to pop, about 3 minutes. Immediately transfer to a bowl to cool.

Place about one-third of the grains in a spice grinder, and process to a fine flour, 30 to 45 seconds. While processing, shake the spice grinder up and down to distribute the grains. Repeat with the remaining grains. You should have about 1½ cups of teff flour.

Place the teff flour in a large bowl and combine it with the baking powder, white sugar, salt, baking soda, and cinnamon.

In another bowl, lightly beat the eggs, 1¼ cups buttermilk, butter, and molasses.

Stir the liquid ingredients into the dry ingredients until barely blended. Do not overmix. If the batter is too thick to easily spread over the waffle iron, or thickens while standing, stir in the remaining buttermilk.

If you plan to serve the waffles all at once, preheat the oven to 200°F.

Heat a waffle iron according to the manufacturer's instructions. When a drop of water thrown on the waffle iron sizzles, spoon on enough batter to cover three quarters of the surface. Close the lid and bake until the waffle is golden brown and the edges are crisp. Since teff contains no gluten, the waffles will be fragile, so remove them gently by prying up one corner with a fork and then sliding a spatula underneath to lift them up.

Serve immediately or, to keep the waffles warm, place them in a single layer on a rack in the oven.

To serve: Set a waffle on each plate and top with caramelized banana. Garnish with raspberries, if you wish. Pass maple syrup or honey at the table.

VARIATION
Add 3 tablespoons sesame seeds and/or 2 tablespoons dried currants to the batter.

PORRIDGE, HASH, AND GRANOLA

oatmeal for connoisseurs

Generous pinch of salt, or more to
taste

1 cup old-fashioned rolled oats

Hulled, raw, unsalted sunflower seeds
or slivered almonds, toasted, for
garnish

Milk, to serve at the table

Honey, maple syrup, or brown sugar,
to serve at the table

Ah, oatmeal. Eating a steaming bowlful is surely one of the
most comforting ways to ease into the day. Here is a toothsome way to prepare oatmeal that has an interesting texture with
minimal gumminess. The trick is to steep the rolled oats in a
frugal amount of just-boiled water and to restrain yourself from
stirring more than once.

Use this approach to prepare any amount of oatmeal. For each
cup of rolled oats, add 1 cup plus 2 tablespoons of water.

SERVES 2 TO 3

Bring 1 cup plus 2 tablespoons of water and the salt to a boil in a
small, heavy saucepan. Sprinkle in the oats and stir only once.
Cover, turn off the heat, and let sit for 5 minutes. Spoon into individual bowls and garnish with sunflower seeds. Serve with milk and
honey.

VARIATIONS

• Use half water and half milk, or all milk instead of water.

• Add 1/3 cup raisins, dried currants, or dried cranberries when
you add the oatmeal.

GRAIN EXCHANGE

Use rolled Kamut, barley, wheat, spelt, or triticale instead of oats.
If the rolled grains are not tender enough after the 5 minutes of
steeping, add a few more tablespoons of boiling water, cover, and
simmer until done.

5-minute steel-cut oats with gingered fruit compote

FOR THE COMPOTE

3 cups mixed dried fruit, such as figs, prunes, apricots, and apple rings

½ cup dried cranberries

2 to 3 tablespoons chopped crystallized ginger

½ cup whole almonds

FOR THE OATS

Generous pinch of salt (optional)

1 cup steel-cut oats

Pinch of ground cinnamon

½ cup milk (optional)

If you enjoy oatmeal, you are bound to love steel-cut oats, with their satisfying texture and big oat flavor.

Steel-cut oats take 20 to 30 minutes to cook, so they are usually reserved for the weekends. However, if you soak them overnight, they require less than 5 minutes of simmering the next morning.

Prepare the compote in advance and refrigerate it for up to a week. Heat it before serving.

SERVES 4

To make the compote: In a small saucepan, combine 4 cups of water with the mixed dried fruit, cranberries, ginger, and almonds. Bring to a boil. Cover, reduce the heat to low, and simmer until the fruits are soft, 15 to 20 minutes.

To make the steel-cut oats: Bring 4 cups of water and the salt (if using) to a boil in a heavy 2-quart saucepan. Stir in the oats and cinnamon. Turn off the heat. Cover and let sit overnight.

The next morning, stir well. Bring to a simmer over medium heat. If all of the water has been absorbed, stir in milk (if using) or additional water. Cover and cook over low heat until the oats are tender, about 5 minutes.

To serve: Divide the oats among four bowls. Spoon the compote on top.

last-minute steel-cut oats

Instead of soaking the oats overnight, follow the instructions above and simmer, covered, for 18 to 25 minutes, depending upon desired texture. Add more water if the mixture becomes too thick before the porridge is done. Alternatively, if the porridge is too thin, boil it uncovered to achieve the desired consistency.

grits with cranberries, toasted almonds, and orange zest

1 cup non-corn grits (also called
   cracked grains or meal), such as
   barley, wheat, millet, or rye

⅛ teaspoon salt

½ cup dried cranberries or cherries

¼ cup slivered almonds, toasted

Grated zest of 1 orange

1 to 3 tablespoons honey, plus more
   to pass at the table

1 tablespoon unsalted butter, cut
   into bits

Milk or cream, to serve at the table
   (optional)

Honey, maple syrup, or brown sugar,
   for garnish or to serve at the table
   (optional)

While most of us think of corn grits when "grits" are mentioned, the same word is used to refer to any type of coarsely ground grain. Corn grits take a good hour to soften, but most other grits take only about 20 minutes.

For this breakfast porridge, you can use one type of grain or a combination. Wheat, millet, and barley grits are mellow and slightly sweet, while rye grits have a barely detectable sour edge.

Don't be concerned if the package directions for the various grains suggest different cooking times and liquid requirements. Just cook the porridge until all of the grits are tender. A little bit of butter dramatically enhances the flavor of any grits.

Leftovers reheat well in the microwave.

SERVES 4

Bring 2½ cups of water to a boil. Reduce the heat and stir in the grits and salt. Cover and simmer for 10 minutes, stirring occasionally to prevent the grits from settling to the bottom.

Stir in the cranberries. Cover and continue cooking until the grits are tender, usually 5 to 10 additional minutes. If the mixture becomes dry before the grits are thoroughly cooked—or if you prefer a thinner porridge—stir in water as needed.

When the grits are tender—they should be soft, but you will always be aware of some texture— stir in the almonds, orange zest, honey, and butter. Garnish with milk and honey at the table, if you wish.

VARIATIONS

• Cook the grits in 1 cup milk and 1½ cups water instead of all water.

• Use raisins or diced figs instead of cranberries, and chopped hazelnuts instead of almonds.

amaranth breakfast porridge

1 cup amaranth
½ tablespoon unsalted butter
1 to 1½ tablespoons honey
⅛ teaspoon salt
Pinch of ground cinnamon or freshly
    grated nutmeg (optional)

My assistant Nicole Nacamusi introduced me to the notion of cooking amaranth for breakfast, and I am forever grateful. Amaranth has a mildly sweet, earthy corn flavor that marries beautifully with honey. It makes a very comforting, high-protein hot breakfast cereal. Soaking the amaranth overnight results in a virtually instant breakfast. Leftover amaranth reheats well in the microwave.

SERVES 4

In a small saucepan, soak the amaranth in 3 cups of water for 7 hours or overnight.

Shortly before you are ready to eat, bring the amaranth to a boil in the soaking water over high heat, uncovered. Stir well. Reduce the heat to low, cover, and simmer until all of the water is absorbed and the amaranth is soft and translucent, 3 to 5 minutes. (It will always be slightly crunchy, but shouldn't be hard.) Remove from the heat and stir in the butter, honey, salt, and cinnamon (if using). Serve hot.

last-minute amaranth

Increase the water to 3½ cups and bring to a boil. Whisk in the amaranth. Return to a boil. Cover, reduce the heat to low, and simmer until the amaranth is soft and translucent, 22 to 25 minutes. Add more water if the mixture begins to stick to the bottom of the pot before the amaranth is tender. Remove from the heat and stir in the butter, honey, salt, and cinnamon (if using).

sorghum porridge

⅓ cup whole sorghum

Salt

1 tablespoon hulled, raw, unsalted
    sunflower seeds, toasted

Plain or vanilla yogurt and dark brown
    sugar, for serving

Sorghum makes a potent porridge when ground into a coarse meal that is toasted before simmering. This is not a porridge for anyone who likes a meek and mild breakfast, but serious porridge lovers will consider sorghum a great discovery.

In many parts of rural Africa, sorghum porridge is a staple. The flour is often cooked in sour milk. I find that a dollop of cool yogurt served on top of the cooked porridge adds just the right dose of sourness for the Western palate.

You can toast a one-week supply of sorghum grits and store it in the refrigerator. Or cook a double batch of porridge and reheat portions in the microwave as needed.

SERVES 2

Place the sorghum in a spice grinder and pulse until you've created an unevenly coarse meal resembling grits, usually 40 to 45 times.

Heat a large skillet over medium heat. Add the sorghum and toast, stirring constantly, until the grain releases a toasty aroma, 2 to 4 minutes.

In a small, heavy saucepan, bring 1⅓ cups of water to a boil. Stir in the toasted sorghum and a pinch of salt. Reduce the heat, cover, and simmer until the grits are tender, 10 to 15 minutes. Stir from time to time to prevent the grains from sticking to the bottom of the pan. If the porridge is too thin, cook uncovered to reach the desired consistency. If the porridge is too thick, stir in more water.

Stir in the sunflower seeds. Transfer to bowls and top with heaping spoonsful of yogurt and a sprinkling of brown sugar.

VARIATION

Cook the porridge in milk instead of water.

GRAIN EXCHANGE

Use whole millet or buckwheat instead of sorghum. When grinding, start checking the consistency after 20 pulses.

MAKING PORRIDGE FROM LEFTOVER GRAINS

IT'S EASY to transform last night's leftovers or frozen grains into breakfast porridge if the grains aren't heavily seasoned or salted. Put the grains into a saucepan and add water or milk to cover and a pinch of cinnamon. Bring to a boil. Add raisins or chopped dried fruit, if you wish. Reduce the heat, cover, and simmer until the grains are soft and have soaked up some of the liquid, 6 to 10 minutes. Uncover and simmer, stirring occasionally, until some of the liquid evaporates and the mixture thickens, about 5 minutes. Sweeten to taste with sugar, honey, or maple syrup. Top with granola or yogurt and toasted nuts.

rolled grain porridge with currants, apple, and walnuts

Pinch of salt

2 cups mixed rolled grains (flakes)

2 tablespoons dried currants

$1/8$ teaspoon ground cinnamon

1 large apple, cored and grated

1 tablespoon unsalted butter, cut into bits

$1/3$ cup coarsely chopped walnuts, toasted

Maple syrup or honey, to serve at the table (optional)

Milk or cream, to serve at the table (optional)

If you like oatmeal, you might enjoy making a breakfast porridge with a variety of rolled grains. Some distributors sell multigrain rolled cereals, which is quite handy, but making your own mix is a good way to use up odd amounts.

Because they have been steamed and rolled flat, all rolled grains cook quickly. Most package instructions call for 2 parts water to 1 part rolled grains. I use much less liquid—just a little more water than rolled grains—because I like the flakes to remain firm.

Well-stocked health food stores carry a range of rolled grains (sometimes labeled flakes), such as wheat, rye, Kamut, spelt, and barley. Avoid quinoa and amaranth flakes, which are quite delicate and dissolve the minute they hit hot liquid. Also check the instructions and avoid any cereals labeled "flakes" that don't require any cooking.

Adding a grated unpeeled apple contributes moisture, specks of bright color, and a fresh, clean taste.

SERVES 4

Bring $2 1/3$ cups of water and the salt to a boil. (This is less liquid than most packages recommend, but I like the results.) Reduce the heat and stir in the grains, currants, and cinnamon. Cover and simmer for 4 minutes. Stir in the grated apple and butter, plus a bit more hot water if the mixture seems dry.

Cover and cook over low heat until the flakes are moist and tender and the porridge is heated throughout, 1 to 2 additional minutes. Stir in the walnuts and serve hot. Pass maple syrup and milk at the table, if you wish.

pear-cardamom porridge

Substitute a pear for the apple and a pinch of cardamom for the cinnamon.

granola revisited

2/3 cup dark amber (Grade B) maple
   syrup
1/4 cup peanut or canola oil
1 tablespoon vanilla extract
3 1/2 cups old-fashioned rolled oats
1/2 cup toasted wheat germ (available
   already toasted)
1/2 cup unsweetened shredded
   coconut
1 1/2 cups unsalted mixed whole nuts
   (hazelnuts are elegant), coarsely
   chopped
1/2 cup golden raisins
1/2 cup dried cranberries

Everyone who makes homemade granola swears that his or
her own version is the best. I thought that of mine, too, until
I tasted Verlie Payne's sophisticated rendition below. One of the
secrets is long, slow roasting, which relieves the cook from any
worry about burning and results in burnished, golden oat flakes.

MAKES ABOUT 7 CUPS

Place a rack in the middle of the oven, and preheat the oven
to 225°F.

In a small saucepan, blend the syrup and oil. Cook over low heat,
stirring frequently, until warm, 3 to 5 minutes. Stir in the vanilla
extract. Cover and set aside.

In a large bowl, toss together the oats, wheat germ, coconut, and
nuts. Stir in the syrup mixture until the oats are evenly coated.

Spread the granola mixture evenly onto a large rimmed baking
sheet. Bake until the oats are golden brown, about 1 hour and
30 minutes. Stir the mixture every 15 to 20 minutes, and rotate the
baking sheet so that the mixture will be evenly toasted.

Transfer to a large storage container. When cool, stir in the raisins
and cranberries. Cover and store at room temperature for up to
2 weeks or refrigerate for up to 2 months.

VARIATIONS
• Use dried blueberries or chopped dates instead of the raisins.
• Use rolled barley, spelt, or rye in place of some of the rolled
oats.

buckwheat hash with bacon and eggs

4 strips hickory-smoked bacon, finely
    chopped
1 large onion, finely chopped
1½ cups untoasted whole buckwheat,
    lightly rinsed
¾ pound red-skinned potatoes, cut
    into ½-inch dice (2 cups)
¾ teaspoon salt
4 to 6 large eggs

One day I got to thinking about how buckwheat and potatoes are both favored in Russian and Eastern European
kitchens, and I decided to try them together in a hash. Since diced
potatoes and buckwheat groats require the same cooking time,
the idea became even more appealing.

Top the hash with a slightly runny fried egg, and you have an
almost instant garnish and sauce.

SERVES 4 TO 6

Place the bacon in a large heavy saucepan, and cook over medium
heat until its fat renders, about 5 minutes. Turn the heat to
medium-high and cook the bacon until crisp. Drain the crisped
bacon bits on a paper towel.

Pour off all but about 1 tablespoon of the bacon fat from the
pan. (Reserve the fat for frying the eggs, if you wish.) Add the onion
to the pan and cook over medium-high heat until lightly browned,
about 4 minutes. Stir in the buckwheat and coat with the fat. Stir
in the potatoes, 2½ cups of boiling water, and salt. Stir well to
loosen any browned bits stuck to the bottom of the pan.

Cover and cook over medium heat until the buckwheat and potatoes are almost tender and most of the water has been absorbed,
about 15 minutes. Turn off the heat and let the mixture rest for 10
minutes to complete cooking.

Meanwhile, fry the eggs to your preferred consistency: sunny-
side up, over-easy, or scrambled.

When the buckwheat hash is done, mound it onto four to six
plates. Top each portion with a fried egg. Sprinkle the bacon bits
on top.

VARIATION

Omit the eggs. Serve each portion with a dollop of dill sour cream (see page 128).

GRAIN EXCHANGE

• Use toasted buckwheat (kasha) instead of untoasted. The flavor will be much stronger.

• Use pearl barley instead of buckwheat. Cut the potatoes into 1-inch chunks. Increase the boiling water to 3 cups and the cooking time to 30 minutes, plus 10 minutes standing. Drain off any unabsorbed water.

desserts
and

baked
goods

cookies and confections

crisps, pies, and a cobbler

puddings and a parfait

a whole-grain flour primer

In the recipes that follow, you will see how easy it is to incorporate a variety of wholesome whole-grain flours into delicious baked goods of all sorts. Since there are already numerous excellent whole-grain bread–baking books available, I've concentrated on creating recipes for quick breads, cookies, and desserts. (Whole-grain flours are also used in the waffle and pancake recipes in the breakfast chapter.) You may find, as I have, that when you first prepare these recipes, the motivation is to improve your diet and health. Then, as you start to appreciate the more complex flavor and texture of whole-grain baked goods, refined versions gradually seem either too rich or taste fake and flat by comparison.

The reason that whole-grain flours have more complex flavor and texture is that they are ground from whole grains. Unlike refined white flour, which is ground only from the starchy endosperm, whole-grain flour contains particles of the fiber- and mineral-rich bran and the vitamin- and oil-rich germ.

Whole-grains flours require special care. Once exposed and no longer protected by the bran layer, the germ's heart-healthy oil becomes quite prone to rancidity. Happily, you can avoid this problem in various ways. The best is to grind the grains into flour as needed at home. For small quantities, this is easily done in a coffee grinder reserved for this purpose.

Numerous grains including buckwheat, quinoa, and teff do very well using this approach. Dense, hard grains like wheat berries, oats, and spelt can be home-ground into flour if you have purchased them in flaked or rolled form. Anyone who becomes passionate about whole-grain baking will probably want to consider buying a home mill or placing a standing order for freshly milled flour from Montana Flour and Grain (see page 308).

When selecting flour, opt for stone-ground whenever available. The process of stone grinding creates minimal heat, thereby preserving more of the nutritional value of the germ—especially the heat-sensitive vitamin E, which acts as an antioxidant, keeping the flour fresh for a longer period of time.

Fortunately, stone mills still operate throughout the country and welcome visitors to witness the process. Many, like Bob's Red Mill near Portland, Oregon, started because the owner became fascinated by old millstones and developed a passion for keeping alive this old-fashioned, wholesome way to grind whole grains. (See Mail-Order Sources for the names of mills selling stone-ground flour.)

When buying flours in sealed bags, check the expiration date and buy the freshest available. Read the label to be sure that the flour contains no preservatives or additives—more likely found in supermarket brands than in health food store products. Opt for organically grown grains whenever possible, to promote your own well-being and the health of the environment at the same time.

If purchasing flour from a bulk bin, judge freshness by first sniffing it. If there is either no aroma or the flour smells faintly sweet or nutty, it is fresh. If the flour smells musty or has an "off" odor, it has gone rancid. If in doubt, taste the flour. Any hint of bitterness indicates that it is past its prime.

Because it is so perishable, *as soon as you bring home a batch of whole-grain flour—even if it is in an unopened bag—refrigerate or freeze it in a dated zipper-topped plastic bag.* For optimum flavor and nutrition, use it within a few months. To judge freshness before each use, follow the instructions in the preceding paragraph.

If you find yourself wondering why using whole-grain flour is worth all of this extra effort, take a look at the following chart.

WHOLE-WHEAT VERSUS WHITE FLOUR: NUTRIENT VALUES

	CALORIES	GRAMS PROTEIN	GRAMS TOTAL CARBOHYDRATE	GRAMS FIBER	MG CALCIUM	MG PHOSPHORUS	MG IRON	MG POTASSIUM
whole-wheat flour	330	14	69.1	2.3	36	383	3.1	370
white flour	364	10.5	76.1	0.3	16	87	0.8	95

Based on a 3¹/₂-ounce quantity. Excerpted from the U.S. Department of Agriculture Handbook No. 8.

BAKING WITH WHOLE-GRAIN FLOUR

Many of the recipes for baked goods in health-oriented cookbooks call for half whole-wheat flour and half all-purpose, but I resolved from the start to be a purist and not use an ounce of refined flour in this book.

My baking experiments began with whole-wheat pastry flour, a fine flour ground from soft wheat berries, which I knew to be lighter than standard whole-wheat flour because it contains less protein and therefore less gluten. The pastry flour made delicious pancakes and waffles. But baked goods were another story. After dozens of experiments, I became discouraged. No matter how much butter or extra eggs I added, many of the quick breads and cookies came out too dry, too moist, or too crumbly.

Then I decided to try whole-grain spelt flour. Because spelt is a type of wheat that many people with wheat allergies easily tolerate, it has become quite readily available. And what a joy to work with! In quick breads, spelt flour reacts very much like all-purpose flour. Light in taste and color, it makes an excellent base for moist cakes and delicate cookies.

For those who would like to experiment with adapting their favorite baked goods to whole-grain versions based on spelt flour, I offer the following guidelines:

■ Use spelt flour in an equal amount to the all-purpose flour called for in the recipe.

■ Increase the baking powder by $\frac{1}{4}$ to $\frac{1}{2}$ teaspoon per cup of flour.

■ Include at least $\frac{1}{4}$ teaspoon baking soda plus an acid such as buttermilk or yogurt to create additional leavening action.

■ Increase the liquid by 1 tablespoon per cup of flour.

■ When using whole-grain flours other than spelt, substitute no more than 25 percent of the specialty flour for all-purpose until you experience the taste, texture, and baking qualities of each type.

TRICKS OF THE TRADE

Here are some suggestions to guarantee success with the baking recipes that follow.

■ Measure out the flour by scooping or spooning it into a dry measuring cup, and then leveling it off with a knife.

■ When a range of sweetener is given, use the larger amount if you like your baked goods on the sweet side.

■ Pay attention to the suggested placement of the oven rack.

■ Use an oven thermometer to make sure your oven temperature is accurate.

■ Rotate the baking pans as directed to achieve even baking and browning. Very few home ovens bake evenly.

■ Occasionally the recipe will ask you to ignore the common instructions that a baked good is done when a cake tester comes out clean. To avoid dryness in the finished product, it's sometimes best to halt baking when there are a few crumbs clinging to the cake tester. However, take care to distinguish between crumbs and gooey, uncooked dough. The latter indicates that more baking is required.

NONWHEAT FLOURS AT A GLANCE

TYPE OF FLOUR	TASTE	COLOR	TEXTURE	CONTAINS GLUTEN	EASY TO GRIND*
AMARANTH	Grassy, with faint corn flavor	Caramel	Heavy, slightly gummy	No	Yes, from seeds
BARLEY	Light, faintly sweet	Pale	Pleasing, user-friendly	Yes	Yes, from barley flakes
BUCKWHEAT, TOASTED (Kasha)	Strong, musky, nutty	Mahogany	Heavy	No	Yes, from hulled groats or grits
BUCKWHEAT (untoasted)	Mild	Tan	Heavy	No	Yes, from hulled groats or grits
BROWN RICE	Mild, faintly sweet	Pale	Sandy, dry	No	Yes, from rolled flakes
CORNMEAL, BLUE	Distinct corn flavor	Grayish blue	Dry	No	No
CORNMEAL, YELLOW/ WHITE	Distinct corn flavor	Pale yellow/ ivory	Pleasantly gritty, dry	No	No
OAT	Mild, slightly sweet	Pale	Light, user-friendly	Yes	Yes, from rolled flakes
QUINOA (ivory)	Herbaceous, vegetal	Pale	Smooth, moist	No	Yes, from whole seeds
RYE	Slightly sour	Medium	Heavy	Yes	Yes, from rolled flakes
TEFF	Grassy, with mild corn taste	Dark	Sandy, dry	No	Yes, from whole seeds

*Yes means it is easy to grind to a fine flour in a spice or coffee grinder. No means best to purchase already ground. All flours are available in well-stocked health food stores and online.

QUICK BREADS

oat muffins with currants and fennel seeds

1 to 1¼ cups old-fashioned rolled
  oats

¼ cup light brown sugar

1 cup spelt flour, plus more for
  flouring the muffin cups

2½ teaspoons baking powder

½ teaspoon baking soda

1 teaspoon salt

1 teaspoon fennel seeds, coarsely
  chopped

2 large eggs

1½ cups well-shaken buttermilk

4 tablespoons (½ stick) butter,
  melted, plus more for greasing the
  muffin cups

3 tablespoons honey

1 teaspoon grated orange zest

⅓ cup dried currants

Oat flour gives these fruit-and-nut muffins a silky, moist texture. Fennel seeds, with their natural licorice sweetness, provide exotic companionship to the currants.

MAKES 12 MUFFINS

Place a rack in the top third of the oven and preheat the oven to 400°F. Butter and flour 12 standard muffin cups. Set aside.

In a spice grinder, grind enough of the oats to equal 1 cup of flour. Put the remaining oats in a small bowl and mix in the brown sugar to make the muffin topping. Set the topping aside.

In a large bowl, combine the spelt and oat flours, baking powder, baking soda, salt, and fennel seeds.

In a smaller bowl, lightly beat the eggs. Blend in the buttermilk, butter, honey, and grated orange zest.

Stir the wet ingredients and currants into the dry ingredients until most of the flour is incorporated. Do not overmix. The mixture can be slightly lumpy. Divide the batter among the prepared muffin cups. Sprinkle a heaping teaspoon of the oat–brown sugar mixture on top. Bake until the muffins are golden brown around the edges and spring back to a gentle touch, and a cake tester inserted in the center comes out clean, 14 to 16 minutes.

Set the muffin tin on a rack to cool for 2 minutes. Twist gently to release the muffins, or run a knife around the edges to unmold. Eat warm, or cool to room temperature. If not eating the same day, freeze in a zipper-topped freezer bag for up to 3 months. Thaw at room temperature or in the oven.

date-nut muffins

1½ cups spelt flour

2 teaspoons baking powder

½ teaspoon baking soda

1½ teaspoons ground allspice

1 teaspoon ground cinnamon

¼ teaspoon freshly grated nutmeg

½ teaspoon salt

2 large eggs

⅓ cup (packed) light brown sugar

1½ tablespoons molasses

1 teaspoon vanilla extract

¼ cup plus 1 tablespoon canola oil, plus more for greasing the pans

⅔ cup unsweetened applesauce

½ cup well-shaken buttermilk

1 cup (packed) chopped pitted moist dates

¼ cup chopped crystallized ginger

⅔ cup coarsely chopped walnuts, toasted

I have such fond memories of eating Arnold's date-nut bread when I was a kid that I felt inspired to combine dates and nuts in a low-fat muffin. I couldn't resist adding some crystallized ginger, which really lifts the combination to new heights.

Moist and spicy, the muffins are best eaten warm. They make a great snack and a wonderful addition to brunch.

MAKES 12 MUFFINS

Set a rack in the top third of the oven and preheat the oven to 400°F. Grease 12 standard muffin cups and set aside.

In a large bowl, combine the flour, baking powder, baking soda, allspice, cinnamon, nutmeg, and salt.

In a medium bowl, beat the eggs. Add the brown sugar, molasses, vanilla, oil, applesauce, and buttermilk. Stir until well blended.

Add the liquid mixture, dates, crystallized ginger, and walnuts to the dry ingredients and stir just until combined. Do not overmix.

Divide the batter among the muffin cups. Bake until a cake tester inserted in the center comes out clean, 15 to 17 minutes. Set the muffin tin on a rack to cool for 1 minute. Twist gently to release the muffins, or run a knife around the edges to unmold. Eat warm, or cool to room temperature on a wire rack.

If not eating the same day, freeze in a zipper-topped freezer bag for up to 3 months. Thaw at room temperature or in the oven.

raisin-pecan muffins

Instead of dates and walnuts, use yellow raisins and toasted pecans.

fig-hazelnut muffins

Instead of dates and walnuts, use dried figs and toasted hazelnuts. Omit the crystallized ginger.

■ ■ ■

lemon–poppy seed muffins

2 cups spelt flour

1½ tablespoons poppy seeds

1 tablespoon baking powder

½ teaspoon baking soda

¾ teaspoon salt

2 large eggs

1 cup well-shaken buttermilk

½ to ⅔ cup (packed) light brown
   sugar, to taste

6 tablespoons (¾ stick) butter,
   melted, plus more for greasing the
   muffin cups

1 tablespoon (packed) grated lemon
   zest (from 3 large lemons)

1 tablespoon freshly squeezed lemon
   juice

1 teaspoon vanilla extract

Whoever first thought of combining lemon and poppy seeds was a genius. I've tried to analyze why these two ingredients make such a memorable team. Is it the lemon's tartness and the poppy seed's earthy crunch? Or is it the grayish blue against the pale yellow?

The muffins are usually gone before I've figured it all out. And it's a good thing, because muffins taste best the day they're baked, preferably warm.

MAKES 12 MUFFINS

Place a rack in the top third of the oven and preheat the oven to 400°F. Butter 12 standard muffin cups. Set aside.

In a large bowl, combine the flour, poppy seeds, baking powder, baking soda, and salt.

In a medium bowl, lightly beat the eggs. Whisk in the buttermilk, brown sugar, butter, lemon zest, lemon juice, and vanilla extract. Don't be concerned if the mixture looks curdled or lumpy.

Stir the wet ingredients into the dry ingredients until most of the flour is incorporated. Do not overmix. The mixture can be slightly lumpy. Divide the batter among the prepared muffin cups.

Bake until the muffins are golden brown around the edges and a cake tester inserted in the center comes out either clean or with a few crumbs attached, 11 to 13 minutes.

Set the muffin tin on a rack to cool for 1 minute. Twist gently to release the muffins, or run a knife around the edges to unmold. Eat warm, or cool to room temperature on a wire rack. If not eating the same day, freeze in a zipper-topped freezer bag for up to 3 months. Thaw at room temperature or in the oven.

orange–poppy seed muffins

Replace the lemon juice and lemon zest with orange juice and grated orange zest.

raspberry muffins

Omit the poppy seeds. When combining the liquid and dry ingredients, add 1½ cups fresh or frozen raspberries.

cranberry-pecan muffins

Omit the poppy seeds. Substitute grated orange zest for the lemon zest. When combining the liquid and dry ingredients, add ½ cup chopped dried cranberries and ½ cup coarsely chopped toasted pecans.

savory barley muffins with thyme and romano

1 cup spelt flour

1 cup barley flour

2¼ teaspoons baking powder

½ teaspoon baking soda

1 teaspoon dried thyme

¾ teaspoon salt

2 large eggs

1½ cups well-shaken buttermilk

¼ cup olive oil

2 tablespoons honey

¼ cup grated Romano cheese or a combination of Romano and Parmesan

Serve these unusual savory muffins as an alternative to whole-grain bread when having soup for dinner. They are good split open, with butter or cheese.

You can easily grind the barley flour from barley grits or flakes.

MAKES 12 MUFFINS

Set a rack in the top third of the oven and preheat the oven to 400°F. Grease 12 standard muffin cups. Set aside.

In a large bowl, combine the spelt flour, barley flour, baking powder, baking soda, thyme, and salt.

In a smaller bowl, lightly beat the eggs. Blend in the buttermilk, oil, and honey.

Stir the egg mixture into the dry ingredients, just until most of the flour is absorbed. Do not overmix. Divide the batter among the muffin cups. Sprinkle a generous teaspoon of cheese on top of each muffin. Brush away any cheese that lands outside of the muffin cups.

Bake until the muffins are golden brown around the edges and spring back to a gentle touch, and a cake tester inserted in the center comes out clean, 12 to 15 minutes.

Set the muffin tin on a rack. After 2 minutes, twist the muffins to release them or run a knife around the edges and pop them out. Serve warm.

If not eating the same day, freeze in a zipper-topped freezer bag for up to 3 months. Thaw at room temperature or in the oven.

blue cornmeal muffins with chili

Substitute blue cornmeal for the barley flour. Omit the thyme and substitute 1 teaspoon chili powder and ½ teaspoon dried oregano. Instead of cheese, sprinkle a few hulled, raw, unsalted pumpkin seeds on top of each muffin.

quinoa cake with crystallized ginger

1 cup uncooked quinoa

1 cup spelt flour, plus more for flouring the pan

1 cup (packed) dark brown sugar

1½ teaspoons baking powder

½ teaspoon baking soda

⅛ teaspoon salt

1 cup coarsely chopped Brazil nuts, toasted

4 to 6 tablespoons coarsely chopped crystallized ginger, to taste

½ cup golden raisins

3 large eggs

½ cup orange juice

8 tablespoons (1 stick) unsalted butter, melted and cooled, plus more for greasing the pan

2 teaspoons vanilla extract

I have adapted this recipe from Maria Baez Kijac's fascinating cookbook, *The South American Table*. Cooked quinoa stirred into the batter creates a moist dessert that is surprisingly light. I find the texture of this cake so appealing that I often include cooked quinoa in muffin and pancake batters.

Serve the inch-high cake on its own or set a scoop of *dulce de leche* ice cream on top.

MAKES ABOUT 15 SQUARES

Bring a large pot of salted water to a boil. Add the quinoa and cook until the grains are translucent and tender (there should be no white dot of uncooked starch in the center), 11 to 14 minutes. Drain thoroughly in a fine-meshed strainer. Spread the quinoa out on a large platter to cool.

Set a rack in the middle of the oven and preheat the oven to 350°F. Butter and lightly flour a rectangular baking pan that measures approximately 11 by 7 inches. Set aside.

In a large bowl, combine the flour, brown sugar, baking powder, baking soda, salt, Brazil nuts, ginger, and raisins.

In a small bowl, combine the eggs, orange juice, butter, and vanilla extract.

Stir the liquid ingredients and the quinoa into the dry ingredients just until blended. Transfer to the prepared pan and smooth the top.

Bake until a cake tester inserted in the center comes out clean, 45 to 60 minutes, depending upon the size of the pan. Rotate the pan halfway through for more even baking.

Set the pan on a cooling rack. When cool, cut into fifteen 2-inch squares.

cinnamon-walnut quinoa cake

Instead of Brazil nuts, crystallized ginger, and raisins, use walnuts, ½ teaspoon cinnamon, and ⅓ cup chopped dried apricots.

wheat and oat scones with cranberries

⅓ to ½ cup old-fashioned rolled oats

1½ cups whole-wheat pastry flour, plus more for kneading

¼ to ⅓ cup sugar, to taste, plus more for dusting the scones

1 tablespoon baking powder

¼ teaspoon baking soda

½ teaspoon salt

6 tablespoons (¾ stick) cold unsalted butter, cut into bits

Grated zest of 1 orange

⅓ cup dried cranberries

⅓ cup golden raisins or additional cranberries

1 large egg

½ cup well-shaken buttermilk, plus more for brushing the scones

There are about as many scone recipes as there are scone fans. Scones come in all shapes and sizes, with textures that vary from very dry to moist.

I favor a moderately moist scone in a wedge shape, which is what this recipe delivers. Serve them with clotted cream or butter and jam if you wish, but they are also quite delicious without any adornments.

Scones are best when freshly made and still warm. You can refrigerate the dough for up to 3 days or freeze the wedges for 3 months and pop them directly into the oven. Increase the baking time by a few minutes.

MAKES 12 MEDIUM OR 16 SMALL SCONES

Place a rack in the middle of the oven and preheat the oven to 450°F. Line a baking sheet with parchment. Set aside.

In a spice grinder, grind enough of the rolled oats to make a scant ½ cup of fine flour. Transfer to a large bowl. Blend in the whole-wheat flour, sugar to taste, baking powder, baking soda, and salt.

With a pastry blender or two knives, cut the butter into the flour until the mixture resembles uneven pebbles. Stir in the grated orange zest, cranberries, and raisins.

Whisk the egg into the buttermilk in a small bowl. Pour the liquid into the dry ingredients. With a rubber spatula, lightly stir and fold in the wet ingredients just until the dry ingredients are moistened. Do not overmix.

Turn the dough out onto a floured surface. Gently knead 4 or 5 times, incorporating any loose dough as you go. The dough should be slightly moist. Work in a little more flour if it feels sticky. Shape the dough into 2 rounds about ½-inch thick. Cut each round into 6 or 8 wedges.

Transfer the wedges to the prepared baking sheet, leaving $\frac{1}{2}$ inch between them. Liberally brush buttermilk on top and dust with sugar. Bake until the bottoms are golden, 13 to 15 minutes. Rotate the baking sheet halfway through for even baking.

Transfer the scones to a cooling rack. Eat warm or at room temperature.

apricot-lemon scones

Use scissor-snipped dried apricots in place of the raisins and lemon zest instead of orange zest.

corn bread

1 cup fine yellow cornmeal, preferably
  stone-ground

1 cup whole-wheat pastry flour

3/4 cup sugar

1 1/2 teaspoons baking powder

1/2 teaspoon baking soda

3/4 teaspoon salt

1/4 teaspoon freshly ground black
  pepper

2 large eggs

3/4 cup heavy cream

1/4 cup sour cream

3 tablespoons butter, melted

1 cup fresh or frozen corn kernels

1/4 cup finely diced red bell pepper

1/3 cup hulled, raw, unsalted pumpkin
  seeds

"Corn bread with panache" is how one taster described this moist, sweet quick bread. A generous amount of black pepper creates a subtle layer of heat, giving the corn bread more complex flavor. Make sure that your cornmeal smells and tastes fresh.

MAKES SIXTEEN 2-INCH SQUARES

Place a rack in the center of the oven and preheat the oven to 400°F. Line the bottom of an 8-inch square pan with parchment paper. Set aside.

In a medium bowl, combine the cornmeal, flour, sugar, baking powder, baking soda, salt, and black pepper.

In a large bowl, lightly beat the eggs. Stir in the heavy cream, sour cream, butter, and corn kernels. Fold the dry ingredients into the liquid mixture until most of the flour has been absorbed. Do not overmix.

Pour the batter into the prepared pan and distribute evenly. Scatter the bell pepper and pumpkin seeds on top. Bake until a cake tester inserted in the center comes out with just a few crumbs attached, about 30 minutes.

Transfer the pan to a cooling rack and let sit for 5 minutes. Run a knife along the edges and carefully unmold onto the rack. Peel off the parchment paper. Alternatively, cut into squares and serve hot, right from the pan.

Corn bread tastes best when freshly made, but if well wrapped, it can be refrigerated for up to 3 days and frozen for up to 3 months. Reheat before serving.

Add 1 seeded, minced jalapeño when you add the corn kernels.

savory corn bread
Reduce the sugar to ¼ cup.

corn muffins
Bake the sweet or savory batter in 12 greased standard muffin cups in the top third of the oven until a cake tester inserted in the center comes out with just a few crumbs attached, 15 to 17 minutes.

cornmeal biscuits with sage butter

FOR THE BISCUITS

1½ cups spelt flour

½ cup yellow cornmeal, preferably stone-ground, plus more for dusting the work surface

2 tablespoons (packed) light brown sugar

2 teaspoons baking powder

1 teaspoon salt

¼ teaspoon baking soda

⅛ teaspoon ground chipotle or chili powder

3 tablespoons cold unsalted butter, cut into small bits, plus more for greasing the baking sheet

1 large egg

1 cup well-shaken buttermilk

FOR THE SAGE BUTTER

1 generous tablespoon minced fresh sage

8 tablespoons (1 stick) unsalted butter, at room temperature

Most traditional biscuit recipes don't contain eggs, but when using whole-grain flour, an egg improves the texture significantly. These pale yellow biscuits are absolutely delicious when split open and slathered with sage butter.

MAKES 12 TO 14 BISCUITS

Place a rack in the center of the oven and preheat the oven to 400°F. Lightly grease a baking sheet with butter.

In a bowl, combine the flour, cornmeal, brown sugar, baking powder, salt, baking soda, and chipotle.

Using two knives or a pastry blender, cut the butter into the dry ingredients until the mixture resembles unevenly coarse pebbles.

In a small bowl, whisk together the egg and the buttermilk. Pour the liquid into the dry ingredients, stirring to combine until most of the flour is incorporated.

Sprinkle a work surface lightly with cornmeal. Gently knead the dough until smooth, usually 25 to 35 turns. Shape the dough into a disc.

Sprinkle more cornmeal onto the work surface and more on top of the disc. Roll the dough out to a generous ¼-inch thickness. Fold the dough in half and gently roll to about ½-inch thick.

Use a 2-inch round biscuit cutter or a ¼-cup metal measuring cup to cut out the biscuits. Transfer them to the prepared baking sheet. Roll out scraps to create additional biscuits. (The raw biscuits freeze well, and can be popped into the oven straight from the freezer.)

Bake for 5 minutes. Rotate the pan and continue baking until the bottoms are golden and the tops spring back to a gentle touch, 5 to 7 more minutes, or slightly longer if they were frozen.

While the biscuits are baking, make the sage butter: Mash the sage into the butter in a small bowl. Set aside, or cover tightly and refrigerate until needed.

When the biscuits are done, serve them immediately with the sage butter on the side.

Refrigerate leftover biscuits in a zipper-topped bag for up to 3 days and reheat in a 350°F oven. Baked biscuits do not freeze well.

sesame-corn biscuits

Add 2 tablespoons sesame seeds to the dry ingredients.

cheese biscuits

When the biscuits are about a minute short of done, lightly sprinkle each with 2 teaspoons coarsely grated Cheddar cheese and return to the oven until done.

stuffed cornmeal biscuits

Just before serving, split the biscuits open and fill them with thinly sliced scallion greens, sliced prosciutto or country-smoked ham, and herbed goat cheese.

drop biscuits

Do not knead the dough. Instead, drop the batter by heaping tablespoonsful, about 1 inch apart, onto the prepared baking sheet. Bake as directed.

COOKIES AND CONFECTIONS

anise pignoli cookies

1 tablespoon plus 2 teaspoons whole anise seeds

2 cups whole-wheat pastry flour

½ teaspoon salt

⅛ teaspoon baking soda

12 tablespoons (1½ sticks) unsalted butter, at room temperature

⅔ cup sugar

1 large egg

1 cup (about 5 ounces) pine nuts

This is a charming and sophisticated whole-grain version of the classic Italian pine nut cookie. Pine nuts imported from China are almost as good as Italian ones and generally less expensive.

Unless you have a large oven and several baking sheets, you will need to bake the cookies in two or three batches.

MAKES ABOUT 5 DOZEN 1½-INCH COOKIES

Coarsely chop the anise seeds with a chef's knife or by pulsing them in a spice grinder. Transfer them to a medium bowl and blend in the flour, salt, and baking soda.

In a food processor or with an electric mixer, beat the butter and sugar until smooth and fluffy. Beat in the egg. Add half the flour mixture and process until incorporated. Repeat with the remaining flour. Scatter the nuts on top, and pulse once or twice to distribute them evenly.

Place the processor bowl in the refrigerator until the dough firms up slightly, at least 20 minutes. Meanwhile, set one rack in the center of the oven and a second rack just below, and preheat the oven to 350°F. Line two large cookie sheets with parchment.

Remove half of the dough from the refrigerator and form balls ½ inch in diameter. Place the balls on the prepared cookie sheets, leaving 1 inch between them. Flatten the dough until each cookie is about ½-inch thick. If your hands get sticky, wash them under cold water and dry them well. (You can also rechill the dough for 5 or 10 minutes if it gets too soft.)

Bake until the edges begin to turn light golden for a chewy cookie, 8 to 9 minutes, or ringed with a deep golden border for a crisp cookie, 10 to 12 minutes. Halfway through, rotate the cookie sheets top to bottom and back to front for more even browning.

When done, let the cookies cool on the cookie sheets for 2 minutes. Transfer them to a wire rack and cool to room temperature. Reuse the parchment, if you wish, when making cookies from the remaining dough.

Store for up to 3 weeks in an airtight container in a cool place.

butter pecan cookies

Omit the anise seeds. Add 1½ teaspoons vanilla extract when you add the egg. Use coarsely chopped pecans instead of pine nuts.

■ ■ ■

chocolate chip–hazelnut cookies

2 cups spelt flour

½ cup white sugar

½ cup (packed) light brown sugar

½ teaspoon salt

½ teaspoon baking soda

¼ teaspoon baking powder

1 cup semisweet chocolate chips

1 cup hazelnuts, coarsely chopped and toasted

1 large egg

10 tablespoons (1¼ sticks) unsalted butter, melted and cooled to room temperature

1 tablespoon vanilla extract

When I first tasted these whole-grain cookies, I was reminded of an ancient Roman recipe for an elaborately disguised food that ended with the statement, "No one will know what he is eating." To paraphrase, no one will know they are eating anything but a terrific chocolate chip cookie. Tell them afterward that they've just enjoyed spelt flour.

MAKES ABOUT 3 DOZEN 2½-INCH COOKIES

Place a rack in the upper third of the oven, and preheat the oven to 350°F. Line two large cookie sheets with parchment paper.

In a large bowl, blend the flour, white and brown sugars, salt, baking soda, and baking powder. Stir in the chocolate chips and hazelnuts.

In a small bowl, lightly beat the egg. Whisk in the melted butter and vanilla extract. Stir the wet ingredients into the dry ingredients to create a soft dough.

Use a small melon scoop or a rounded tablespoon (such as a coffee measuring spoon) to form the dough into 1½-inch mounds. Place the balls on the parchment paper a generous 1 inch apart. Gently flatten each ball slightly. Wet your hands if the dough feels sticky.

Bake 1 sheet of cookies at a time until the bottoms are golden brown, about 10 to 12 minutes for soft cookies and 13 to 15 minutes for crisper cookies. Rotate the cookie sheet every 3 minutes for even browning. When they are done, slide the parchment onto a cooling rack. (The cookies may seem a bit fragile but will firm up as they cool.) Bake the remaining cookies. Cool to room temperature.

Store in an airtight container in a cool place for up to 5 days or freeze for up to 3 months.

mocha chocolate chip cookies

Add 2½ tablespoons instant coffee powder to the dry ingredients.

fruit-and-nut oatmeal bars

1¾ cups rolled oats

¼ cup honey

3 tablespoons orange juice
    concentrate

2 tablespoons walnut, hazelnut, or
    canola oil, plus extra for greasing
    the pan

½ teaspoon salt

½ teaspoon ground cinnamon

1 teaspoon baking powder

¼ teaspoon baking soda

⅓ cup chopped dried apricots

⅓ cup dried cranberries

⅓ cup raisins, preferably golden

1 teaspoon grated orange zest

½ cup slivered almonds, toasted

¼ cup hulled, raw, unsalted sunflower
    seeds, toasted

3 tablespoons flax seeds

These moist, chewy bars are chock-full of good stuff and—since they contain no eggs—cholesterol-free. The ingredients are bound together by heart-healthy flax seeds; ground and mixed with water, they develop a consistency similar to egg whites.

MAKES 16 BARS

Place a rack in the center and preheat the oven to 350°F. Lightly oil an 8-inch square baking pan. Distribute 2 tablespoons of the rolled oats on the bottom. Reserve another 2 tablespoons of the oats for sprinkling on top.

In a medium saucepan, bring ½ cup of water to a boil. Turn the heat to low and blend in the honey, orange juice concentrate, oil, salt, and cinnamon. Cover and turn off the heat.

Place ½ cup of the rolled oats in a spice grinder and process into a flour. Stir the oat flour, baking powder, baking soda, remaining cup of oats, apricots, cranberries, raisins, grated orange zest, almonds, and sunflower seeds into the honey mixture in the pot. Cover and let sit for 10 minutes.

Meanwhile, in the spice grinder, process the flax seeds into a fairly fine flour. (Avoid overprocessing, which makes the flour pasty.) Transfer to a medium bowl and add ½ cup of water. Whisk vigorously until the mixture becomes gummy, about 1 minute. Fold the flax seed slurry into the oat mixture.

Pour into the prepared pan and smooth off the top. Sprinkle the reserved oats on top and gently press them into the batter. Bake until the bottom and sides are golden, the center springs back to a gentle touch, and a cake tester inserted into the middle comes out clean, 30 to 35 minutes.

Cool on a rack. Slice the cake down the middle while it is still in the pan. Then cut each half into 1-inch-wide bars. Eat warm, at room temperature, or chilled. You can refrigerate the bars in an airtight container for up to 5 days.

oatmeal-raisin cookies

3 cups old-fashioned rolled oats

1½ cups spelt flour

1 teaspoon ground cinnamon

¾ teaspoon baking soda

½ teaspoon baking powder

½ teaspoon salt

¾ cup (tightly packed) dark brown
   sugar

¼ cup white sugar

12 tablespoons (1½ sticks) unsalted
   butter, at room temperature

2 large eggs

1½ teaspoons vanilla extract

1 cup raisins (yellow are nice)

Crisp on the outside, soft and chewy within, these cookies are made by first lightly toasting the rolled oats, which deepens the "oaty" flavor. It's essential to bake these cookies one batch at time to avoid burning the bottoms.

MAKES 2½ DOZEN 3-INCH COOKIES

Place one rack in the top third and another in the bottom third, and preheat the oven to 400°F. Line a cookie sheet with parchment paper.

Spread the oats out on a large rimmed baking sheet. Bake on the bottom rack for 3 minutes, stir, and continue baking until lightly toasted, 1 to 2 more minutes. Set aside to cool.

Reduce the oven temperature to 350°F.

In a large bowl, combine the spelt flour, cinnamon, baking soda, baking powder, and salt. Stir until blended.

In a food processor fitted with the steel blade, or with an electric mixer, process the brown and white sugars and butter until smooth and fluffy. Add 1 egg and process for about 20 seconds. Add the second egg and vanilla extract and process until the mixture is smooth, about 20 seconds more. Add the egg mixture to the flour mixture and stir until the flour is absorbed. Blend in the toasted oats and the raisins until the oats are all coated with the dough.

Drop heaping tablespoonsful of the dough onto the parchment-lined baking sheet, leaving about 2 inches between the cookies for spreading. Use the back of the spoon or your fingers to gently flatten the cookies roughly into rounds about ½-inch thick.

Bake on the upper rack until the tops and bottoms are nicely browned and the tops spring back to a very gentle touch, 8 to 10 minutes. Rotate the cookie sheet every 3 minutes for even browning. Slide the parchment paper onto a cooling rack. Repeat with the remaining batter, relining the cookie sheet with clean parchment and making sure to let the sheet cool between batches.

Store in an airtight container in a cool place for up to 10 days.

oatmeal ice cream sandwiches

After the cookies have cooled, spoon 2 heaping tablespoonsful of ice cream (cinnamon, maple walnut, and vanilla are all good choices) on the bottom side of a cookie. Place another cookie, bottom side down, on top of the ice cream. Gently press to distribute the ice cream filling. Repeat to make as many sandwiches as you like. Serve immediately.

chocolate chip–oatmeal cookies

Instead of or in addition to raisins, add 1 cup chocolate chips.

oatmeal-cherry cookies

Use dried cherries instead of raisins.

raspberry jam cookies

1 cup old-fashioned rolled oats

1 cup walnuts

1½ cups whole-wheat pastry flour

½ teaspoon ground cinnamon

1 teaspoon baking soda

¼ teaspoon salt

8 tablespoons (1 stick) unsalted butter, melted, plus more for greasing the cookie sheets

½ cup honey

2 tablespoons freshly squeezed lemon juice

1 teaspoon (packed) grated lemon zest

Scant ⅓ cup raspberry jam

These festive, soft cookies have a crimson jam center. Or make a colorfully mixed batch by using a variety of jams.

MAKES ABOUT 2 DOZEN 2-INCH COOKIES

Set racks in the middle and top third of the oven and preheat the oven to 350°F. Grease two large cookie sheets.

Combine the oats and nuts in a food processor fitted with the steel blade. Pulse until the mixture resembles a coarse meal. Add the flour, cinnamon, baking soda, and salt, and pulse a few times to mix well.

Add the melted butter, honey, lemon juice, and zest. Pulse a few times to create a soft, moist dough. Refrigerate the dough for 15 minutes.

Using your hands, roll the dough into smooth balls about 1½ inches in diameter. Place the balls 2 inches apart on the prepared cookie sheets. Gently press the balls to flatten them slightly. Smooth the edges. With your index finger, make a well in the center of each cookie. Fill each hollow with ½ teaspoon of the jam. Wipe off any jam that spills onto the cookie sheet.

Bake the cookies until lightly browned on the bottom, 13 to 16 minutes, reversing and rotating the top and bottom sheets halfway through for even browning.

Let the cookies cool for 5 minutes on the cookie sheets before transferring them to a cooling rack. When cool, store in an airtight container in a cool place for up to 1 week or freeze for up to 3 months.

orange marmalade cookies

Substitute grated orange zest for lemon zest and orange marmalade for the raspberry jam.

spelt gingersnaps

1²/₃ cups spelt flour

½ teaspoon baking powder

¼ teaspoon baking soda

½ teaspoon salt

¾ cup (packed) dark brown sugar

4 tablespoons (½ stick) unsalted
butter, at room temperature

2 large eggs

3 tablespoons molasses

¼ cup coarsely chopped crystallized
ginger

This unusual caramel-colored crisp cookie calls for crystallized ginger instead of ground. For best flavor and texture, chop the ginger coarsely enough to let its presence be felt in every bite.

MAKES ABOUT 2 DOZEN 2-INCH COOKIES

Place the rack in the middle and preheat the oven to 325°F. Line a cookie sheet with parchment.

Place the spelt flour in a medium bowl. Stir in the baking powder, baking soda, and salt.

In a food processor fitted with the steel blade, or with an electric mixer, beat the sugar and butter together until fluffy. Add 1 egg and process for 20 seconds. Add the second egg and process an additional 20 seconds. Add the molasses and process until the mixture is smooth.

Add the flour mixture and process until completely incorporated. Add the ginger and pulse once or twice to distribute it evenly.

Drop tablespoonsful of dough on the prepared cookie sheet, leaving 1 inch between the mounds for spreading. Bake for 12 to 15 minutes for soft cookies, and 19 to 21 minutes for crisp ones. Let the cookies cool for 1 minute on the cookie sheet before transferring them to a cooling rack. Cool completely.

Store in an airtight container in a cool place for up to 10 days.

popcorn-almond-caramel balls

1½ cups sugar

2 tablespoons freshly squeezed lemon
 juice

1 tablespoon unsalted butter

½ teaspoon baking soda

5 cups popped Basic Popcorn
 (page 40)

1 cup almonds, coarsely chopped

Oil for rolling balls (optional)

These are like Cracker Jack for grown-ups…kids will love
them too.

MAKES ABOUT 2½ DOZEN 2-INCH BALLS

Spread out an 18-inch length of waxed paper on a work surface.

Place the sugar in a heavy 4-quart saucepan. Stir in the lemon
juice and ⅓ to ½ cup water—enough to give the mixture a texture that resembles wet sand. With a wet pastry brush, wipe down
any sugar sticking to the sides of the pan.

Place the pan over medium-high heat. Bring the mixture to a boil
and continue boiling to evaporate the water. When the color begins
turning from light to dark amber, after about 8 minutes, swirl the
pan to distribute the amber section. Continue cooking and swirling
the pan until the mixture is a few shades darker, about 2 minutes.
Immediately stir in the butter and baking soda, but stand back and
be careful, as the mixture will splatter.

Turn off the heat. Working very quickly, stir in half of the popcorn
and nuts and stir to coat well. Stir in the remaining popcorn and
nuts and coat well.

Still working quickly, set heaping tablespoonsful of the mixture
on the waxed paper. When the mixture is cool enough to handle,
shape each mound into something that resembles a ball. (If your
hands get sticky, oil them.)

When the balls have cooled completely, transfer them to an airtight container and store in a cool, dry place for up to 1 week, but
not in the refrigerator, where they will get soggy.

NOTE: To wash the saucepan, fill it with water and boil until any
caramel stuck to the bottom and sides dissolves.

VARIATION
Use unsalted peanuts or walnuts instead of almonds.

millet-chocolate crunch

2 bars (3.5 to 4 ounces each)
   bittersweet chocolate
1½ to 2 cups unsweetened puffed
   millet
⅓ to ½ cup dried currants
⅓ to ½ cup hulled, raw, unsalted
   sunflower seeds

I tried making this confection on a whim and was surprised at how easy it was to execute. The crunch is based on puffed millet, which is normally used as a breakfast cereal but when coated with chocolate becomes a sweet treat.

You can throw the crunch together in under 15 minutes—the kids will love helping—but you need to allow at least 30 minutes freezer time for it to harden.

MAKES ABOUT 25 SMALL PIECES

Line a baking sheet that will fit into your refrigerator or freezer with heavy-duty aluminum foil.

Break up the chocolate into squares. Place them in a medium bowl and heat in the microwave for 1 minute at 20% power. Stir well and microwave until melted and smooth, about 1 minute more at 20% power. (Alternatively, melt the chocolate in the top of a double boiler.) Let cool for 5 minutes.

Stir in the millet, currants, and sunflower seeds until coated with the chocolate. (Use the smaller amounts for 3.5-ounce bars.) Drop spoonfuls onto the foil. Leave them in irregular mounds or use your fingers and the spoon to shape the pieces into 1½-inch-round "cookies." (The mixture will be quite sticky at this point.)

Set in the refrigerator or freezer until the chocolate hardens, 30 minutes to 1 hour. Remove the crunch from the foil and refrigerate it in an airtight container for up to 2 weeks. Serve cold.

VARIATIONS

• Transfer mixture to foil and press into an irregular shape about 1½ inches thick. Break into pieces after chocolate hardens.

• Use milk chocolate instead of bittersweet.

• Use any puffed grains instead of millet.

• Use chopped toasted walnuts or hazelnuts instead of sunflower seeds.

whole-wheat almond biscotti

2 cups unblanched almonds, toasted

2 cups whole-wheat pastry flour

1⅓ cups sugar

1 tablespoon grated orange zest
   (from 3 oranges)

1 teaspoon baking powder

½ teaspoon baking soda

1 teaspoon ground cinnamon

¼ teaspoon ground cardamom

½ teaspoon salt

2 large eggs

½ teaspoon vanilla extract

½ teaspoon almond extract or
   additional vanilla

In these thick, almond-studded biscotti, ground almonds provide nutty richness. By leaving some of the almonds coarsely
chopped, you end up with a rustic and very crunchy cookie.

MAKES ABOUT 2½ DOZEN 1-INCH-THICK BISCOTTI

Set a rack in the middle of the oven, and preheat the oven to 350°F.
Line a large cookie sheet with parchment paper.

Place 1 cup of the almonds and 1 cup of the flour in the bowl of
a food processor. Process until the almonds are finely ground. Transfer to a large bowl. Coarsely chop the remaining almonds and add
them to the bowl. Stir in the remaining flour, sugar, orange zest,
baking powder, baking soda, cinnamon, cardamom, and salt.

In a small bowl, lightly beat the eggs. Beat in ¼ cup of water, and
the vanilla and almond extracts. Add the egg mixture to the dry
ingredients. Stir until all of the flour is absorbed. Knead a few times
if that makes it easier to incorporate the flour. The dough will be
firm and sticky.

Set the cookie sheet so that the long side is facing you. Wet your
hands and transfer half of the dough to the top half of the parchment. Shape the dough into a log about 14 inches long and 2 inches
wide. Shape the remaining dough into a second log on the bottom
half of the parchment, leaving at least 2 inches between the logs to
allow for spreading. Bake, rotating the cookie sheet every 10 minutes, until the top feels firm and a cake tester inserted into the center comes out clean, 20 to 25 minutes.

Remove the logs from the oven. Slide the parchment onto a cooling rack. Reduce the oven temperature to 250°F.

When the logs are cool, slide the parchment onto a cutting
board. With a serrated knife, gently cut ¾-inch-thick slices on the
diagonal.

Stand the biscotti about ¼ inch apart on the baking sheet. Bake until they become drier, 18 to 20 minutes for soft, chewy biscotti, and 40 to 45 minutes for dry, crisp biscotti. Transfer to a cooling rack. (Biscotti will become crisper as they cool.) Store in an airtight container in a cool place for up to 1 month.

GRAIN EXCHANGE
Use spelt flour instead of whole-wheat pastry flour.

chocolate-hazelnut biscotti
Substitute hazelnuts for the almonds. Reduce the flour to 1½ cups. Add ½ cup unsweetened cocoa powder and increase the sugar to 1½ cups. Stir ½ cup semisweet chocolate morsels into the dry ingredients. Omit the almond extract.

CRISPS, PIES, AND A COBBLER

pear-cranberry oat crisp

FOR THE OAT TOPPING

¾ cup old-fashioned rolled oats

⅓ cup whole-wheat pastry flour

½ cup coarsely chopped pecans

⅓ cup (packed) dark brown sugar

¼ teaspoon ground cinnamon

⅛ teaspoon allspice

¼ teaspoon salt

6 tablespoons (¾ stick) unsalted butter, melted, plus more for greasing the pan

FOR THE FILLING

2½ pounds ripe Bosc pears (5 large), quartered and cored

⅓ cup dried cranberries

¼ cup (packed) light brown sugar

¼ cup coarsely chopped crystallized ginger

1 teaspoon grated lemon zest

2 tablespoons freshly squeezed lemon juice

This lovely, old-fashioned whole-grain dessert has never gone out of favor. I've given it a fresh twist by adding crystallized ginger to the filling. Serve it warm on its own, or with a scoop of vanilla ice cream or yogurt.

SERVES 8

Set a rack in the lower third of the oven and preheat the oven to 375°F. Butter an 8-inch square baking pan. Set aside.

To prepare the oat topping: In a bowl, combine the oats, flour, pecans, dark brown sugar, cinnamon, allspice, and salt. Stir the mixture as you drizzle on the butter. Continue stirring until the dry ingredients are coated with the butter.

To prepare the filling: Cut the pears crosswise into ¼-inch slices. Place them in a bowl and add the cranberries, light brown sugar, ginger, lemon zest, and lemon juice. Toss gently to distribute the ingredients. Transfer the mixture to the prepared pan. Distribute the oat topping over the fruit.

Bake the crisp uncovered until the pears are tender when pierced with the tip of a knife and the topping is lightly browned, 45 to 60 minutes. If the topping threatens to burn before the fruit is tender, loosely cover the crisp with aluminum foil.

Remove from the oven and let cool slightly before spooning onto plates or into bowls.

GRAIN EXCHANGE

Use rolled spelt, triticale, or Kamut instead of oats.

upside down peach-berry cobbler

FOR THE FRUIT

4 medium-size ripe peaches, pitted
  and sliced (peeling is unnecessary)
1 cup frozen or fresh ripe mixed
  berries
½ cup coarsely chopped pecans
¼ to ⅓ cup (packed) dark brown
  sugar, to taste
2 teaspoons grated lemon zest
1 tablespoon cornstarch
2 teaspoons freshly squeezed lemon
  juice

FOR THE CAKE LAYER

¾ cup whole-wheat pastry flour
¼ cup fine yellow cornmeal,
  preferably stone-ground
⅓ cup white sugar
1¼ teaspoons baking powder
¼ teaspoon baking soda
¼ teaspoon salt
½ teaspoon ground cinnamon
¼ teaspoon ground allspice
¼ teaspoon ground anise
½ cup well-shaken buttermilk
3 tablespoons unsalted butter, melted,
  plus more for greasing the pan
1 large egg
1 teaspoon vanilla extract

This classic American dessert is served upside down so that the colorful fruit is on top. Enjoy it warm, with some sweetened whipped cream or a scoop of vanilla ice cream or coconut sorbet.

SERVES 6 TO 8

Set a rack in the middle and preheat the oven to 350°F. Lightly butter an 8-inch square baking pan. Set aside.

Place the peaches and berries in a large bowl. Add the pecans, brown sugar, and zest. Dissolve the cornstarch in the lemon juice and gently toss it with the fruit. Transfer the fruit mixture to the prepared pan. Set aside.

To prepare the cake layer: In a large bowl, blend the flour, cornmeal, white sugar, baking powder, baking soda, salt, cinnamon, allspice, and anise.

In the bowl used for tossing the fruit, whisk together the buttermilk, butter, egg, and vanilla extract. Fold the wet ingredients into the dry ingredients, just until incorporated. Do not overwork the batter. Use a rubber spatula to spread the batter evenly over the fruit.

Set the pan on a rimmed baking sheet to catch any bubbling fruit juice. Bake, rotating the pan every 15 minutes, until the top of the cake is lightly browned and the center of the cake springs back to a gentle touch, 35 to 45 minutes.

Set the pan on a rack and let cool for 5 minutes. Run a knife around the edges. Invert a large platter on top of the pan and turn the pan over onto the platter to release the cobbler. Scrape any fruit clinging to the bottom of the pan onto the top of the cobbler. Serve warm.

VARIATION
Use 6 to 8 nectarines or plums instead of peaches.

tarrragon-scented rustic nectarine tart

FOR THE TART DOUGH

2 cups whole-wheat pastry flour, plus
   more for rolling

¼ cup sugar

½ teaspoon salt

12 tablespoons (1½ sticks) cold
   unsalted butter, cut into bits

1 to 4 tablespoons ice water

FOR THE TART FILLING

¼ cup walnuts

6 tablespoons sugar, or to taste

2 tablespoons whole-wheat pastry
   flour

1½ pounds nectarines, pitted and
   thinly sliced

1 tablespoon minced fresh tarragon,
   plus more for garnish

½ cup fresh blueberries

When soft fresh fruit is in season—and even when it isn't (see the Frozen Peach and Blueberry Tart, opposite)—consider making this stunning dessert—a free-standing tart that requires no special equipment. The dough is easy to handle, so even beginning bakers are guaranteed good results.

Fresh tarragon adds a hint of licorice and comes as an unusual surprise.

MAKES ONE 10-INCH TART; SERVES 8

To make the dough: Put the flour, sugar, and salt in a medium bowl. Cut the butter into the flour with a pastry blender or your hands until the mixture resembles pebbles.

Gently stir in the ice water 1 tablespoon at a time, using the minimal amount needed to make the dough clump together. Do not handle the dough more than necessary. Form the dough into a 5-inch disc. Wrap in plastic wrap and refrigerate until firm but not hard, about 30 minutes.

When it's time to roll out the dough, line a large baking sheet with parchment. Flour the work surface and rolling pin to prevent sticking. Roll the dough out until it's about ¼-inch thick and 12 inches in diameter. Carefully roll the dough onto the rolling pin and lay it out on the parchment. If time permits, refrigerate for 30 minutes or longer. (Refrigerating the dough at this point minimizes shrinkage while the tart is baking, but it is not essential.)

Place a rack in the lower third of the oven and preheat the oven to 400°F.

To make the filling: In a mini processor or food processor, grind the walnuts with 2 tablespoons of the sugar and the flour. Evenly distribute the mixture on top of the tart dough, leaving 1 inch around the perimeter uncovered.

In a large bowl, toss the nectarines with the remaining 4 tablespoons sugar, or to taste, and add the tarragon. Arrange the nectarine slices on the tart, again leaving 1 inch uncovered around the perimeter. Scatter the blueberries on top of the nectarines. Fold the 1-inch border of dough over the fruit, crimping it as you go. (This will create a barrier that prevents the fruit juices from escaping while the tart is baking.) If the dough tears, patch it together.

Bake the tart until the edges are richly browned, 27 to 30 minutes. (Rotate the baking sheet every 10 minutes for even browning.) Slide the parchment paper and tart onto a cooling rack and let cool for 15 minutes before slicing and serving. Sprinkle with a little more tarragon and serve warm.

VARIATION

Use fresh basil instead of tarragon.

frozen peach and blueberry tart

Use 1 pound frozen sliced peaches instead of the nectarines and substitute frozen blueberries for the fresh. There is no need to defrost the fruit before baking the tart.

pumpkin pie with pumpkin seed crust

FOR THE CRUST

1 cup spelt flour, plus more for rolling
  the dough

¼ cup hulled, raw, unsalted pumpkin
  seeds

2 tablespoons (packed) light brown
  sugar

¼ teaspoon salt

4 tablespoons (½ stick) cold unsalted
  butter, cut into bits

1 teaspoon apple cider or raspberry
  vinegar

FOR THE FILLING

2 large eggs

1 can (15 to 16 ounces) unsweetened
  pumpkin puree

1¼ cups 2% milk

¾ to 1 cup light brown sugar, to taste

1½ teaspoons ground cinnamon

1 teaspoon freshly grated nutmeg

½ teaspoon ground allspice

½ teaspoon salt

1 teaspoon vanilla extract

Sweetened whipped cream, for garnish
  (optional)

I love the way the smooth, mellow filling contrasts with the nutty crust in this updated version of an American favorite. I also love using pumpkin seeds in the crust, since it makes such good use of the other edible and nutritious part of the vegetable.

MAKES ONE 10-INCH PIE; SERVES 8

To make the crust: Put the flour, pumpkin seeds, brown sugar, and salt into the bowl of a food processor fitted with the metal blade. Process until the pumpkin seeds are finely ground.

Add the butter and pulse until the mixture resembles coarse meal. Add 3 tablespoons of cold water and the vinegar, and pulse until the mixture clumps together into a mass. Remove the blade and gather the dough into a ball. Press into a flattened disc. Wrap with plastic wrap and chill until firm, about 30 minutes.

Place the rack in the center of the oven and preheat the oven to 400°F.

On a lightly floured surface, roll the dough into a circle about 12 inches in diameter. Sprinkle flour on the top of the dough, if necessary, to facilitate rolling. Transfer the dough to a 10-inch pie plate and press it into the bottom and almost to the top of the pie plate. Prick with a fork in several places. Press a sheet of foil onto the crust and weight it down with pie weights or dried beans. Bake for 15 minutes. Pour out the weights. Set the pie plate on a cooling rack and remove the foil. Reduce the oven temperature to 375°F.

To prepare the filling: In a food processor or electric mixer, combine the eggs, pumpkin, milk, brown sugar, cinnamon, nutmeg, allspice, salt, and vanilla extract. Process until smooth. Pour the mixture into the prepared crust. Trim off any exposed crust to avoid burning.

Bake until the filling doesn't jiggle when you gently move the pie from side to side, 35 to 45 minutes.

Set the pie on a cooling rack. Serve at room temperature or chilled with whipped cream, if desired.

VARIATION

Use hulled, raw, unsalted sunflower seeds or walnuts instead of the pumpkin seeds.

PUDDINGS AND A PARFAIT

bulgur pudding with honey and dates

1 cup fine bulgur

1 cup 2% milk

¼ to ⅓ cup honey, to taste

1 teaspoon ground cinnamon

1 teaspoon ground ginger

¼ teaspoon salt

1 cup walnuts, toasted and chopped

1 cup pitted dates, chopped

⅓ cup dried currants or raisins

Ice cream or sweetened whipped
  cream, for garnish (optional)

I have adapted this earthy, comforting bulgur pudding from Gil Marks's *The World of Jewish Desserts*. According to Marks, it is a Sephardic pudding (alternately called *prehito, moustrahana*, and *belila*) that is common among the Jews of Turkey, who serve it to celebrate the fall holiday of Sukkot.

This dessert cooks in a flash and can be served warm or chilled. Leftovers make a delicious breakfast.

SERVES 6 TO 8

Combine the bulgur and 2 cups of water in a medium saucepan. Bring to a boil over high heat, reduce the heat to medium, and cook uncovered, stirring frequently, until the water is absorbed, 3 to 5 minutes.

Stir in the milk, ¼ cup honey, cinnamon, ginger, and salt. Bring the mixture to a boil. Reduce the heat to medium and continue cooking, uncovered, at a gentle boil, stirring occasionally, until the mixture develops the consistency of porridge, about 5 minutes. Stir in the walnuts, dates, and currants. Sweeten with additional honey, if desired. Serve warm in bowls. Top with a scoop of ice cream, if you wish.

GRAIN EXCHANGE

For a more coarsely textured pudding, use medium bulgur instead of fine. Instructions and cooking time remain the same.

bulgur-date pudding cake

Pour the hot pudding into a buttered 8- or 9-inch square pan. Cool it to room temperature. Cover with plastic wrap and refrigerate for at least 3 hours. Cut the pudding into 6 or 9 portions and set them on plates. Garnish each portion with ice cream, if you wish.

hazelnut-fig pudding

Use hazelnuts instead of walnuts and figs instead of dates.

brown basmati rice custard pudding

Butter, for greasing the pan

3 cups whole milk

½ cup sugar

2 tablespoons honey

½ teaspoon ground cinnamon

¼ teaspoon salt

3 large eggs, lightly beaten

1½ teaspoons vanilla extract

2 to 2½ cups cooked Basic Brown
Basmati Rice (page 63)

When you are in the mood for a rich, custardy rice pudding, here's the ticket. Brown basmati is a good choice for a creamy whole-grain pudding since the cooked bran layer is quite soft.

If you include the full 2½ cups of cooked rice, you'll end up with a ½-inch layer of custard on top. If you use less rice, you'll have a thicker layer of custard.

SERVES 8

Place the rack in the bottom third of the oven and preheat the oven to 350°F. Grease a 2-quart baking dish. Have ready an ovenproof pan that is large enough to hold the baking dish with some room to spare.

In a medium saucepan, combine the milk, sugar, honey, cinnamon, and salt. Set over medium-high heat and bring almost to a boil, stirring occasionally to dissolve the sugar. (Watch for boil-overs, which can happen in a flash.) Turn off the heat. Let cool for 5 to 10 minutes.

In a large bowl, whisk the eggs with the vanilla extract. Whisk ½ cup of the hot milk mixture into the eggs. Gradually whisk the eggs into the hot milk. Stir in the rice.

Pour the mixture into the prepared baking dish. Place the uncovered dish into the larger pan. Pour enough water into the larger pan to come halfway up the sides of the dish.

Bake until the center of the pudding feels set when gently pressed with the back of a spoon, 55 to 80 minutes. Serve warm or chilled.

VARIATIONS

• Use maple syrup instead of honey.

• Add ½ cup raisins along with the rice.

• Substitute 1 cup cooked wild rice and use 1 to 1½ cups of basmati.

coconut–black rice pudding

1 cup Thai black sticky rice, rinsed

Pinch of salt

1 can (14 to 15 ounces) unsweetened
coconut milk

2 to 4 tablespoons sugar, to taste

1 can (8 ounces) lychees, for garnish
(optional)

Thai black rice makes a stunning rice pudding. The grain has a natural sweetness and gives off a gorgeous burgundy color as it cooks. The starch is silky, and the bran layer becomes very soft, so the pudding is creamy in the tradition of white rice puddings.

SERVES 6

In a heavy 2-quart saucepan, bring 1¾ cups of water to a boil. Add the rice and salt and return to a boil. Cover, reduce the heat, and simmer until the rice is tender, 25 to 30 minutes. It's all right if there is some unabsorbed water.

Stir in the coconut milk and sugar to taste. Bring to a boil. Reduce the heat and boil gently, uncovered, stirring occasionally to prevent sticking, until the rice absorbs most of the coconut milk, about 10 minutes. Leave the mixture slightly soupy since the rice will continue to absorb the coconut milk as it sits.

Spoon into individual dessert bowls or use martini glasses for special effect. Garnish with lychees and a bit of their syrup, if you wish. Serve warm, room temperature, or chilled.

VARIATION

Garnish with canned mandarin oranges instead of lychees.

GRAIN EXCHANGE

Use Chinese black rice instead of Thai.

creamy wheat berries with honey

3 cups milk (2% is fine, but don't
   use skim)
3 tablespoons honey, plus more
   to taste
3 cups cooked Basic Wheat Berries
   (page 94)
Generous pinch of ground cinnamon
Pinch of salt
1/3 cup pitted, chopped dates
Sweetened whipped cream, for garnish
   (optional)

In many cultures dating as far back as the Middle Ages, crunchy, toothsome wheat berries have been sweetened and served for holiday celebrations. In Russia, poppy seeds, walnuts, and raisins are added for a dish called *kutya*. In Turkey, a similar dish is called *kofyas*, and in Greece it's known as *koliva*.

The combination of wheat, honey, and dates has survived so long because it is heavenly. Serve small portions as it's quite filling.

SERVES 6

In a heavy 3-quart saucepan, combine the milk and honey and bring to a boil. Stir in the wheat berries, cinnamon, and salt. Return to a boil, then reduce the heat and cook at a gentle boil for 30 minutes, stirring occasionally. Skim off and discard the skin that forms on top.

Stir in the dates and continue cooking at a gentle boil, stirring occasionally, until the mixture becomes quite thick, about 15 minutes longer. Add more honey, if you wish.

Serve hot in small bowls. Garnish with whipped cream, if you wish.

VARIATIONS

• Use raisins or dried currants instead of dates.
• Stir in 1/2 cup chopped, toasted nuts just before serving—or use the nuts as a garnish.
• Press the cooked mixture into timbales and unmold onto dessert plates. Surround with pear or apple slices.

barley and rhubarb pudding

1 pound rhubarb, trimmed and cut
   into 1-inch pieces (3 cups)
2½ cups orange juice
1 cup barley flakes
Honey to taste (optional)

Combining whole grains and fruit for a dessert is more common around the world than it is in America, and this is a shame since the natural sweetness and mild flavor of grains invites the thought of dessert puddings.

Barley becomes sweeter still when cooked in orange juice. Since you'll be using barley flakes, and rhubarb cooks in a matter of minutes, this tart-sweet pudding cooks very quickly.

An alternative to serving it on its own is to use the pudding—which is thinner than most—as a topping for vanilla yogurt or ice cream.

SERVES 6

Combine the rhubarb and orange juice in a nonreactive 2-quart saucepan. Bring to a boil, cover, and reduce the heat. Simmer for 5 minutes. Stir in the barley flakes. Cover and simmer until the barley is tender, about 7 minutes. Add honey to taste, if you wish.

The mixture will thicken as it sits, but if you would like to thicken it immediately, boil uncovered until thickened to your liking. Serve warm or refrigerate until needed, up to 5 days.

GRAIN EXCHANGE
Used old-fashioned rolled oats or rolled Kamut instead of barley.

farro parfait with ricotta, oranges, and mint

1 container (15 ounces) ricotta

2 tablespoons plain yogurt

3 to 4 tablespoons orange marmalade, to taste

1/3 cup (packed) fresh mint leaves, plus more for garnish

3 navel oranges, peeled

1 1/2 cups cooked Basic Farro (page 96)

The idea for creating this unusual parfait came from *The Italian Country Table* by Lynne Rossetto Kasper. When Lynne described how mountain farmers mix cooked farro with fresh ricotta, honey, and a sprinkling of cinnamon, my imagination was off and running.

I've made my version more elegant by whipping the ricotta and sweetening it with marmalade. Then I've created a parfait by alternating the ricotta mixture with farro and orange segments. I use strawberries in the summer, and mangoes whenever I spot a good one (see opposite).

The parfait looks especially striking when served in 8-ounce martini glasses. Otherwise, you can use clear dessert bowls.

SERVES 6

Blend the ricotta, yogurt, and 3 tablespoons of marmalade in a food processor until creamy, about 1 minute. If you wish, blend in more marmalade to taste. Add the mint and pulse until it is distributed and coarsely chopped.

Cut each orange into 3/4-inch slices. Separate each slice into segments.

To assemble the parfaits: Place a heaping spoonful of the ricotta mixture on the bottom of each glass or bowl. Distribute a heaping tablespoon of farro on top. Add a layer of orange segments. Repeat with a second layer of ricotta, farro, and oranges. Top with 3 table-spoons of ricotta. Garnish with a mint leaf.

GRAIN EXCHANGE

Use coarse bulgur or cracked wheat instead of farro.

farro parfait with strawberries and anise

Omit the mint. Use strawberry jam instead of orange marmalade. Add 1½ teaspoons anise seeds to the ricotta mixture. Use sliced strawberries instead of oranges.

farro parfait with mango and crystallized ginger

Stir ¼ cup chopped crystallized ginger into the ricotta mixture. Use diced fresh mango instead of orange segments.

further reading

websites

BOTANY

www.botanical.com
Here in its totality, the delightful Mrs. Grieve's *A Modern Herbal,* first published in England in 1931, full of the legend and lore of whole grains and other edible plants

GRAIN MILLING

www.countrylivinggrainmills.com
A good starting place for those who want to make their own rolled grains and grind their own flour

NUTRITION AND DIET

www.mypyramid.gov/pyramid/grains.html
Ways to make sure you are getting the USDA-recommended amount of whole grains into your diet with a diagram of the anatomy of a grain

www.nal.usda.gov/fnic/dga/index.html
USDA Food and Nutrition Center with links for the Food Pyramid and the latest dietary guidelines

www.nal.usda.gov/fnic/foodcomp/search
Nutritional breakdown of grains and other ingredients

www.whfoods.com
The website of the nonprofit George Mateljan Foundation, discussing the nutritional and health-promoting benefits of various foods, with emphasis on grains

www.wholegrain.umn.edu/
Nutritional studies on whole grain by researchers at the University of Minnesota

www.wholegrainscouncil.org
A consortium of scientists, dietitians, industry members, and educators dedicated to getting more whole grains onto the American dinner plate and into schools

SPROUTING

www.waltonfeed.com/grain/sprouts.html
Detailed instructions for sprouting many types of grain

books for background reading and cooking

Alford, Jeffrey, and Naomi Duguid. *Flatbreads & Flavors*. New York: William Morrow, 1995.
A prose and photographic study of flatbreads and accompaniments from around the world, some using whole-grain flour

Figoni, Paula. *How Baking Works*. Hoboken, NJ: John Wiley & Sons, 2004.
Clear and thorough book on this complicated subject

Kijac, Maria Baez. *The South American Table*. Boston: The Harvard Common Press, 2003.
Includes many traditional and contemporary recipes for amaranth, quinoa, and various forms of corn

Lawrence, Sue. *Scots Cooking*. London: Headline Book Publishing, 2000.
Contemporary interpretations of Scottish cooking, including interesting recipes using oats

London, Sheryl and Mel. *The Versatile Grain and the Elegant Bean*. New York: Simon & Schuster, 1992.
Half of the book is devoted to the whole and refined forms of each grain, including background and recipes

Muir, Jenny. *A Cook's Guide to Grains*. London: Conran Octopus Limited, 2002.
Innovative grain recipes from a British food journalist

National Research Council. *Lost Crops of Africa, Vol. 1: Grains*. National Academy Press: Washington, DC, 1996.
Discusses various types of millet, sorghum, teff, and other grains indigenous to Africa, including their potential uses worldwide

Pitzer, Sara. *Whole Grains*. New York: Garden Way, 1981.
A good basic primer on how to grow, harvest, and cook whole grains

Sass, Lorna. *Lorna Sass' Complete Vegetarian Kitchen*. New York: William Morrow, 2002.
Many vegan recipes using whole grains

Stoskopf, Neal C. *Cereal Grain Crops*. Reston, VA: Reston Publishing, 1985.
A very readable textbook on the botany, growing, seed production, and quality of grains, including chapters on individual grains

Uvezian, Sonia. *Recipes and Remembrances from an Eastern Mediterranean Kitchen*. Northbrook, IL: The Siamanto Press, 2001.
An impressive, well-researched, and illustrated study of the foods of this area, with many traditional recipes, including a substantial section on bulgur kibbe

Wolfert, Paula. *Mediterranean Grains and Greens*. New York: HarperCollins, 1998.
Focuses on traditional uses of grains specific to the area

————. *Couscous and Other Good Food from Morocco*. New York: William Morrow, 1987.
The classic on the subject

specific grains

AMARANTH

www.kokopelli-seed-foundation.com/
amaranths.html
History of cultivation, nutrition, and uses

www.hort.purdue.edu/newcrop/1492/
grains.html#Canihua
Botanical description and cultivation of Andean
grains

Cole, John. *Amaranth from the Past for the Future.*
    Emmaus, PA: Rodale Press, 1979.
A detailed study of history, traditional uses, and
the Rodale Institute's experiments growing
amaranth in this country, with recipes

CORN

Fussell, Betty. *The Story of Corn.* New York: Knopf,
    1992.
Social, historical, magical, and sacred aspects of
this all-important food

KAMUT

www.kamut.com
History, development of crops in this country, and
products

POPCORN

Smith, Andrew F. *Popped Culture: A Social History
    of Popcorn in America.* Washington, DC:
    Smithsonian Institution Press, 2001.
A thoroughly researched study by a culinary historian, including a substantial selection of historical
recipes

QUINOA

www.hort.purdue.edu/newcrop/
proceedings1993/V2-222.html
History, nutritional value, and cultural practices

RICE

Alford, Jeffrey, and Naomi Duguid. *Seductions of
    Rice.* New York: Artisan, 1998.
The use of rice all over the world, divided into
chapters by country and illustrated with evocative
photos taken by these well-travelled food writers

RYE

http://rye.vtt.fi/chapter1.htm
A detailed scientific analysis of rye and its effects
on health

SPELT

www.purityfoods.com
Background on spelt with good links

TEFF

www.ethnomed.org/cultures/ethiop/teff.html
Use of teff in Ethiopia

www.marilee.us/teff.html
Good links for this grain

WILD RICE

Hauser, Susan Carol. *Wild Rice Cooking.* New York:
The Lyons Press, 2000.
An affectionate history of wild rice, with recipes

mail-order sources

To mail-order the grains mentioned in this book, check the websites and telephone numbers listed below. I have not given sources for the very common grains unless there is a distributor of a very special variety.

The websites frequently provide interesting background, articles, recipes, and links. Many offer a range of other ingredients as well. Printed catalogues and e-mail newsletters are often available by request.

general

www.bobsredmill.com
(800) 349-2173
Wide range of organic and nonorganic whole grains, grits, and flours in various-size packages (also distributed nationwide in health food stores and many supermarkets). You can visit the mill and on-site store near Portland, Oregon.

www.goldminenaturalfood.com
(800) 475-FOOD
An impressive selection of heirloom varieties of organic grains carefully chosen by owner Jean Richardson, most sold in one-pound packages

www.indianharvest.com
(800) 346-7032
Wide range of whole grains and grain blends in eight-ounce packages

www.kalustyans.com
(800) 352-3451
Large variety of whole and cracked grains sold in one-pound bags; also a wide selection of international ingredients

www.kingarthurflour.com
(802) 649-3361
A wide range of organic whole-grain flours and whole grains, primarily geared for bakers

www.montanaflour.com
(406) 622-5436
Flour milled from organic whole grains on request

www.shopnatural.com
(520) 884-0745
This online health food store carries a wide range of organic packaged and bulk whole grains and whole-grain products

particular grains

AMARANTH

www.nuworldamaranth.com

(630) 369-6819

Run by Larry Walters and his family, who have been growing and selling amaranth and amaranth products since 1982

BARLEY

BLACK BARLEY

www.goldminenaturalfood.com

(800) 475-FOOD

www.indianharvest.com

(800) 346-7032

HULL-LESS BARLEY

www.andale.com/stores/sf_home.jsp?
mode-1&sfUrl=CowboyFoods

(800) 759-5489

Bud Clem carries golden waxy, bronze nugget, and treasure state varieties under the label NuBarley

BUCKWHEAT

www.ployes.com/Products.htm

(800) 239-3237

Acadian light buckwheat flour and pancake mix

CORN

CHICOS

www.loschileros.com

(888) EAT-CHILE

Also sells a variety of blue and white corn products

www.ranchogordo.com

(707) 259-1935

Also sells hominy and heirloom dried beans

CORN PRODUCTS

www.nativeseeds.org

(866) 622-5561

A small selection of heirloom grains indigenous to the Southwest, including white posole and blue cornmeal

CORN, SWEET DRIED

www.theamishcountrystore.com

(877) 787-9657

Sells John Cope's products

www.sensiblefoods.com

(888) 222-0170

CORNMEAL AND GRITS

www.ansonmills.com

(803) 467-4122

Fine and coarse yellow and white stone-ground cornmeal and grits, including quick grits; coarse grits contain germ; also sells polenta and farro

www.hoppinjohns.com

(800) 828-4412

Stone-ground cornmeal, speckled-heart grits, and flour

HOMINY (POSOLE)

www.redcorn.com

(800) 280-9745

Red, white, and blue hominy

MASA (FRESH)

www.ansonmills.com

(803) 467-4122

JOB'S TEARS

www.goldminenaturalfood.com

(800) 475-FOOD

Organic pearled Job's tears

www.simply-natural.biz

(888) 392-9237

Job's tears with more bran intact (yuuki hato mugi)

MILLET

KIBBI MILLET

www.simply-natural.biz

(888) 392-9237

MILLET FLOUR

www.bobsredmill.com

(800) 349-2173

MILLET GRITS

www.bobsredmill.com

(800) 349-2173

MILLET PUFFS

www.shopnatural.com

(520) 884-0745

OATS

www.scottishgourmetusa.com

(877) 814-FOOD

Pinhead and porridge oats

POLENTA

www.ansonmills.com

Includes red and white polenta

www.chefshop.com

Various kinds imported from Italy, including yellow and white, and a northern Italian specialty polenta with buckwheat

QUINOA

www.bobsredmill.com

(800) 349-2173

Packages Inca Organics quinoa and distributes to health food stores nationally

www.incaorganics.com

A wholesaler that imports organic quinoa from Ecuador—the best-tasting I've found. The website provides retail sources

www.quinoa.bigstep.com

(310) 217-8125

Ancient Harvest brand quinoa flakes and pasta, Bolivian red quinoa

www.whitemountainfarm.com
(800) 364-3019
Tan and black organic quinoa. The black quinoa, developed by Colorado farmer Ernie New, is actually a tasty tricolor mix of black, red, and ivory seeds.

RICE

BASMATI BROWN RICE
www.indiaspicehouse.com
(407) 226-2727
Imported from Pakistan; quality varies

www.southernbrownrice.com
(800) 421-7423
Also carries short-grain brown rice, long-grain brown rice, and rice blends, all organically grown in Arkansas. Highly recommended.

BHUTANESE RED RICE
www.lotusfoods.com
(866) 972-6879

CAMARGUE RED RICE
www.kalustyans.com
(800) 352-3451
Sporadically in stock

www.zingermans.com
(734) 663-DELI
Sporadically in stock

CHINESE BLACK RICE
www.lotusfoods.com
(866) 972-6879
Lotus Foods calls this product Forbidden Black Rice

COLUSARI RED RICE
www.goldminenaturalfood.com
(800) 475-FOOD

www.indianharvest.com
(800) 346-7032

HIMALAYAN RED RICE
www.lotusfoods.com
(866) 972-6879

ITALIAN BLACK RICE
www.manicaretti.com
(800) 799-9830
Grown in the Po plain, Principato di Lucedio's black rice is a cross between Italian and Chinese rices. The rice keeps its color while cooking and has the pleasing aroma of freshly baked bread.

ITALIAN WILD RED RICE
www.chefshop.com
(877) 437-6269

JASMINE BROWN RICE
www.importfood.com
(888) 618-THAI
Jasmine brown rice imported from Thailand

www.lotusfoods.com
(866) 972-6879
Packager of the light, flavorful brown jasmine rice grown by Lowell Farms; also sold in bins in some large health food stores and labeled accordingly

KALIJIRA BROWN RICE
www.lotusfoods.com
(866) 972-6879

THAI BLACK STICKY RICE

www.importfood.com
(888) 618-THAI
Also carries imported Thai red jasmine and brown jasmine

www.indianharvest.com
(800) 346-7032

www.kalustyans.com
(800) 352-3451

SORGHUM

www.twinvalleymills.com
(402) 279-3965
Sells whole grain and flour

TEFF

www.teffco.com
(888) 822-2221
Brown and ivory teff, whole grains and flours

WHEAT

BULGUR
www.kalustyans.com
(800) 352-3451
Four grinds plus Lebanese bulgur, which has a slightly smoky taste

www.sunnylandmills.com
(559) 233-4983
Four grinds of excellent quality

COUSCOUS (WHOLE-WHEAT)

www.shopnatural.com
(520) 884-0745

FARINA
www.bobsredmill.com
(800) 349-2173
Finely ground whole wheat good for breakfast porridge

FARRO
www.chefshop.com
Imported from Italy

www.gustiamo.com
(877) 907-2525
The Latini line of artisanal farro pasta is available in many shapes and size and is much esteemed by pasta connoisseurs.

www.igourmet.com
Organic farro imported from Italy

www.manicaretti.com
(800) 799-9830
Offers cracked and semi-pearled farro, farro pasta, and farro flour as well as a variety of regional polentas. The grains are grown under organic conditions but are not certified organic.

FRIKA (GREEN SPELT)
www.kalustyans.com
(800) 352-3451
Immature (green) wheat imported from the Middle East; some broken grains, must be washed several times (see also Gruenkern)

GRUENKERN (GREEN SPELT)

www.germandeli.com

Beautiful, very clean product with shiny whole olive green kernels, from Germany; also available in cracked form (see also Frika)

KAMUT PUFFS

www.shopnatural.com

(520) 884-0745

SPELT

www.purityfoods.com

Sells whole-grain spelt and spelt products

WILD RICE

www.goldminenaturalfood.com

(800) 475-FOOD

High-quality organic product imported from Saskatchewan

www.indianharvest.com

(800) 346-7032

Wild rice flour, wild rice and grain blends

SPICES AND SPICE BLENDS

www.penzeys.com

(800) 279-3965

Every dried herb and spice you can imagine; I recommend their garam masala blend

THAI CURRY PASTE AND OTHER ETHNIC INGREDIENTS

www.ethnicgrocer.com

(630) 860-1733

Also chipotle in adobo and most anything else you can't find locally

WHOLE-WHEAT PHYLLO

www.fillofactory.com

(800) OK-FILLO

Whole-wheat and spelt phyllo shipped frozen; also available in some health food and gourmet stores

miscellaneous

HONEYS AND MUCH MORE

www.igourmet.com

(877) 446-8763

Wide selection of gourmet foods, including a variety of honeys, smoked sea salt, farmhouse cheeses, and interesting vinegars

acknowledgments

BOOK IDEAS ARE LIKE GRAINS, waiting to be sown and tended with care so that they can nourish. I am grateful that the idea for this book was successfully planted by Pam Krauss, Senior Vice President and Executive Editor at Clarkson Potter, and that my editor, Rica Allannic, has tended it with such care.

Writing cookbooks is a happy combination of stove and desktop. The desktop aspects are solitary, making stovetop companionship that much more welcome and precious. The voluntary help I received was offered with great generosity and enthusiasm by culinary students and young professionals eager to learn. It was a joy to work with them all, and their contributions and good cheer have enriched this book immeasurably.

My first assistant, Kristin Donnelly, brought impressive competence to the initial grain testing and organization of the book. Kristin was also so knowledgeable about wine that I invited her to select and write the recommendations that you'll find in the entrée chapter. Heartfelt thanks, Kristin, for giving me such a running start.

Ilana Morady arrived next and took great initiative in learning about whole-grain baking. Her many experiments gave me an excellent head start with the cookies and quick breads. Verlie Payne continued to retest and improve the baked goods with dedication and passion. Michele Rickert and Veronica Sylvester brought their advanced baking skills to refining the quick breads and cookies even further.

Cathy Roberts has maintained her long-standing record of testing every recipe prepublication and mailing me regular reports on her experiences accompanied by specially selected cartoons to give me a laugh. Others whose ideas and diligence have enriched this book and my life include Tarra Bathurst, Jennifer Benerofe, Judy Bloom, Heather and Gerhard Bock, Sarah Breckenridge, Laurie Cooper, Altagracia de Lara, Aviva Epstein, Robert Fargher, Robin Gotch, Stacey Isaacs, Jennifer Iserloh, Marcelle Kaskawits, Livia McAllister, Denise Michelson, Nicole Nacamuli, Susan Nobel, Asya Ollis, Wendy Ramunno, Elizabeth Schneider, Barbara Spiegel, Teri Tsang, Jane Tunks, and Rita Yeazel.

I have special gratitude for Amy Quazza of the Institute for Culinary Education and Rosemary Serviss of the Natural Gourmet Cooking School for sending so much help my way. And how could I have managed without my good neighbor Betsy Lawson, who so graciously allowed me to store my overflow of grains in her refrigerator?

Thank you to David Prince for the gorgeous photographs and to food stylist Megan Schlow and her assistant Laure Leber for interpreting my recipes with such flair. At Clarkson Potter, I would like to acknowledge the dedication of Maggie Hinders, Senior Designer, and the enthusiasm of Sydney Webber, Director of Marketing, and Jean McCall, Associate Director for Special Markets. Copy editor Suzanne Fass was ruthless in her quest to vanquish the gremlins. Sarah Jane Freymann of the Sarah Jane Freymann Literary Agency openheartedly advised on contractual matters large and small.

Many growers and distributors of whole grains were exceedingly generous in providing both information and grain samples for recipe testing. Heartfelt thanks to Anson Mills, Birkett Mills, Dennis Gilliam and Matt Cox of Bob's Red Mill, Bouchard Family Farms, Carpenters Mills, Tim Mar of Chefshop.com, John Clough of Garden Spot Distributors and Shiloh Farms, Bud Clem of Cowboy Foods, Ellis Stansel Gourmet Rice, GermanDeli.com, Gibbs Wild Rice, Jean Richardson of Goldmine Natural Foods, Gourmetchef.com, Grey Owl Wild Rice, igourmet.com, Mike Holleman of Indian Harvest, Caryl Levine of Lotus Foods, Lundberg Family Farms, Andre Giles of Montana Flour and Grains, Larry Walters of Nu-World Amaranth, Steve Sando of Rancho Gordo New World Specialty Food, Anne Robinson of ScottishGourmetUSA.gourmetfoodmall.com, Southern Brown Rice, Spectrum Naturals Oils, Mike Orlando of Sunnyland Mills, Twin Valley Mills, War Eagle Mills, and Ernie New of White Mountain Farm. Special thanks to Le Creuset and Emile Henri Cookware for providing high-quality Dutch ovens in various sizes for recipe-testing.

And who got me to the wheat fields of Montana but the indefatigable Maria Emmer-Aanes, former marketing director of Great Harvest Bread Company and now with Nature's Path? Thanks to Maria, I visited Montana farmer Ed Aanes and got to ride on a combine and have my picture taken in amber waves of grain, and I joined an unforgettable tour of northern Montana with Kamut grain farmer and visionary Bob Quinn. Bob founded the Kamut Association of America, which generously provided the Kamut wheat that brings such natural beauty to these pages.

My fine experience of the wheat harvest in Montana prompted me to join Midge and Bob Leventry of Inca Organics on their mission to inspect the quinoa harvest in Riobamba, Ecuador, another experience of a lifetime for this city girl. The value of traveling to the source was instilled in me by the Oldways Preservation Trust, founded by K. Dun Gifford. Oldways has created extraordinary opportunities for journalists to experience traditional foods in their land of origin, and thanks to Dun and Executive Vice President Sara Baer-Sinnott, I have tasted the traditional foods of Tunisia, Crete, Liguria, and Apulia. I am also grateful to Oldways for taking the initiative to create the Whole Grains Council, a consortium of industry members, scientists, and chefs dedicated to increasing consumption of whole grains to provide better health for all.

Finally, I would like to thank dear friends who provided love and support during what sometimes felt like a never-ending process: Jane Assimacopoulos, Michela Biasutti, Judy Bloom, Joyce Curwin, Erin Elliot, Maria Emmer-Aanes, Jennifer Iserloh, Susan Johnston, Dan Macey, Karen Muchnick, Cathy Roberts, and Elizabeth Schneider.

index

conversion chart
EQUIVALENT IMPERIAL AND METRIC MEASUREMENTS

American cooks use standard containers, the 8-ounce cup and a tablespoon that takes exactly 16 level fillings to fill that cup level. Measuring by cup makes it very difficult to give weight equivalents, as a cup of densely packed butter will weigh considerably more than a cup of flour. The easiest way therefore to deal with cup measurements in recipes is to take the amount by volume rather than by weight. Thus the equation reads:

1 cup = 240 ml = 8 fl. oz. $\frac{1}{2}$ cup = 120 ml = 4 fl. oz.

It is possible to buy a set of American cup measures in major stores around the world.

In the States, butter is often measured in sticks. One stick is the equivalent of 8 tablespoons. One tablespoon of butter is therefore the equivalent to $\frac{1}{2}$ ounce or 15 grams.

LIQUID MEASURES

Fluid Ounces	U.S.	Imperial	Milliliters
	1 teaspoon	1 teaspoon	5
$\frac{1}{4}$	2 teaspoons	1 dessertspoon	10
$\frac{1}{2}$	1 tablespoon	1 tablespoon	14
1	2 tablespoons	2 tablespoons	28
2	$\frac{1}{4}$ cup	4 tablespoons	56
4	$\frac{1}{2}$ cup		120
5		$\frac{1}{4}$ pint or 1 gill	140
6	$\frac{3}{4}$ cup		170
8	1 cup		240
9			250, $\frac{1}{4}$ liter
10	$1\frac{1}{4}$ cups	$\frac{1}{2}$ pint	280
12	$1\frac{1}{2}$ cups		340
15		$\frac{3}{4}$ pint	420
16	2 cups		450
18	$2\frac{1}{4}$ cups		500, $\frac{1}{2}$ liter
20	$2\frac{1}{2}$ cups	1 pint	560
24	3 cups		675
25		$1\frac{1}{4}$ pints	700
27	$3\frac{1}{2}$ cups		750
30	$3\frac{3}{4}$ cups	$1\frac{1}{2}$ pints	840
32	4 cups or 1 quart		900
35		$1\frac{3}{4}$ pints	980
36	$4\frac{1}{2}$ cups		1000, 1 liter
40	5 cups	2 pints or 1 quart	1120

SOLID MEASURES

U.S. and Imperial Measures		Metric Measures	
Ounces	Pounds	Grams	Kilos
1		28	
2		56	
$3\frac{1}{2}$		100	
4	$\frac{1}{4}$	112	
5		140	
6		168	
8	$\frac{1}{2}$	225	
9		250	$\frac{1}{4}$
12	$\frac{3}{4}$	340	
16	1	450	
18		500	$\frac{1}{2}$
20	$1\frac{1}{4}$	560	
24	$1\frac{1}{2}$	675	
27		750	$\frac{3}{4}$
28	$1\frac{3}{4}$	780	
32	2	900	
36	$2\frac{1}{4}$	1000	1
40	$2\frac{1}{2}$	1100	
48	3	1350	
54		1500	$1\frac{1}{2}$

OVEN TEMPERATURE EQUIVALENTS

Fahrenheit	Celsius	Gas Mark	Description
225	110	$\frac{1}{4}$	Cool
250	130	$\frac{1}{2}$	
275	140	1	Very Slow
300	150	2	
325	170	3	Slow
350	180	4	Moderate
375	190	5	
400	200	6	Moderately Hot
425	220	7	Fairly Hot
450	230	8	Hot
475	240	9	Very Hot
500	250	10	Extremely Hot

Any broiling recipes can be used with the grill of the oven, but beware of high-temperature grills.

EQUIVALENTS FOR INGREDIENTS

all-purpose flour—plain flour
baking sheet—oven tray
buttermilk—ordinary milk
cheesecloth—muslin
coarse salt—kitchen salt
cornstarch—cornflour

eggplant—aubergine
granulated sugar—caster sugar
half and half—12% fat milk
heavy cream—double cream
light cream—single cream
parchment paper—greaseproof paper

plastic wrap—cling film
scallion—spring onion
shortening—white fat
unbleached flour—strong, white flour
zest—rind
zucchini—courgettes or marrow